yellow const
black

1 roll of brown

army green

LUDWIG TRUTNAU

NONVENOMOUS SNAKES

63 Color Photographs

BARRON'S

New York/London/Toronto/Sydney

Front cover photos: Brown Water Python *(Liasis fuscus)* by L. Trutnau. (bottom left) Reticulate Python *(Python reticulatus);* (bottom center) California Mountain King Snake *(Lampropeltis zonata);* (bottom right) Tiger Ratsnake *(Spilotes pullatus).* Back cover: Gray-banded King Snake *(Lampropeltis mexicana).*

U.S. Scientific Consultant: Herndon Dowling, Ph.D.

First English language edition published in 1986 by Barron's Educational Series, Inc.

©1979, 1981 Eugen Ulmer GmbH & Co., Stuttgart, Germany

The title of the German edition is *Schlangen 1.*

All inquiries should be addressed to:

Barron's Educational Series, Inc.
250 Wireless Boulevard
Hauppauge, New York 11788

Library of Congress Catalog Card No. 86-22181

International Standard Book No. 0-8120-5632-9

Library of Congress Cataloging-in-Publication Data

Trutnau, Ludwig.
    Nonvenomous snakes.

    Translation of: Ungiftige Schlangen, v. 1 of the author's 2 v. work Schlangen im Terrarium.
    Includes index.
    1. Snakes as pets.   2. Snakes.   I. Title.
SF459.S5T78413   1986   639.3'96   86-22181
ISBN 0-8120-5632-9

PRINTED IN HONG KONG
89   490   9876543

CONTENTS

FOREWORD

Snakes are creatures much like other animals, but our behavior toward them in most cases is dominated by unrecognized psychological factors.

Throughout history snakes have been regarded as symbols of evil in practically all cultures. The conviction that these creatures are malicious, dangerous, and deadly is deep-rooted and largely determines our attitude toward them today. Most people pursue and kill snakes thoughtlessly, indeed almost instinctively, wherever they are to be found, whether this makes sense or not. The common killing of harmless European Grass Snakes (*Natrix natrix*) or American Gartersnakes (*Thamnophis sirtalis*) is a case in point. Unfortunately, it is extremely difficult if not impossible to convince our fellow human beings to give up such prejudices that were absorbed in early childhood as a result of misguided teachings. I hardly need mention that most people are unwilling to make an effort to find out the truth about these unjustly despised and persecuted creatures. In practically all the countries in the world snakes are senselessly hunted and destroyed, and almost the only justification for this is that these animals are born in a shape that is distasteful to humans and that, lacking external limbs, they move by slithering. For the great majority of those not versed in the natural sciences this alone is reason enough to annihilate beings that have been a part of nature's ongoing act of creation for more than 100 million years.

For more than twenty-five years the author has kept and bred both harmless and venomous snakes in captivity, observed and collected them in their natural habitat, and thus had a chance to study their ways of life and behavior. He sees it as a sad but nevertheless necessary duty to help dispel the negative feelings associated with these fascinating creatures and to counteract the general ignorance on the subject of their real nature. But this book is addressed not only to the layperson who would like to find out basic facts, but also especially to those with a keener interest who are looking for information on how to keep, care for, and breed snakes in captivity.

In the past a snake keeper's main concern was to keep his/her charges alive and in good health with a minimum of technical equipment. Offspring were produced more or less incidentally. But in recent years, interest in the deliberate breeding of snakes has been on the rise. There is little doubt but that the planned breeding of snakes over many generations and under conditions reflecting those of nature will continue to gain in importance in times to come. The reasons for this are obvious: irresponsibility and the desire for profit are resulting in an ever-increasing destruction of natural habitats with the inevitable consequence of reduced populations and the threat of extinction of almost all reptiles. Snakes bred in captivity have the added advantage that they generally adapt better to the conditions of captivity than do animals caught in the wild. It would also be desirable that snakes used in laboratories for scientific studies of animal behavior and other experiments would no longer be taken from nature but rather raised in captivity. The breeding of snakes on a large scale, particularly the breeding of poisonous snakes for the production of snake venom, could become an enterprise of both economic and scientific importance. However, any potential keeper of venomous snakes should be urgently warned never to handle these animals without taking all the proper precautions.

While the breeding of most aquarium fish has become quite routine, the art of producing reptilian offspring is still new, and much more and broader experience will be required before snake keepers will achieve successes comparable to those scored by aquarists. I hope that my book will prove a valuable contribution to this field, as well.

Finally, I have the pleasant task of thanking Bernd von Schoeders, Dr. Heinz Schroder, Bernd Schulz, Maurice Vanderhaege, and Norbert Wittman for their help and advice in some specific matters. I also owe thanks to Wulff Frick for making some slides available to me. And last but not least I am grateful to Dr. Heinz Wermuth and the Eugen Ulmer Verlag without whose encouragement and help this book would never have come into being.

Ludwig Trutnau

Altrich, March 1979

SNAKES IN NATURE

GENERAL BIOLOGY

There are approximately 2,400 species of snakes in the world. Although they vary greatly in size and habits, they share a basic body plan and have many of the same basic environmental requirements.

Approximately 20% of the known snake species are poisonous.

BODY STRUCTURE AND FUNCTION

Snakes are characterized by an elongated body, the absence of limbs, and jaw bones that are remarkably mobile and allow the jaw to expand. We distinguish three parts in the body of a snake: the head, the body proper, and the tail. The neck is not externally apparent; or if so, it is only by a slight tapering toward the head. The external shape is smooth and without visible segments because of the structure of the snake's skeleton, which consists of a skull, a vertebral column—made up of up to 560 vertebrae, depending on the species—and ribs. The entire animal is covered with a solid layer of overlapping scales somewhat like shingles of a roof.

Skin and Molting
The skin is made up of three layers of which the innermost is the thickest. It contains the pigment cells. The middle layer is very thin and consists of continually forming cells that are pushed outward as they mature. There they soon die, harden, and thus form the outermost layer of the skin, a keratinous epidermis that envelops the whole body. Periodically a liquid is secreted between the middle and outer layers of the skin, giving the snake a dull and somewhat milky look. Even the eyes are affected, and the snake's ability to see is reduced. This lasts for several days until the "molting secretion" is absorbed by the skin and the milky look disappears. At this point the snake rubs its snout against some rough object and peels the old skin off, inside out and in one piece. In this way the outermost skin, which needs to be replaced periodically because of growth and wear, is renewed.

Internal Organs
The lungs of snakes have undergone a unique transformation. While the more primitive species have two lungs (the right lung larger than the left) snakes at a higher stage of development have only the right lung. The posterior part of this single lung serves as an air chamber, while the anterior part functions as a respiratory organ. To conform to the long thin shape of the body, other internal organs of the snake, such as the liver, kidneys, stomach, and intestines, are elongated. Paired organs such as kidneys and testes also are offset, with one being ahead of the other, to allow a slender body.

Sense Organs
Snakes have immovable eyelids that form solid, transparent "glasses" in front of the eyes. Snakes therefore cannot blink, but there is no such thing as the fixed stare that is so often mentioned in connection with snakes. Instead, the eyes are fully mobile and move independently of each other. The ability to see is developed to different degrees in different snakes. In blind snakes or worm snakes (Typhlopidae) the eyes are vestigial, whereas many arboreal snakes have extremely sharp vision. Snakes' eyes are most sensitive to the movement, rather than the color or form, of their surroundings.

Snakes do not possess external openings for hearing. They do not hear high sounds, but they perceive even the slightest vibrations of the ground and are capable of hearing low sounds.

A remarkable feature of snakes is the Jacobson's organ, which is located in a pair of pits in the palate toward the front of the mouth that contain many nerve endings. With the aid of the tongue the snake picks up scent molecules and brings them to the openings of the Jacobson's organ. In this way a snake is able to follow the track of its prey. This curious organ serves the snake not only in finding prey but also in seeking out suitable hibernating quarters, finding sexual partners, and recognizing a particular partner during mating season.

Some snake families (boas and pit-vipers) also have heat sensitive organs located in pitlike depressions on the head which sense the body heat of warm-blooded animals, and thus make it possible for the snake to detect prey in total darkness.

Musculature and Locomotion

The body muscles are attached to the ribs. They insert on broad ventral scutes, which push in leverlike fashion against uneven places on the ground for locomotion. This forward motion in a straight line, which resembles that of a centipede, is used by most snakes primarily when they shed their old skins; many vipers, however, especially members of the genus *Bitis*, often move this way at other times, too. The sinuous motion from side to side that we think of as the typical mode of serpentine locomotion is seen most clearly when a snake hurries along over uneven ground, moves around on trees, shrubs, or rocks, or swims in the water. In this type of locomotion the snake reaches forward with the ventral scutes on one side and simultaneously pushes back with those on the other side. Many snakes that live in desert sand—among them the North African horned vipers (genus *Cerastes*) and the horned rattlesnakes of the American Southwest (*Crotalus*)—move very fast in a process called "sidewinding." In this mode the anterior part of the body is raised and moved diagonally ahead while the rest of the body is moved up. The snake touches the ground in only two places, leaving behind characteristic hooklike prints in the sand. These movements are executed in rapid succession and can be kept up for a long time, allowing the snake to cover great distances.

Snakes living in the ground move by digging and burrowing. Vestigial pelvic bones are still found in the most primitive forms of these burrowers, proof of how closely related these animals are to lizards. Some sea snakes have vertically flattened tails that help propel them through the water. Snakes that are exclusively arboreal have ventral plates with clearly visible angles that assist them in fleeing along the branches of trees at great speed.

GROWTH RATE AND SIZE

Mammals generally stop growing when they reach sexual maturity. Most reptiles, however, keep increasing in size throughout their lives not always at the same rate. Periods of rapid growth are followed by times when the animals barely grow at all. Snakes grow faster in youth than they do in old age, and hibernation inhibits growth partially or completely. The conditions necessary for growth are sufficient food and adequate temperatures and light. Since the food supplies and the temperatures in a terrarium differ vastly from the conditions prevailing in the natural habitat, the size of captive snakes does not allow us to draw conclusions about how large wild snakes get. A Reticulate Python (*Python reticulatus*) I acquired in October 1968 grew from 6½ feet to 16 feet (2 m-5 m) in the course of nine years, and my African Rock Python (*Python sebae*) increased from 4 feet to 14½ feet (1.2-4.5 m) over a period of ten years. Young Boa Constrictors (*Boa constrictor*) measure 16 to 20 inches (40-50 cm) shortly after hatching, and by the time they are one year old, they are about 32 inches (80 cm) long. Corn Snakes (*Elaphe guttata*) are about 8 to 10 inches (20-24 cm) long at birth and can, if well fed, grow to over 4 feet (120 cm) in three years.

Herpetologist Clifford H. Pope kept some of the most detailed records we have on the growth rate of the Burmese Python (*Python molurus bivittatus*). On February 10, 1946, Pope's specimen of this giant serpent was 40 inches (102 cm) long. One year later it measured 69 inches (175 cm), and by the end of September 1947, it was 99 inches (251 cm). By the end of May, 1948, the snake was over 10 feet long (3 m). After that the growth slowed down. In October 1956, after eleven years in captivity, the snake measured 12 feet (360 cm), and in January 1960, when it was measured for the last time, it had gained another foot, adding up to a total of 13 feet (390 cm).

Another snake expert, Volsoe, gives the following data for the growth rate of the Common Viper (*Vipera berus*): a young viper was 6¼ inches (16 cm) long in August and about ½ inch longer (17 cm) by the following winter. One year later it measured 10¼ inches (26 cm), the next year, 14 inches (35 cm), and the year after that, 17 inches (43 cm). Two years later, when the snake was five years old, it measured 18½ inches (47 cm). According to herpetologist Klauber, Prairie Rattlesnakes (*Crotalus viridis*) grow from 11 inches (28 cm) to 36 inches (90 cm) in the course of four years and ten months. Some Eastern Diamondback Rattlesnakes (*Crotalus adamanteus*) the author observed grew from about 14 inches (35 cm) at birth to lengths ranging between 3 feet 4 inches and 4 feet (100-120 cm) in three years.

It is possible to estimate the length of a live snake fairly accurately when it crawls along a glass panel or wall of its cage. Still, measurements of live and moving snakes are often quite unreliable, and even snake skins fail to yield accurate measurements of a snake's length because they twist and stretch, especially when they are freshly shed. Estimates of snakes seen in the wild usually exaggerate the animals' lengths.

Just how big do snakes grow? This is a question that is often asked, but is not easy to answer. The biggest snakes belong to the family of nonvenomous giant serpents (Boidae). But only a few species of this group gain lengths greater than 20 feet (9 m); the majority of them are of only moderate or small size. Anacondas (*Eunectes murinus*) and Reticulate Pythons (*Python reticulatus*) grow to over 33 feet (10 m) only in rare cases. Indian Pythons (*Python molurus*) and African Rock Pythons (*P. sebae*) may measure up to 23 feet (7 m) or a little over. The Boa Constrictor (*Boa constrictor*), probably the most famous of all the giant snakes, hardly ever grows longer than 15 feet (4.5 m). There are reports of Anacondas that were supposedly 50 feet (16 m) long. But it is doubtful that these reports reflect reality because thus far there has been no substantiated evidence of an Anaconda measuring even 33 feet (10 m). Many years ago the New York Zoological Society offered a prize of 5,000 dollars to anyone who could produce an Anaconda 33 feet (10 m) long, but the prize has not been claimed to this day.

The largest poisonous snakes are the King Cobra (*Ophiophagus hannah*), the Black Mamba (*Dendroashis polylepis*), and the Taipan (*Oxyuranus scutellatus*), which can reach lengths of over 16 feet (5 m), 13 feet (4 m), and 10 feet (3 m), respectively. The Bushmaster (*Lachesis mutus*) and the Eastern Diamondback Rattlesnake (*Crotalus adamanteus*) grow to over 10 feet (3 m) and 8 feet (2.5 m) only occasionally.

The most diminutive snakes are found among the blind snakes of the genera *Leptotyphlops* and *Typhlops*. Many of these small snakes do not get any bigger than 8 or 12 inches (20-30 cm). As is to be expected, many snakes living in tropical regions are larger than their relatives from temperate zones. In the tropics the climate is ideal for reptiles and the food plentiful, thus creating optimal conditions for continual growth all through the year.

LONGEVITY

The longevity of snakes varies from species to species. Large snakes tend to live longer than smaller ones. We do not have much reliable data on the life expectancy of snakes living in the wild, but we are better informed about species that are kept in captivity, such as the following: Boa constrictor (*Boa constrictor*), 38 years; Mexican Python (*Loxocemus bicolor*), 32 years; Ball Python (*Python recius*), 30 years; Black-lipped Cobra (*Naja melanoleuca*), 29 years; Anaconda (*Eunectes murinus*), 28 years; Rainbow Boa (*Epicrates cenchria maurus*), 27 years; Cottonmouth (*Agkistrodon piscivorus*), 21 years; Corn Snake (*Elaphe guttata*), 21 years; African Rock Python (*Python sebae*), 27 years; Northern Copperhead (*Agkistrodon contortrix mokasen*), 29 years; Western Diamondback Rattlesnake (*Crotalus atrox*), 25 years; Louisiana Milksnake (*Lampropeltis triangulum amaura*), 20 years; Northern Pacific Rattlesnake (*Crotalus viridis oreganus*), 17 years; San Diego Gopher Snake (*Pituophis melanoleucus annectens*), 20 years; Massasauga (*Sistrurus catenatus*), 14 years; Black Rat Snake (*Elaphe obsoleta obsoleta*), 20 years; Rosy Boa (*Lichanura trivirgata*), 18 years; and a subspecies of the Grass Snake (*Natrix natrix natrix*), 11 years. A White-lipped Pit Viper (*Trimeresurus albolabris*) kept by the author has been living in captivity for 18 years.

DIET AND FEEDING

In contrast to many lizards and turtles, snakes are exclusively carnivorous. Depending on their species, they feed on mammals, birds, amphibians, and fishes, as well as invertebrates such as insects, spiders, myriapods, scorpions, worms, and snails. Some feed almost entirely on reptiles and, as typical snake eaters, will sometimes consume weaker members of their own species. While many snakes eat quite a varied diet, some kinds specialize in certain specific foods and would rather starve to death than eat anything else. The egg-eating snakes of the genera *Dasypeltis* and *Elachistodon* are famous examples of this. They eat nothing but eggs. Some members of the Dipsadinae, a subfamily of arboreal snakes, live exclusively on snails.

Unlike the warm-blooded mammals and birds, snakes, whose body temperature varies with that of the environment, are less dependent on a regular intake of food. Their more sluggish metabolism allows them to wait for suitable prey for weeks or even months.

SUBDUING PREY

The skull of a snake is very mobile, the bones being held together by flexible tendons, hinges, and muscles. It can thus function as a system of levers and is ideally suited for swallowing large prey. The prey animal is caught with lightning speed and held fast by the needle-sharp teeth which slant slightly inward and backward. Most snakes have two rows of teeth in the upper jaw and one row in the lower. The harder the captured animal struggles to get free, the deeper the snake's teeth bite.

The sensing, hunting, and killing of prey is done in different ways. Natricine, or water, snakes have good eyes and are alert to movement. They catch sight of a hopping frog or a swimming fish instantly, give chase immediately, and swallow the victim alive. Smell plays practically no role at all. Members of the *Elaphe* genus kill small mammals and birds with the pressure of their jaws or by pressing them against the ground. Larger and stronger mammals are subdued by the snake's wrapping itself around them in several loops. This is the way many colubrids and giant serpents kill their prey.

Venomous snakes have an extremely effective weapon with which to paralyze and kill their victims. The venom is produced in two glands located on the sides of the head just behind the eyes. The chemical composition of venom is not at all uniform. Snake venoms consist of different, highly complex combinations of enzymes. Generally there are two components that affect the victim: one attacks the nervous system and the other, the blood and tissues. In the case of the venomous elapids and sea snakes, the poison that affects the nerves usually predominates (death through paralysis of the respiratory system); the venom of vipers and pit vipers acts primarily on the victim's tissues. The venom also initiates the digestive process and thus corresponds to the saliva of mammals. Venom glands are, in fact, modified saliva glands. The colorless, yellowish, orange, or greenish venom is injected into the victim through two needle-sharp poison fangs within fractions of a second. Sometimes the bite happens so fast that it is almost impossible to see. In some snakes the poison fangs stick straight down from the upper jaw; in others they are located farther back in the mouth and are practically immobile. Other types of snakes can raise the fangs or hide them away in folds of the mucous membrane.

Most poisonous and nonpoisonous colubrids use their eyes and their sense of smell to detect and follow prey while the majority of vipers and pit vipers, as well as many giant snakes, lie patiently in wait. When an unsuspecting animal passes by, the snake strikes and kills it either with a poison bite or by wrapping its body around it in a deadly grip.

SWALLOWING AND DIGESTION

The dead animal is then swallowed head first or, more rarely, from the other end. Potent stomach juices initiate the actual process of digestion and carry it through to the end. The enzymes in the stomach juices break down proteins, fats, and carbohydrates into simpler components that the body can absorb and use. Being a chemical process, digestion is affected by temperature. Snakes are able to digest more quickly and more thoroughly at 77° to 90°F (25°-32°C)—optimal temperatures for them —than at 59° to 68°F (15°-20°C).

After a meal snakes like to retreat to a quiet, protected spot of the right warmth to digest in peace. Normally a healthy snake digests its food in no more than three to eight days, even if it excretes the remains much later. This delayed defecation is typical of snakes of the genera *Bitis*, *Boa*, and *Python* among others. Depending on the surrounding temperature, mushy excrements are produced one to several days (sometimes weeks or even months) after the snake has eaten. Indigestible parts of the prey, such as hair, feathers, toenails, teeth, scales, and egg membranes are found in these excrements.

Snakes eat only infrequently, something that is no doubt connected to their ability to consume a large amount of food at one meal. Information on how often snakes eat in their natural habitat is scarce and not very specific. The size of the animals eaten affects the frequency of food intake. From snakes living in captivity we know that young specimens need an adequate feeding at least once a week. Adult snakes stay healthy for years when fed once every two to four weeks. I have found that slight underfeeding is better than constant overfeeding. Overfeeding will bring animals to record length and weight in a shorter time but tends to shorten life span and inhibits reproduction.

LIFE CYCLE

In snakes as in other reptiles, fertilization of the eggs takes place inside the body of the female. Both in the northern and southern hemisphere, reproduction is tied to certain seasons of the year and is determined by the fluctuations in temperature that accompany them. Although snakes do sometimes mate in the fall, matings normally take place in the spring after hibernation. Under very favorable conditions snakes may reproduce every year, but a two-year cycle is more normal. Snakes are solitary animals and do not engage in any special social behavior, but many individuals of both sexes often congregate in certain places at mating time. Snakes that otherwise stay within a given territory undertake longer or shorter journeys before this time in search of partners.

SEX DIFFERENCES

It is often far from easy to tell the sexes apart at first glance because the sexual organs of snakes are inside the body. In fully grown snakes there are some external signs that may give a hint as to sex. In males, the tail, which starts at the cloaca, is longer than in females, and males often are not only more brightly or differently colored than females but are longer and more stoutly built. The sexual organs of male snakes are located in the base of the tail just behind the cloaca. There is always a pair of organs, which are called hemipenes. The hemipenis has spines or folds on the outside, and along the center of the organ there is a groove for the passage of the sperm. During copulation only one hemipenis is inserted into the female's cloaca, where the spines anchor it for several minutes to several hours. During this time the male vibrates his body against the female and both animals are visibly excited.

COURTSHIP AND MATING

The two sexes recognize each other not only by the scent emanating from skin glands but also by optical signs and especially by inborn (i.e., hereditarily transmitted) behavior patterns that are typical of the species. Every mating is preceded by some form of courtship behavior.

In the case of some species—for example, the Aesculapian Snake (*Elaphe longissima*) and the Dark Green Racer (*Coluber viridiflavus*)—the male keeps hold of the female's neck with his teeth during copulation. In many species a clear courtship ritual can be observed. When two or more males meet, they engage in ritualized contests that are reminiscent of the tournaments of medieval knights. These combat dances are performed only by males and often last for hours. Such a test between rivals is a remarkable spectacle. Neither of the snakes is ever hurt in the process. The two opponents crawl over each other and wrap their tail ends around each other. Then they raise the anterior part of the body up at an angle, press their heads against each other, and try to tire each other out by pushing down strongly to one side or the other. Eventually the weaker party concedes.

Before copulating, the male crawls along next to the female or moves across her back while making varied pulselike motions or twitching with body and head. He also rubs his head along the female's back, examines her all over with his flicking tongue, and appears highly agitated. The female responds to his touchings with a slight twitching of the body and rapid movements of the tail. At the point of copulation, the two snakes lie next to or on top of each other, stretched out full length. The male wraps his tail around that of the female and positions it in such a way that he can introduce his hemipenis into her cloaca.

15

Copulation can last anywhere from a few minutes to several hours or, in exceptional cases, even for days. While they are locked together, the two partners seem to be filled with subdued excitement. Often they lie stretched out straight, heads pointed in opposite directions. When the female moves, the male slides along adeptly without disengaging himself from her. In undulating movements the two animals continually wind themselves around each other and unwind again. Many females stop eating sooner or later after the mating and do not resume feeding until after the eggs are deposited or the young snakes born.

EGG-LAYING

The white or grayish-white eggs are usually elliptical in shape and covered with a tough, parchmentlike membrane. This membrane consists of nine to ten layers which are organized in such a way that the filaments of each layer are at right angles to those of the one below. Depending on the species, the eggs can measure up to several inches in length. Inside of them there is enough yolk to feed the growing embryo.

The eggs are usually laid four to sixteen weeks after the mating. The number in a clutch depends on the species. In the case of giant serpents there may be over one hundred. When egg laying time approaches, the female often gets restless and starts crawling around ceaselessly in search of a suitable spot for the eggs. Once she finds such a spot, she pushes the eggs out one at a time at shorter or longer intervals with sinuous movements of the lower body. In many species the eggs are covered with a sticky liquid and thus adhere to each other firmly. Usually the female deposits her clutch on the ground in sand, soil, or moss, in heaps of old leaves, peat, or even compost or manure, under rocks, in rock fissures, in cracks in walls, under logs or old wood, under termite hills, or in any kind of hidden spot where the temperature and humidity are conducive to the development of the embryos. After the eggs are laid, the female crawls away and pays no further attention to them.

With few exceptions—pythons and some poisonous and nonpoisonous colubrids—snakes do not engage in parental care. Pythons do brood their eggs. The mother wraps her body and head around the clutch. Some species use periodic muscle contractions to create a higher incubating temperature. The body temperature of these snakes, which are otherwise cold-blooded animals, rises several degrees during brooding. Temperature readings have shown that the temperature between the coils of a brooding Indian python's body may be as much as 13°F (7°C) higher than that of the surroundings.

DEVELOPMENT OF THE EGGS

Chance determines the fate of the eggs. Temperature affects the progress of the embryos' development. Incubation, which lasts two to three months on the average, can extend to as much as six or seven months, as in the case of the Boomslang (*Dispholidus typus*). The egg contains enough nourishment for the growing organism. Inside the egg an umbilical cord connects the embryo to the yolk sac which contains the food reserves. The yolk is surrounded by a liquid called the amnion. Yolk and amnion are in turn contained in the allantois, an entodermal pouch of the embryo's hindgut. As the embryo develops, the yolk sac shrinks, and the allantois increases in size, now also serving as an embryonic bladder and aiding in the exchange of gases. Another membrane, the chorion, envelops the allantois, amnion, yolk sac, and embryo.

Toward the end of the incubation period, folds and vertical cracks in the surface of the egg show that the snakes are getting ready to hatch. The unborn snakes now develop a sharp point on their snouts—the egg tooth—with which they are able to slice open the egg shell and thus make their way out of the egg. Soon the newborn snakes shed their skins and are now ready to start life on their own without any protection or aid from parents.

LIVE-BEARING SPECIES

In a number of species the females do not lay eggs but instead retain them inside the body where they mature. These snakes thus bear fully developed, "live" young. When they are born, the young are enveloped in a transparent egg membrane which they soon break out of. Since they are fully developed they are small replicas of their parents in all essential physical and behavioral aspects. This kind of development is characteristic of some colubrids and all boas, true vipers, and pit vipers. We assume that this unusual procedure evolved to provide protection against various environmental factors that would otherwise threaten the survival of the species. In the temperate zones of northern Europe, for instance, a gravid Smooth Snake (*Coronella austriaca*) or Common Viper (*Vipera berus*) can warm up in the sunshine as needed and thus regulate her body temperature for the optimal development of the young inside her.

HIBERNATION

Most snakes living in temperate and subtropical zones with marked temperature differences between summer and winter have a period of dormancy in the winter which, depending on how long the weather stays cold, can last anywhere from two to nine months. This dormancy of snakes is not simply a slowing down of the life processes in response to the growing cold, as is often assumed. I am not at all of the opinion that hibernation is caused merely by the season's low temperatures, because even before winter temperatures begin, the metabolism of snakes changes in response to certain hormonal changes that occur seasonally. These hormonal and metabolic changes initiate dormancy well before winter starts. The snakes of many species stop eating in late summer. They are filled by a deep restlessness and start wandering in search of suitable wintering places. In terrariums, too, this behavior can be observed every year.

Being cold-blooded organisms, snakes are unable to regulate their body temperature, and in order to survive they have to find a sheltered place well before the winter cold approaches. These wintering places, where temperature and humidity remain relatively constant, are usually found underground, tucked away in root holes, walls, rock crevices, slopes of loose rock, etc. This is where snakes spend their winters. All the vital functions, such as heart beat, breathing, and the entire metabolic process are dramatically reduced. During their active period the animals have stored extra food in connective tissue in the form of fat. These fat reserves together with the slowed metabolism allow them to survive very well for months without food in temperatures just above freezing. But if the temperature dips much below freezing they die. Hibernation is not necessarily a continuous process. Especially in southern regions it is often broken on warm days, and one can see snakes sunbathing briefly near their hibernating quarters, which they immediately dart back into at the slightest sign of danger.

Many snakes hibernate by themselves, but others seem to favor congregating for the winter, often in close communion with snakes of other species. This is especially true in places that offer favorable conditions for wintering over. In the course of excavacations, winter quarters have been uncovered that contained Smooth Snakes (*Coronella austriaca*), Ringed Snakes (*Natrix natrix*), and Common Vipers (*Vipera berus*) all in one place. The largest number of snakes hibernating together was found in Norway, where there were said to be about 800 Common Vipers. Similar aggregations of dormant snakes have been found in North America. In Manitoba, for instance, 148 Smooth Greensnakes (*Opheodrys vernalis*), 101 Red-bellied Snakes (*Storeria occipitomaculata*), and 8 Plains Gartersnakes hibernating together were dug up.

Mating normally takes place in the spring.

(Brief mention should be made, too, of aestivation. In very hot and dry summer weather snakes retreat from the heat into dark, moist, and cooler nooks.)

DISTRIBUTION

Snakes occur in almost all parts of the world, but they are subject to the general laws of distribution. In northern Europe they have penetrated into the polar zone in Scandinavia, but they hardly occur north of the 67th degree of latitude. In the southern hemisphere their distribution extends to about the 44th degree of latitude. In some tropical seas, snakes are found only in certain locations. On some islands there are a great many of them, on others none at all. There are no snakes on the Azores, Bermuda, Hawaii, in Ireland, Iceland, Antarctica, or New Zealand. The geographic distribution of extant snakes is determined largely by climatic conditions, among which temperature is the prime factor. The higher up one gets in the mountains, the fewer snake species one finds because average temperatures decrease as altitude increases. But snakes live up as high as 15,000 to 16,000 feet (4500-4900 m) above sea level. The small Himalayan viper (*Agkistrodon himalayanus*), for instance, is found in Nepal at heights of 16,000 feet, and the Mountain Bush Viper (*Atheris hindii*) occurs in the Kinangop and Aberdare Mountains of Kenya as high as 10,000 feet (3100 m). The author has collected Dusky Rattlesnakes (*Crotalus trisertiatus*) in the vicinity of El Limon Totalca near Orizaba Mountain in Mexico at altitudes above 10,000 feet, and one encounters the Mexican Gartersnake (*Thamnophis scalaris*) at 13,000 feet (4000 m) and higher.

In general, however, most snakes live in the lowlands, hilly country, and low mountains. The closer one gets to the Equator, the richer the variety of snakes becomes. The greatest number of species and the greatest contrasts in appearance are found in tropical areas where largely constant temperatures, humidity, and daylight as well as abundant food and hiding places create optimal living conditions for snakes. In these habitats tiny species live alongside giant ones.

The distribution of snake species is determined, on the one hand, by the physical make-up of the snakes in question and the conditions necessary for their survival and, on the other, by the age of the species and by the climatic and geographical changes the earth has undergone over the ages. It is therefore not surprising that every continent has its own particular snake fauna, but on each continent, mountain ranges, large rivers, inlets of seas, and changes in climate set natural limits to the snakes' ability to wander.

Scientists distinguish six to eight zoogeographic regions. Each of these is characterized by animal orders, families, subfamilies, or markedly different genera that do not, in our present era, occur in other regions. I should like to briefly describe these zoogeographic regions and mention the snakes that are typical of them and sometimes endemic to them. ("Endemic" means occurring only in a particular locality.)

ZOOGEOGRAPHIC REGIONS

One major zoogeographic region is the Holoarctic region, which comprises the temperate and cold zones of the Northern Hemisphere. This region is often divided into the Nearctic, which includes temperate North America, and the Palearctic which is made up of temperate Asia, Europe, and Saharan Africa. Other major zoogeographic regions are the Ethiopian, Madagascan, Oriental, Indoaustralian, Australian and Neotropical.

Holoarctic Region

As said above, the *Holoarctic region* comprises the temperate and cold zones of the northern hemisphere. The snakes characteristic of these areas belong to the family Colubridae with its many genera. Some of these genera, such as *Natrix*, *Thamnophis*, *Coluber*, *Elaphe*, *Lampropeltis*, and others, are in turn composed of large numbers of individual species. Europe, Africa, and Asia are characterized by a large variety of true vipers (Viperidae), whereas pit vipers (Crotalidae) are found primarily in North America and the Far East. Some species have amazingly extensive ranges while others occur only in specific places that are sometimes separated by great distances. The Ringed Snake (*Natrix natrix*) and the Diced Water Snake (*Natrix tessellata*) provide a good example of the former. The Ringed Snake is found throughout Europe and western Asia; the Diced Water Snake occurs from central Europe to western China. The Common Viper (*Vipera berus*), too, has a huge, almost unbroken range stretching from the Iberian Peninsula to central and northern Asia. The Aesculapian Snake (*Elaphe longissima*) and especially Orsini's Viper (*Vipera ursinii*), on the other hand, occur only in scattered localities in central and southern Europe and in western Asia.

Some colubrids are also widely distributed across the North American continent. The Common Garter Snake (*Thamnophis sirtalis*), the Ringneck Snake (*Diadophis punctatus*), the Common Kingsnake (*Lampropeltis getulus*), and the American Racer (*Coluber constrictor*) are examples of snakes that inhabit practically all of the United States, large areas of Mexico, and even parts of southern Canada. On the other hand, the Striped Crayfish Snake (*Regina alleni*) and the Short-tail Snake (*Stilosoma extenuatum*) are found only in Florida.

Ethiopian Region

The *Ethiopian region* includes Africa south of the Sahara as well as southern Arabia. Typical of this region are a large number of blind snakes (*Typhlops*), slender blind snakes (*Leptotyphlops*), pythons (*Python*), burrowing pythons (*Calabaria*) and sand boas (*Eryx*). There are also a great number of snakes of the family Colubridae. Poisonous snakes are represented in the Ethiopian region by sea snakes (Hydrophiidae), members of the family Elapidae, and Old World vipers (Viperidae). Snakes typical of this region are mambas (*Dendroaspis*), cobras of the genera *Hemachatus* and *Naja*, burrowing vipers (*Atractaspis*), Bush vipers (*Atheris*), night adders (*Causus*), and puff adders (*Bitis*), to mention a few. The pit viper family (Crotalidae) is not represented in this region at all.

Madagascan Region

The *Madagascan region* includes the island groups north of Madagascar and is the home of a number of colubrids. The Boid genera *Sanzinia* and *Acrantophis* occur exclusively in this region. Poisonous snakes are completely unknown here, as are slender blind snakes (Leptotyphlopidae). A number of snakes found on Madagascar show remarkable similarities to some species found in South America, which suggests a close relationship between the two groups.

Oriental Region

The *Oriental region* includes southern Asia and the Malay archipelago. The snake fauna of southern Asia has much in common with that of the Ethiopian region. Both areas have blind snakes (*Typhlops*), slender blind snakes (*Leptotyphlops*), sand boas (*Eryx*), pythons (*Python*), racers (*Coluber*), sand snakes (*Psammophis*), cobras (*Naja*), and saw-scaled vipers (*Echis*). Especially characteristic of the fauna of southern Asia are rat snakes (*Ptyas*, *Zaocys*), the genus *Dendrelaphis*, wolf snakes (*Lycodon*), flying snakes (*Chrysopelea*), kukri snakes (*Oligodon*), Oriental whipsnakes (*Ahaetulla*), and the strange mock vipers (*Psammodynastes*). Some primitive snakes like the pipe snakes (Cylindrophiidae), sunbeam snakes (Xenopeltidae), and shield-tailed snakes (Uropeltidae) are also characteristic of this region. Poisonous snakes are represented by members of the families Hydrophiidae, Elapidae, Viperidae, and Crotalidae.

Indoaustralian Region

To the southeast of the Oriental region lies the *Indoaustralian* border area, comprising the

Celebes, the Lesser Sunda Islands, and the Molucca Islands. Apart from some endemic forms, the snake fauna here shows elements of both the Australian and the Oriental regions. Overall the Oriental forms predominate, though they diminish toward the east as the share of Australian fauna increases.

Australian Region

The *Australian region* includes not only Australia itself but also New Zealand, New Guinea, Melanesia, and some of the South Sea Islands. There are an especially large number of endemic species and genera found here. The snake fauna of this region is indeed unique. There are not only blind snakes (Typhlopidae) and giant snakes (Pythonidae), but also quite a few snakes of the family Colubridae. But even more remarkable for the region as a whole is the number of sea snakes (Hydrophiidae). The most outstanding aspect of the Australian region, however, is the large variety of poisonous serpents (Elapidae), which make up about two thirds of all the snakes found here. There are over 120 poisonous species. True vipers (Viperidae) and pit vipers (Crotalidae) are unknown in this region.

Neotropical Region

The *Neotropical region*, which extends from Central to South America, also has a great wealth of different snakes. Nonpoisonous colubrids are especially common. Some genera like the night snakes (*Hypsiglena*), black-headed snakes (*Tantilla*), lyre snakes (*Trimorphodon*), and kingsnakes (*Lampropeltis*) are found both in the Neotropical region and in Holarctic North America. Snakes endemic to Central and South America include lined snakes (*Leimadophis*), spindle snakes (*Atractus*), false coral snakes (*Erythrolamprus*), mussuranas (*Clelia*), and anacondas (*Eunectes*). The worm snakes of the families Leptotyphlopidae and Typhlopidae, which are distributed in all tropical regions, are found here, too, as are a number of giant snakes (Boidae) of which I will mention here only the famous Boa Constrictor. Pipe snakes

(Aniliidae) are represented only by one genus with a single species. This species, the reptile-eating false coral snake, *Anilius scytale*, occurs in Guyana, eastern Peru, northern Brazil, and Colombia. The poisonous Elapidae are represented by the genus *Micrurus*, and many nonvenomous snakes, the so-called false coral snakes, mimic their strikingly colorful markings as protection against potential enemies. One sea snake (Hydrophiidae) also occurs off the Pacific Coast of South America, and there is a remarkable variety of pit vipers, especially of lance-head snakes or fer-de-lances (*Bothrops*).

FACTORS IN THE HABITAT

Different species inhabit all kinds of environments that meet their needs and to which they have adapted in the course of time. Temperature, light, air, soil, and moisture are the determining factors for choosing a specific biotope. Many snakes live exclusively above ground while others burrow into the ground and surface only occasionally. In the humid and hot tropics with their lush vegetation we find many species that live in trees and shrubs. Others are found exclusively in various bodies of water which they leave only rarely. A snake's habitat also has to supply hiding places and the kind of food the snake lives on.

The more varied the landscape of an area is, the more snakes there are. Areas without any snakes at all are rare. Snakes usually stay in one place and do not range very far. They are extremely reluctant to abandon the location they have adopted. Usually they inhabit wild areas far from human traffic, but this is not always the case. If they find favorable conditions, are left alone, or have adequate hiding places they sometimes live quite close to human habitations and sometimes even penetrate into towns and cities. In tropical countries snakes, especially those that are active at dusk, sometimes enter houses and can represent a danger if they happen to belong to a poisonous species. The author has caught both poisonous and nonpoisonous snakes in many places inhabited or frequented by people. The following is a list of such places: a military drill field; the edges of a tennis court and a golf course in Louisiana; many neglected gardens in Europe and North America; behind hotels and restaurants and at rest stops along highways; in abandoned houses and barns; along the roadside under piles of old wood, cardboard, roofing metal, and rusty tin cans; in barrios; under the wooden roofs of log cabins; in city walls and ruins; in vineyards and orchards; along railroad tracks; in many parks; in villages; in many cities such as Miami, Atlanta, Houston, and San Antonio; frequently along highways; along the edges of fields and on cow pastures; and once even in a pig sty. All of these places offered plenty of opportunities for hiding.

The distribution of snakes in the various parts of the earth depends primarily on the climate. Through adaptation over millions of years snakes have not only adjusted to the climate of their habitat but have also come to depend on the annual weather cycle there. Different local weather patterns create many different micro-climates in a given area; and this is reflected in the distribution and composition of the area's snake fauna.

Every area has a certain type of climate. Similar climatic types combine to form a climatic zone. Since mountains, proximity to or distance from seas, and ocean currents can affect climate in many different ways, each climatic type has a number of subforms that are hard to define exactly and between which it is hard to draw exact boundaries. Of the seven climatic zones that are generally recognized, five are inhabited by snakes with the most varied needs for survival. These zones are:
1. the equatorial zone
2. the zone of equatorial monsoons
3. the two high-pressure zones with trade-winds
4. the subtropics
5. the temperate latitudes.

Climate results from the interaction of a number of factors. The most important of these for the survival of snakes are temperature, length of daylight, precipitation, air currents, air humidity, and soil moisture.

Temperature

The body temperature of snakes depends on that of their environment. If the environment cools down beyond a certain point, the entire metabolism of the snake slows down and muscular activities cease. The snakes barely move any longer, they stop eating, and digestion comes to a halt. But a snake's body temperature is determined less by the air temperature than by the warmth of the substrate. A number of the author's observations support this point: once he saw Common Vipers near melting snow in air temperatures barely above freezing. The warm March sun had heated up the surface of the ground which consisted mainly of pine needles and dry leaves, and the snakes' bodies benefited equally from the sun. And in the spring of 1959 he saw a considerable number of Ringed Snakes. There had been a frost during the night, and every pond and puddle was covered with a thin sheet of ice. Although the sun was shining, the air was still very cold. The snakes were sunning themselves on the slopes next to the ponds, apparently just having left their winter dens. Since the nights are still cold in the spring, one usually finds snakes outside their hiding places only during the day. But they do not become active at dusk or nighttime until the surrounding temperature rises above 77° to 86°F (25°-30°C). Behavior similarly dependent on temperature is especially common among desert snakes. At night they often travel for miles, leaving behind their characteristic sidewinding tracks in the fine desert sand. One can get an idea of the extent of these nighttime journeys by driving on roads that lead through snake country. The animals are attracted by the heat of the asphalt and are run over by passing cars. In Florida and Texas I have seen hundreds of snakes killed on the road during the night. Similar reports come from Africa, Asia, and Australia.

Many species of the *Natrix* genus leave the land and retreat into water when the air temperature gets too high. Other snakes withdraw to refuges on land that offer more comfortable temperatures; they hide under stones, rocks, logs, bark, roots, or in the ground. Scarlet Milk Snakes (*Lampropeltis triangulum elapsoides*) and Corn Snakes (*Elaphe guttata*) love to hide under the loose bark of dead pines where they find warmth and moisture. The bark also offers protection against enemies and against the yearly floods of some areas. In addition, there is plenty of food to be found here because many small lizards (*scincella laterale, Anolis carolinensis*) also hide under the bark where they live on many insects and their larvae. In the spring, many snakes, such as the Diced Water Snake (*Natrix tessellata*), the European Whipsnake (*Coluber viridiflavus*), Lataste's Viper (*Vipera latasti*), and the Sand Viper (*Viper ammodytes*), that ordinarily live on the ground sometimes crawl onto low shrubs or even into trees to bask there.

Some snakes expose their anterior bodies to the sun and leave their tail ends in mouse holes or under rocks. This keeps them from overheating. Such behavior is especially common among Sand Vipers (*Cerastes cerastes*) and Sidewinders (*Crotalus cerastes*). Some blind snakes (Leptotyphlopidae and Typhlopidae) as well as the Shovel-nosed Snakes (*Chionactis*) bury the anterior and posterior parts of their bodies to different depths to achieve the desired body temperature.

The range of temperatures in the temperate latitudes also affects reproduction and the development of the young. Many genera (e.g., *Coronella, Vipera, Nerodia,* and *Thamnophis*) bear live young. All the baby snake has to do upon birth is to push its way out of the transparent egg skin and it is ready to crawl off into the world. This type of reproduction is called ovoviviparous. The advantage of ovoviviparous species over egg-laying ones is that the pregnant female can seek out as much sun warmth as she needs and thus not only regulate her own body temperature but also accelerate the development of the embryos

inside her. The surrounding temperatures under rocks or bark would in these regions often be too cool to bring the deposited eggs to maturation.

The ovoviviparous character is not always immutably determined through heredity. In species with a wide area of distribution the trait of bearing fully developed young can change in conformance to climatic conditions. *Vipera lebetina*, for instance lays eggs in southern regions but is said to bear live young in the northern parts of its area of distribution.

The length of snakes, too, is affected by climate. Species living in cool regions are usually small. A small body heats up faster after a cold night than a large one. Small snakes are therefore better adapted to northern climates than big ones. Perhaps this is the reason why large snakes are found mostly in tropical and subtropical regions.

Daylight

Daylight is not as crucial to survival for snakes as temperature. Many snakes are both diurnal and nocturnal. Some species, however, stay hidden during the day and are active only at night. Among these are the mud snakes (*Farancia*) and the kraits (*Bungaras*), which tuck their heads under their bodies when they are exposed to daylight. *Elaphe taeniura ridleyi* lives in large caves near Kuala Lumpur. As in other cave-dwelling creatures, the loss of pigment has affected its coloration; this subspecies is lighter than *E. t. taeniura*. This snake lives mainly on bats.

Daytime activity in many species is dependent both on the snake's age and on the season of the year. Thus the juveniles of many species are only rarely seen moving about in broad daylight while the adults will frequently be met away from their dens. And many snakes that are diurnally active during the spring and fall emerge from their hiding places only at night during the summer.

Light plays a significant role in the development of the eyes and especially of the shape of the pupils. The nocturnal cat snakes (*Boiga*), for example, have enlarged eyes as a result of adaptation to dim light. In burrowing species that live exclusively in dark places, the eyes have regressed completely in the course of time. Species active in the dusk and at night often have vertically elliptical pupils that can narrow to slits in bright light. Examples here are pythons, and boas, vipers (Viperidae), pit vipers (Crotalidae), and some colubrids (Colubridae). In some tree-dwelling genera like the Oriental vinesnakes (Ahaetulla) and African Bird snakes (Thelotornis) the pupils have become narrowed down into long, horizontal slits. Since in these species the skull tapers considerably toward the front, the eyes stand out slightly on the sides of the head. The pupils are wider at the back and narrow down toward the nose. Most likely these snakes have three-dimensional vision, since the optical waves emanating from a distant object would hit the retinas of both eyes and can be assembled into a single image by the brain. With increasing light the pupils contract like the shutter of a camera; some species, like *Elaphe flavirufa*, can narrow them down to tiny dots.

Precipitation, Humidity, and Soil Moisture

Water is also an important factor in the lives of snakes. A number of species occur only in or near lakes, swamps, streams, rivers, or other wet areas. Sea snakes live primarily in tropical oceans. Some species occasionally leave the water to bask in the sun or to deposit eggs, and they are generally quite adept at moving on land. The humid and hot tropical forests harbor snakes of the most varied sort. Species living on or near the ground have adapted to constant high air humidity while those that inhabit the tops of trees are exposed to fluctuations in humidity. Since many forests of

the tropics and subtropics contain bodies of water that rise above their banks in certain seasons and flood large areas, many snakes shift back and forth between terrestrial and aquatic life. This may be how anacondas (*Eunectes*) and water cobras (*Boulengerina*) have evolved into snakes of largely aquatic habits. The much feared Cottonmouth (*Agkistrodon piscivoris*) of the southern United States is found almost exclusively in or near water, as are a number of harmless water snakes.

The Java Wart snake (*Acrochordus javanicus*), a snake which inhabits fresh, brackish, and salt water in the coastal areas of the Indoaustralian islands, is able to stay underwater for hours at a time without breathing. These amazing animals probably hardly ever leave the water unless they are forced to. Their skin, which is often covered with algae that grow on it, is rough and wartlike. Although some herpetologists classify wart snakes with the family of colubrids, their way of moving and general habits make them seem more akin to sea snakes from which they differ, however, in being harmless.

A change in air humidity and soil moisture brought on by rainfall often awakens a sudden urge to travel in terrestrial snakes and causes them to emerge in droves from their hiding places to which they have been confined by excessive heat and dryness. Some species have learned to adapt to living in regions that are extremely arid. These snakes hardly ever drink, obtaining enough liquid from the body fluids of their prey. Many of these snakes have very small nostrils to prevent evaporation and to protect them against fine flying sand. While some desert snakes depend on a very dry environment, other species can live in both wet and dry biotopes.

SNAKES AND HUMANS

SNAKES AND HUMANS

ANTIPATHY AND VENERATION

Ever since man's expulsion from paradise, man and snakes have been enemies. Satan, in the shape of a snake, led first Eve and then Adam to disobey God. And God said to the snake: "Because thou hast done this, thou art cursed above all cattle, and above every beast of the field; upon thy belly shalt thou go, and dust shalt thou eat all the days of thy life. And I will put enmity between thee and the woman, and between thy seed and her seed; it shall bruise thy head, and thou shalt bruise his heel."

But the Bible is not the only book to represent snakes as the prime symbol of evil. The writings of many non-Judeo-Christian peoples depict snakes in a similar light. And, in fact, there is hardly any animal that has suffered as much at the hands of people as the snake. With the possible exception of the crocodile no other reptile evokes as much fear and antipathy as the snake. If we persist in this attitude it is quite likely that snakes will some day disappear from the face of the earth. Many people would not care in the least if this happened.

However, in recent years these "outcasts of the animal world" have been judged a little more objectively than in the past. There is more of an attempt to get away from the old prejudices and accept snakes, like other animals, as nature has created them. The old rule "Kill any snake you run across"—which is unfortunately still adhered to all too often—is gradually giving way to the more tolerant attitude of "Leave them alone" or "Let them go."

Today's awareness that many animal species are on the point of being eradicated or in danger of extinction has resulted in a more rational attitude toward snakes. People are beginning to understand better how these animals function and to feel less of an impulse to kill them. The chances of survival for the snakes we have would be considerably improved if the habit of leaving them alone and letting them go were generally adopted.

USES AND ABUSES OF SNAKES

Quite a number of snake species have proven very useful to humans in combating the problem of rodents, especially rats and mice. This is the reason why in places like Brazil, Southeast Asia, and southern and western Africa the presence of boas and pythons in houses and storage places is considered desirable. It is also why all Indian states have recently curtailed the export of snakes.

Millions of snakes are killed every year so that their skins can be turned into unnecessary and very expensive fashion articles for which other materials could just as well be used. In some places snake meat is eaten, which is not altogether safe if one considers how often snakes are infested with parasitic worms that penetrate into the muscles as well as into body organs.

In the Production of Snake Antiserum

A large number of poisonous snakes are kept on snake farms and in research laboratories for the production of venom. A model institution of this sort is the Pentafarm in Basel, Germany where various species of *Bothrops* have been bred in captivity so that there is no longer any need to import these snakes. The venom is obtained by letting the snakes bite through a rubber membrane and collecting the colorless or greenish to orange venom in a glass vial. (But no layperson should attempt to collect snake venom.)

Snake venom is a mixture of different enzymes and represents a radically modified form of saliva. It is used by the pharmaceutical industry as an ingredient in expensive but highly effective medications. It finds another use in the production of snake serums. The venom is injected in minute and gradually increasing dosages into horses, cattle, or sheep. These mammals then develop antibodies in their blood against snake poison. The mammal's serum is then separated from the blood cells, purified and sold either in 10 cubic centimeter vials or as a powder that can be reconstituted in liquid form when needed. These snake serums are the only antidote against bites from highly poisonous snakes.

According to the World Health Association 30,000 to 40,000 people die annually as a consequence of snake bites. If one considers how many venomous snakes there are in some places of the world this number is really quite low. The danger of snake bites is often much exaggerated and bears little relation to reality. There is thus no need for excessive fear, and many sensational reports in the media turn out to be unfounded horror tales on closer examination.

In Circuses and Shows

Snakes have become popular in zoos and in the terrariums of private fanciers as well as in circuses and nightclub shows. The exhibited animals are usually boas or pythons. These snakes offer two advantages. They are non-poisonous and of impressive size. Snakes are by nature limited in their reactions and cannot be trained as easily as mammals. That is why the success of a "snake number" depends entirely on the personality of the tamer. He or she has to be intimately familiar with the snakes' reactions in order to convey to the audience the illusion that the snakes are active partners in the show. Only in rare cases are poisonous snakes trained for such performances and if they are, the animals' poisonous fangs are removed as a precaution. Nevertheless the author knows of a case that happened in a nightclub in Miami. A strip-tease dancer was bitten by a South African Cape Cobra (*Naja nivea*) in the course of a "snake dance." The woman refused to have a serum injection and died within a half hour.

Private keepers of snakes, too, are often tempted to throw caution to the winds when demonstrating their poisonous snakes, and they sometimes pay for this recklessness with their lives. One example of this is the story of Grace Olive Wiley, a well-known American keeper and "tamer" of snakes. Miss Wiley, a pleasant, rather small, older lady, tamed all her snakes and was especially fond of the poisonous ones, which thrived under her loving care and demonstrated their wellbeing by producing numerous offspring. Long and patient observation of her snakes' reactions was the key to her astonishing ability to pick up venomous snakes without any kind of protection. Miss Wiley was chronically short of money, and in order to buy some food for her pets she would show off her snakes for a fee. In 1948 a journalist came to see her. He wanted to write a feature about the legendary Grace O. Wiley. Grace displayed her snakes to her visitor and was bitten by a newly acquired King Cobra in the process. A few hours later she was dead.

Many an Oriental snake charmer has met a similar fate. Snake charmers commonly use Asian Cobras (*Naja naja*) or Egyptian Cobras (*N. haje*). Of course, for a few coins, some tricksters let their snakes dance with their venom fangs removed or with their mouths sewn shut, but true masters of this rare and remarkable art which, by the way, is passed on from father to son in India, let their animals dance in woven baskets. The snakes are left in their natural state and in full command of their powers. The snake charmer plays a melody on his flute and rocks back and forth rhythmically. The snake follows all the movements of its master with its eyes. Gradually it raises the upper third of its body and spreads the neck ribs, making the throat swell sideways like a pancake. The body sways back and forth in time to the melody, creating the impression that the snake is listening to the music. But this is not so. Snakes are unable to hear most sounds. The snake is simply following the movements of the presumed attacker with its eyes—the head moving along with the eyes—in order to be ready to defend itself by striking when necessary. In Burma women give similar performances with huge King Cobras (*Ophiophagus hannah*) that measure several yards. The climax of such a show, which becomes almost like a religious ritual, is often accentuated with a kiss on top of the cobra's head.

In many Oriental market places one can occasionally see contests between cobras and mongooses (*Herpestes edwardsi*). In most of these fights the mongoose wins because it is quicker than the cobra. After killing the snake it proceeds to eat it in front of the spectators. American roadside zoos generally feature live snakes including many poisonous kinds. Usually their teeth have been removed so that the attendants who handle the animals are not exposed to the danger of snake bite. Most often these snakes are not properly cared for and the hygienic conditions are abominable. It is no wonder that animals thus mistreated no longer show any interest in food and die slow and miserable deaths. These losses are then simply replaced with new snakes caught in the wild.

In Religious Ceremonies

Snakes still play an important role among North American Indians and not just as food. They are the object of religious veneration. One of the most famous rituals is the snake dance of the Hopi Indians which attracts many tourists to Arizona every year. These dances have a real ritualistic function. They are meant to ensure the goodwill of the rain gods, and plenty of rain is necessary for a good harvest. The snake dance, which lasts for nine days, is performed by two groups of priests—the "snake priests" and the "antelope priests." In the course of the first four days the rattlesnakes are caught and housed in underground cages where the priests guard them. In the next few days all kinds of ceremonies, including purifications and secret rituals, take place. The public is admitted on the eighth day. The actual dance is performed in the evening by the priests. They carry the snakes with dancing steps, touch them with their lips, take them in their mouths, and even hold them by the neck with their teeth. After the ritual is over the Indians carry the snakes off in the four directions of the winds and release them. Up to now no Hopi priest has yet been killed through the bite of a rattlesnake because, at least in some cases, the poisonous fangs as well as the reserve fangs are removed before the ceremonies.

Snakes are worshipped like gods not only by the American Indians but also among some tribes in Africa, Asia, and Australia. They are seen as symbols of cunning, wisdom, duplicity, seductiveness, and the power to heal. They can signal luck or bring disaster. They were revered in antiquity, and even today annual snake processions are held in some remote villages in central Italy.

In Crime

Snakes have also played a role in crime throughout the ages. Among many peoples poisonous snakes have been used to get rid of disagreeable individuals. In Africa, for instance, a highly poisonous mamba might be hidden in a room to which the victim was then lured, or some other means of contact between the two would be devised.

It is clear that human beings have used—and abused—snakes for their own purposes in all kinds of ways. Responsible keepers of reptiles should therefore always remember that snakes, too, are creatures of nature and not objects which humans can use as they see fit.

PURCHASING OR CATCHING SNAKES

Particularly in recent years the trade in live snakes for terrariums has become a lucrative business. Pet dealers mail price lists to potential customers almost every month, and the selection of different species is often surprisingly large. Prices tend to be inflated, and the cost of shipping is always charged to the receiver who also assumes the risk of damage during transport. Sick animals can almost never be returned, and even if the snakes are dead on arrival there is usually only partial reimbursement.

Sometimes it happens that a dealer has too large an inventory of reptiles and amphibians so that he or she simply cannot take care of them properly. This inevitably means the natural needs of the animals are sacrificed. If there is a shortage of space the containers are hopelessly overcrowded with snakes of all species from every corner of the world. The drinking water is contaminated with decomposing excreta. The air stinks and is full of disease-carrying microorganisms. The temperature is either too high or too low. Often there is no lighting at all. Dead animals are sometimes overlooked and start to decay. Such a state represents cruelty to animals. Luckily the picture is not this grim everywhere. Nevertheless the author has repeatedly witnessed such scenes at various dealers. It is hardly surprising that snakes that have been kept under such conditions are sick when they are sent out. Customers usually order by mail or by telephone, and they have no chance to look over the snakes they are about to buy.

In my twenty-seven years of experience in this area I have collected a fair amount of evidence. About 25 % of the animals mailed to me were in excellent condition; the rest were more or less sick. Some of the snakes had mouth rot or other infections were evident from their wide-open mouths. Others had intestinal infections caused by bacteria or amoebas, and died after a short time. Many suffered from skin diseases or mites. Infestation of the alimentary canal with parasitic worms was frequent. In the case of dead animals, I often found worms in the muscles, the liver, and the kidneys, as well as in all the other organs.

These are the reasons why it is a very good idea to visit the premises of a pet dealer if one is planning to buy a snake or any other reptile or amphibian.

Another way to acquire snakes is to catch them oneself, but this is often an extremely expensive as well as difficult enterprise, especially if one has one's heart set on species that live in faraway countries. In recent years, too, the export of reptiles and amphibians from a number of non-European countries has been made illegal by the Washington Convention. The collector therefore first has to obtain permission from the appropriate officials of the country in question before he or she can embark on a venture. Finding snakes is often not so easy if one is not totally familiar with just where a given species is likely to occur. There is also a certain risk involved in catching large, fast-moving elapids, and no one lacking the appropriate experience should attempt it.

Small, nonvenomous snakes can be seized with the hand without any danger. Thick leather gloves are useful for catching larger nonvenomous snakes and small venomous ones. For large venomous snakes, such as large vipers and rattlesnakes, one needs a sturdy metal snake hook with a long handle. The snake hook is U-shaped at the end and is slid under the snake. Then the animal is lifted up and allowed to slide into a cloth bag of appropriate size. The bag, which should be held by a second person, hangs from a metal hanger that also has a handle. Then the bag is tied securely. For catching quick-moving colubrids a 6-foot (1.8 m) square rod with a very sturdy leather thong at the end is used. The leather thong, which should be at least 6½ feet (2 m) long, is thrown like a lasso over the snake's head and is then tightened very gently. The numbers of most reptiles and amphibians are rapidly shrinking primarily because of the destruction of habitat, and we should limit our catches to a very few specimens.

Although buying snakes is much simpler, catching them in the wild has the great advantage that we can be almost certain of obtaining healthy animals. Once the snakes are caught they are placed in absolutely clean and tight cloth bags from which there is no way of escape. For travel these bags are put in solid wooden or styrofoam boxes which will keep the animals insulated against sudden rises or drops in temperature.

SNAKES AND ENVIRONMENTAL PROTECTION

The progress of civilization and the attendant changes in the environment have a great impact on the animal world and make more and more inroads on it. Amphibians and reptiles are especially hard hit. In recent years snake populations all over the world have shrunk. The reasons for this decline must in almost all cases be chalked up to humans. Many large snakes are hunted primarily for their skins. The profit-hungry reptile-leather industry and its clientele that continues to provide a market for luxury items made of snake skin, together with the pet trade, are mainly responsible for the declimation of large snake species. Many smaller snake species have been brought to the point of extinction by the reduction of habitat, irresponsible collection, and the widespread use of pesticides. They have become rare or have disappeared altogether in large parts of their former ranges. But it is amazing with what tenacity some snakes cling to existence and defend themselves against the spreading influence of man. Those species that need large, undisturbed tracts of land for survival show the greatest negative effects when people invade their territory.

Because many species of animals, quite a few of which used to be abundant, have become extinct or are threatened with extinction, an international agreement to protect endangered species was signed on March 3, 1973, in Washington, D.C. This agreement with the official title "Washington Convention on International Trade in Endangered Species of Wild Fauna and Flora" has since been supplemented by two appendices. Species listed in Appendix I are fully protected and may be traded only in exceptional cases and with special permission.

The following snakes fall under the rules of Appendix I: *Epicrates inornatus inornatus, E. subflavus,* and *Python molurus molurus. Species listed in Appendix II may be bought or sold if an official permit from the country of origin is presented.* Appendix II applies to the following species: *Epicrates cenchria cenchria, Boa constrictor constrictor, Eunectes notaens,* all the *Python* species not listed in Appendix I, *Cyclagras gigas, Clelia clelia, Elachistodon westermanni,* and *Thamnophis elegans hammondi* or, more properly, *T. couchi hammondi* (author's emendation). Some countries have already drawn up a third appendix that establishes protection for some snakes that occur within their boundaries.

KEEPING AND CARING
FOR SNAKES

HOUSING AND GENERAL CARE

SETTING UP A SNAKE TERRARIUM

A terrarium for snakes should meet all the needs of its occupants. It should be built very solidly and not have any holes or cracks through which the animals could possibly escape. In order to keep unauthorized persons out, any door to the terrarium should be equipped with a lock. There are containers on the market that are quite suitable for housing snakes though not every terrarium you will see is adequate for this purpose.

Reptiles and snakes should be housed only in square or rectangular containers. Any other shape, such as round or triangular, is inappropriate and should not be considered. If you are handy with tools you can build a terrarium yourself without great difficulty and at considerably less cost. Since a number of other publications contain instructions on how to build your own terrarium, I shall not cover this topic here. Any fair-sized terrarium should be equipped with a sturdy but not wide metal frame that has to be protected against rust with a coat of enamel paint. The wooden frames that used to be standard in earlier times are not as practical because they are more subject to damage by moisture and warp easily. For the bottom and the back panel it is best to use a synthetic material that will not rust and is resistant to moisture and temperature fluctuations. Large glass areas should be incorporated into the terrarium so that its occupants get plenty of light, especially daylight. The animals benefit from several hours of sunlight every day.

Ventilation

The air in the terrarium should always be fresh and odorless. The prerequisites for this are painstaking cleanliness, adequate size of the terrarium, and above all good ventilation.

For the ventilation of large terrariums rust-free wire mesh is recommended. Mesh of various sizes and grades is available at hardware stores. Only the best quality products should be used. For smaller terrariums, nylon mesh is adequate. If all four sides of a terrarium consist of glass or some synthetic material and are thus airtight, wire or nylon mesh has to be used for the entire top to insure proper ventilation. If the top is covered partially or entirely with glass, both sides have to have ventilation panels of mesh or perforated metal making up one quarter to one half of the terrarium height.

Size

Of what size and proportions should a terrarium for snakes be? There is no simple answer to this question. It depends entirely on the size and needs of the occupants. Many snakes move very little and therefore have only modest space requirements. Snakes 3 to 5 feet (100-150 cm) long will do very well in a terrarium measuring 40 × 32 × 24 inches (100 × 80 × 60 cm). Smaller snakes measuring from 16 to 32 inches (40-80 cm) can be kept without problems in a space of 20 × 16 × 12 inches (50 × 40 × 30 cm). Large and very solid terrariums with thick glass walls about 3/8 inch (8-10 mm), are required for giant serpents. A container of 8 × 5 × 5 feet (2.5 × 1.5 × 1.5 m) is adequate for an Indian Python measuring 10 feet (3 m). But these are only general guidelines based on my own experience and can be adjusted up or down. Deciding the exact dimensions of your terrarium is largely up to you. Strangely enough there is some evidence that snakes often eat and thrive better in small terrariums than in larger ones.

Heating

In order for the substrate in part of the terrarium to have the right temperature, a bottom heater is required. The commercially available heating cables that are encased on lead or plastic serve quite well for this purpose. Heating cables of different wattage are sold. For a medium-sized container, 15 to 30 watts are appropriate. If you have snakes that like to burrow it is a good idea to cement the cable into the bottom. The cable warms the surrounding area gently and evenly. It is also possible to connect the heating cable to a thermostat. This insures that the temperature will never rise too high. If a terrarium is not too large, has a glass bottom, and if the bottom material is not too deep or consists merely of a layer of disposable paper, then the heating cable can be placed under rather than inside the terrarium. If you choose this method the terrarium should stand on four styrofoam strips about 3/4 inch (2 cm) thick in such a way that a tight air chamber is created by the strips between the terrariums support and its floor. A heating cable of 15 to 30 watts, depending on the size of the container, is then placed inside this chamber. The warm air in the heating chamber will stay trapped there and spread gradually and evenly to the glass bottom and through its covering. I have successfully employed this method of heating in four terrariums standing side by side on a shelf on the wall. Similar heating chambers that warm the air can be constructed inside terrariums, too. Or a heating pad can be used to similar effect, warming a certain area of the terrarium slightly. For a number of snakes from subtropical and tropical regions where the temperature is largely static, no bottom heat is necessary if the room temperature remains fairly constant between 75° and 86°F (24°-30°C) both day and night.

Light

Light is important for the wellbeing of snakes, though not as crucial as warmth. Direct sunlight is best, but acting on this principle and using the sun as a primary light source is not practicable for more indoor terrariums. Placing the snakes close to windows is almost always beneficial. However, you have to make sure that the animals always have enough hiding places so that they can avoid overexposure to sun and light. Snakes need very little ultraviolet light, which plays an important role in the production of vitamin D in the body. Possible artificial sources of light that also give off more or less heat are incandescent bulbs, and ultravoilet lights. For smaller terrariums the so-called "growth-lights" that are used by aquarists are also suitable. In addition to the light sources mentioned, it is advisable to make use of fluorescent lights which not only conserve energy but also resemble natural daylight most closely. I have had very good success with fluorescent tubes of such brands as Osram-L warm tone, Sylvania, Gro-Lux, and Osram-Fluora. (Osram-Fluora has the additional benefit of giving off ultraviolet rays.) Depending on the time of year, the lights should be on 10 to 14 hours a day. An automatic timer can regulate both heater and lighting.

Bottom Material

Other items you may need for setting up your terrarium are some kind of litter or bottom material, stones, pieces of rock, tree limbs or small tree stumps, roots, tree bark, and tubes of decorative cork.

The simplest covering for the bottom is newspaper or paper towel. A terrarium lined this way does not look particularly attractive, but it is very hygienic because potentially harmful bacteria have little chance to develop on the dry paper. Old, dirty paper can easily be replaced in a few minutes. The slightly damp bottom can be wiped and if necessary—as when there are sick snakes in the terrarium—be sterilized. Unlike humans, snakes are indifferent to the aesthetic aspects of their surroundings. Their health and comfort depend much more on the cleanness of their quarters and on proper temperatures. In quarantine terrariums, where cleanliness is so important, I prefer paper lining and cardboard snake boxes.

If you decide against paper you can choose from a number of different bottom materials depending on the snake species you are keeping. Possible materials are sand, gravel, a mixture of sand and forest soil or peat, forest soil mixed with plenty of bark and dry leaves, loam, or vermiculite. Each material has its advantages and drawbacks in terms of appearance, ability to absorb feces, urine, and other moisture. To prevent bacterial decomposition, areas where excrement has been deposited must be cleaned up promptly.

Stones and rocks can be piled in such a way as to provide necessary hiding places. It makes sense to cement these stones firmly together because snakes that burrow can upset piles of loose rocks. Spaces under branches, tree bark, and logs, as well as tubes of cork also make good refuges. Arboreal snakes need climbing trees. They often seek out the crotches of tree limbs to rest in.

Plants

Plants can also offer hiding places to the occupants of a terrarium. Plants help give the terrarium a natural and attractive appearance and make it look less like a cage. Many plants need conditions that cannot be met in a terrarium, but quite a few house plants thrive there and may last for years if properly looked after. It is best to pot them in large plastic pots that prevent rapid evaporation of the moisture in the soil. Ornamental use can be made of bark and stones to disguise the rims of the pots.

Some examples of suitable plants for a terrarium with snakes caught in the area and snakes from temperate regions are English ivy (*Hedera helix*), blackberry (*Rubus fruticosus*), rasperry (*R. idaeus*), or juniper (*Juniperus communis*). In a desert terrarium, succulents such as sansevieria (e.g., *S. trifasciata*), small agaves (e.g., *A. verschaffeltii*), euphorbia (e.g., *E. resinifera*), or aloes (e.g., *A. brevifolia* or *A. striata*) can be incorporated. Various kinds of cacti also belong in a desert terrarium. For a heated, humid terrarium the best plants are rubber trees (*Ficus elastrica*), philodendrons (*P. erubescens* or *P. scandens*), split-leaf philodendron (*Monstera deliciosa*), various kinds of palms, many bromeliads, and other epiphytes. These are just a few examples

of the great many plants from all parts of the earth than can be planted in terrariums. If a terrarium is set up properly with the right kinds of plants and animals it can look just as much like a small corner of nature as a well-planted aquarium. But a terrarium with large, heavy snakes should not contain plants because they would soon get crushed by the weight of the animals.

Other Needs

Every terrarium has to have a dish with water that is always fresh. Aquatic snakes need a fairly sizable container of water where they will often spend hours or even days. And no terrarium should be without a thermometer and hygrometer so that you can always check humidity and temperature. These two devices can be mounted on a side wall. You will also need to spray water into the terrarium, and for this a plant sprayer of plastic or metal can be used.

For removing the snakes' excreta you should have a separate, long-handled spoon for each container.

To feed your snakes live or dead prey you will need tongs at least 12 inches (30 cm) long.

A SNAKE BOX

Most snakes like to spend some time now and then in small dark retreats. You can take advantage of this propensity of snakes if you have a snake box, a small temporary home for your snake. The snake box also provides you with a place for your snake when you need to clean the terrarium. Water has to be changed frequently in a terrarium and droppings removed, and the immediate presence of the snakes when performing these and other chores is often not only a hindrance but sometimes a positive danger. It is reassuring to know that your snakes are in their box when you have to do any work in the terrarium.

A snake box is simply a square wooden box with a removable top. Being able to take off the top makes cleaning the inside of the box easy and quick. The front of the box has a hole through which the snakes enter and which can be shut with a board on runners. Such a snake box can be attached either inside the terrarium or outside. If it is outside the terrarium, it does not interfere with the visual appearance of the terrarium. But you have to take precautions that nobody can open the box and give the snakes a chance to escape. A snake box inside the terrarium can be camouflaged with rocks and bark. Of course, you then have a problem when both the terrarium and the box need cleaning at the same time.

GENERAL CARE

Once the terrarium is all set up and the snakes are acclimated it takes only a few minutes a day to keep everything in good shape. Excrement has to be removed promptly, and there always has to be fresh water in the water dishes. Check temperature and air humidity every day, and make sure the lighting and bottom heater are functioning properly. When the time of molting approaches, the snakes should be sprayed with water more often than usual. The plants also need regular watering.

Providing Proper Temperature and Light Conditions

Since the body processes of a snake function properly only in a specific range of temperature, the temperature in the terrarium has to be set at a level that corresponds to the needs of the occupants. Consistently wrong temperatures—whether too high or too low—harm the animals; they either refuse to eat or they regurgitate partially digested food. Proper digestion and passage of food through the intestines takes place only within a certain range of temperature. If the temperature is too low—and if it is too high as well—snakes generally come down with infections of the respiratory system; they are also unable to reproduce under these conditions.

Most snakes are active when the temperature is between 59° and 90°F (15°-32°C). Within this range, all physical functions increase as the temperature increases. As it gets cooler, the activities slow down. At the low end the critical temperature is just below freezing; at the upper end, it is around 105°F (40°C). Snakes do not have sweat glands, and unlike most mammals they are unable to respond to excessively high external temperatures physiologically by sweating or panting, and thus regulate their own body temperature. Although the preferred temperature of many snakes is very close to the upper limit of what their bodies can stand, few species can live permanently in temperatures much above 90°F (32°C) without harm.

Snakes like to spend their time lying in the morning or afternoon sun or under a heat lamp or on a slightly heated surface. When their bodies heat up beyond a genetically programmed optimum temperature they retreat into the shade of a hiding place. For nocturnally active species, the favored temperature is generally somewhat lower than for diurnally active ones. The same is often true for snakes of subtropical or tropical regions that live in the mountains at higher altitudes. Such "cool-forms" feel comfortable at 65° to 75°F (18°-24°C); if their terrarium is warmer than 77°F (25°C), they languish and die prematurely.

What are the ideal temperatures to keep snakes healthy and encourage them to reproduce? The answer to this question depends on the geographic distribution, the altitude, the habitat, and the special microclimate in which the species in question is found.

Since in tropical areas the temperature is by and large constant, most snakes that live there are active all year round. Such snakes that are used to constant high temperatures are kept all year at 77° to 86°F (25°-30°C) with only minor fluctuations. It would be a mistake to offer them hibernating conditions.

Snakes from temperate zones and subtropical areas require daytime temperatures between 68° and 86°F (20°-30°C) during their active period. This active period usually lasts from March to November, but with this kind of snake only a limited area of the terrarium floor should be warmed slightly above the temperature in the rest of the terrarium. Continual overheating is harmful because these animals' preferred temperature is already quite high and is good for them only for short periods. The snakes always have to be able to seek out or to leave the heated area. Depending on the snakes' place of origin the terrarium temperature is set higher or lower. At night it has to be a few degrees cooler to keep the snakes in top condition by imitating the natural temperature fluctuations.

How long the lights should be on in the terrarium depends on the time of year. If the terrarium is located in a dark place, 10 to 14 hours of artificial light are in order in the summer; in the spring and fall 6 to 8 hours, depending on the month, are adequate.

Providing Water and Proper Humidity

As I have already mentioned, the water container should always be full of absolutely clean fresh water which must not be too cool. On warm days the terrarium should be sprayed with water once or twice because most reptiles live in habitats with high air humidity. It is also quite common that not all snakes satisfy their thirst by drinking water from a dish. Many absorb only the drops of water dripping from leaves and rocks after a thorough drenching with the spray bottle. Needless to say, the plants, too, need regular watering and spraying. It is best to use soft water for this because otherwise the water can leave ugly calcium stains on the leaves.

WINTERING OVER

In the fall snakes from the temperate regions and from Mediterranean countries seem to be filled with an inner restlessness that makes them crawl around ceaselessly. The animals stop eating and pay no attention to their usual hiding places. These are signs that the snakes

are getting ready to hibernate. Before the snakes are allowed to settle into their winter sleep it is important to make sure that they have emptied their bowels. If there are any rotting remains left in the intestines they can cause harm or even death to the snake during hibernation. Lower the temperature in the terrarium, but do not do it abruptly. Reduce it gradually over the course of a week. If you have an entire room that is reserved for your snakes, open the windows wide in the fall. Install a sturdy screen in front of the window opening as protection against intruding animals. Then the cold air can flow in and create temperature conditions resembling those of the outdoors. This method has the advantage that the snakes can stay in their usual quarters and do not have to adjust to the new surroundings and different conditions of a wintering-over box.

Depending on the kind of the snakes you keep, the bottom material in the hibernating container is kept dry or moderately damp. Some snakes need fairly dry soil and high air humidity while others prefer high moisture in soil and air. The terrarium or other container in which the snakes are wintering over should be checked two or three times a week and sprayed with water if the bottom has dried out too much. There should be plenty of dry leaves, moss, and sheets of bark so that the snakes have a chance to hide. The water dishes in the hibernating container always have to be full of fresh water.

The hibernating quarters of many European and North American snakes as well as those from northern and central Asia may drop in temperature to almost freezing. Healthy juvenile snakes survive such low temperatures just as well as adult animals, but it is best not to let weakened animals hibernate because they usually die.

Depending on their area of distribution, snakes from central Europe, North America, and central Asia should be kept at a steady temperature between 36° to 59°F (2°-15°C) for four to five months during the winter. Hibernation lasts from late October or early November to late March or early April. For snakes from the southern parts of Europe and North America, from northern Africa and other areas with similar climates, wintering-over temperatures between 50° and 59°F (10°-15°C) are appropriate, and hibernation should last three to four months, from about mid-November to mid-March. You should be careful never to let the temperature in the hibernating container rise above 59°F (15°C) in order not to stimulate the much reduced metabolism of the snakes unnecessarily at the wrong time. Snakes are not always in a state of total immobility while they hibernate. They occasionally move about slowly and look for better retreats. The container should always be kept dark to let the snakes settle down.

Snakes can be successfully wintered over in plastic containers in a refrigerator that is used exclusively for this purpose. The plastic containers are partially filled with soil, moss, dry leaves, and bark, and they have to have several air holes. Here, too, the snakes need a dish with water and the amount of air humidity they are used to. You can regulate the temperature in the refrigerator so that it resembles natural winter conditions, and the refrigerator also offers the necessary darkness. Open the refrigerator door every second or third day for a short time to air the inside.

When spring approaches the snakes are gradually roused from their sleep. Light is restored, and the surrounding temperature gradually raised. During the first few days the heater and the lighting are turned on only for a few hours. This period is extended a little day by day. After eight to ten days the lighting and heating schedule will be up to normal.

Generally snakes slough their skins for the first time in the spring one to three weeks after they emerge from hibernation. By that time they have absorbed enough liquid and completely emptied their bowels. Female snakes start eating again soon after this, but males often do not take any food until after mating. Amphibians and reptiles from temperate regions will reproduce successfully only if they have been allowed to hibernate in cold temperatures and dark surroundings. Sperm cells and egg cells can only mature if they have been exposed for a while to low temperatures. Living in warm surroundings all year round imposes sterility on many kinds of snakes.

FOOD AND FEEDING

WHAT KIND OF FOOD?

Snakes do not eat plants; they live on animals. Their natural prey is small mammals, birds, reptiles, amphibians, fish, and various kinds of invertebrates. Some highly specialized species live on eggs or snails. Some eat only mammals or only birds. Others are used to a wide range of different prey including all sorts of vertebrates as well as invertebrates. There are even snakes that like raw beef and some will eat canned sardines. In the case of most snakes that feed on mammals, procuring food for them presents no great problem. Mice and rats can usually be obtained for little money or are sometimes given away free by laboratories. Or you can decide to raise your own rabbits, guinea pigs, rats, mice, or hamsters and will then have available food animals of whatever size for your snakes whenever you need them.

Field mice are particularly popular with snakes because of their smell and because they dart around quickly. They can often be found in considerable numbers along the edges of fields and meadows and in the woods as well as in other places. They are easy to catch either alive or dead with traps you can purchase.

It is better to stay away from black rats and Norway rats because they may carry dangerous disease-causing agents that can be transmitted to both humans and snakes. Old laying hens and male baby chicks usually cost very little at poultry farms. Fish can sometimes be bought from a hobby fisherman or, if you want larger amounts, from a commercial fisherman or from a fish market. Snakes that eat amphibians accept aquatic and terrestrial frogs, toads, and newts as well as their larvae. Catch only as many frogs as you need at any given time. It would be even better, in the interests of protecting wildlife, to go out after a night's rain to a road that is often crossed by amphibians and collect all the frogs and toads that have been run over. Lizards should be used as snake food only if a snake cannot be induced to accept any other prey animals. Do not in any case go out and catch indigenous northern lizards because their habitat is shrinking and some species are getting rarer and rarer. Use lizards from southern Europe or Florida instead, where some species are still quite plentiful. Pet dealers usually carry lizards and snakes intended for snake feed. Almost all snakes will get used to dead meat. Leftovers as well as stockpiles of the prey animals mentioned can be stored for months in a freezer and then thawed and fed to the snakes as needed.

FEEDING

Snakes react in different ways to being fed. Some accept live or dead prey immediately after having been purchased while others go on a hunger strike that may last days, weeks, or even months and in some exceptional cases over a year. One snake will eat only live mice while another of the same species will consume only dead ones. There are snakes which refuse to eat white mice or rats but accept normally colored mice. As already mentioned, field mice are preferred by all snakes because they move so quickly and have a pleasant earth smell. Quite a lot of snakes will eat several prey animals one right after the other at one feeding, but some will consume only one for a meal. The time of day also affects how snakes react to food. The best feeding time is late afternoon or early evening. In fact, there are some snakes that refuse food during the day and eat only in the evening.

Some snakes are inhibited by the presence in the terrarium of other snakes of their own or of another species and fast for this reason. If such a snake is placed in isolation it will accept food the very next day.

Many kinds of snakes have seasonal fasting periods during which they cannot be induced to eat as usual in any way. This is true particularly before hibernation. Keepers of snakes have to accept these suspensions of food intake as an unalterable fact of nature. Male snakes often reject all food during the mating season, and females do so during gestation. Another time when snakes often refuse food is just before shedding their old skins.

If you feed several snakes in the same terrarium you always have to watch carefully that two or three snakes do not go after the same prey. If this happens, their heads may collide and then the strongest snake will often proceed to eat not only the prey animal but also the other snake. I have lost a number of valuable snakes this way because of insufficient vigilance. In captivity, individual snakes of many species that normally do not eat snakes may become cannibalistic. Keeping several snakes in one container is never advisable. The smaller ones often lose out at a feeding and languish if they are not moved to another container in time. These snakes then have to be paid special attention and fed small to medium-sized prey which is easier on the digestive system and is digested better and faster than larger prey.

In spite of a caretaker's best efforts some snakes simply will not take to any customary food. Sometimes you discover by chance that a specific snake has specialized exclusively on one certain prey animal that is not normally part of that species' food at all. It is also quite mysterious why some snakes will go on a hunger strike in a terrarium that is perfectly set up and start eating almost instantly after being moved to another container offering identical conditions of heat, light, and hygiene. One lesson of experience is that snakes often do better and eat more readily in smaller containers.

Food from a freezer must be thawed and allowed to reach the snake's body temperature before it is offered. The thawed mouse or rat or other prey is then picked up with long tongs and always placed in exactly the same spot in the terrarium.

How often should you feed your snakes? The answer depends on the age and size of the snakes and on how well-fed they are. Baby snakes should be fed at least once a week; juvenile ones, every ten days to two weeks; and fully grown ones, every three to four weeks. At every third or fourth feeding, one or two drops of a multivitamin should be added. This can be smeared over the prey animal or injected into it.

Snakes should not eat too often and not too much at one time. They move about less in captivity than they do in the wild and therefore do not use up the food as fast. Also, mice and rats that have been bred in laboratories are much fatter than small mammals found in nature. Too much food leads to a fattening of important organs in the snake's body and shortens the animal's life span. Overfed snakes show less interest in mating and are therefore less promising for raising snakes. Snakes that are healthy and have adjusted to life in captivity come up to the opened door as soon as you pick up the tongs to hold the prey animal. Habit has taught them in the course of time to expect food to turn up in this way. They eagerly get hold of the prey animal and wolf it down quickly.

Depending on the size of the snake and of the meals, the entire process of digestion normally lasts from two to ten days in optimal temperatures. You can easily tell how long it takes by watching for the excretion of the remains. Snakes that have just eaten are especially sensitive to temperature fluctuations. They should be left in peace during this time. Disturbances or temperatures that are too high or too low can lead a snake to regurgitate an undigested or only partially digested meal.

FORCE-FEEDING

Snakes that are healthy and hungry usually consume the offered food right away. However, a change in routine, the wrong temperature or humidity, or other negative factors can cause a prolonged refusal of food. Once mistakes are remedied and flaws in the set-up removed the snakes' interest in food usually revives.

Sick animals lack appetite. The problem is more complex if snakes that appear perfectly healthy and are kept under ideal conditions fast or refuse food for an exceptionally long time, lose weight, and begin to show slack skin on their sides because the fat tissue is disappearing. In such a case the organism's resistance is lowered, and it is time to do something about the situation. It is time to start force-feeding.

To force-feed you remove the snake from the container and lay it on a foam rubber mat or some other soft surface and press the head down with your hand. Smaller snakes that do not resist too much can also be held between thumb, fore-, and middle finger. Then you take blunt tweezers, a tongue depressor, or probe, and gently open the snake's mouth, and push a small prey animal or a piece of heart down the gullet. Before actually administering the food, make it slippery with some egg white or lukewarm water. Once the food is far enough down in the snake's gullet, the automatic swallowing reaction will take over.

If you use mice for force-feeding you should first peel the skin off down to the legs. They go down even more easily if they are then dunked into some egg white. You should always remove the incisors of a dead mouse before feeding it because these teeth as well as the dry fur can damage the snake's esophagus and other internal organs. A very humane method of force-feeding is to make a runny mixture of egg yolk and finely chopped meat and administer it through a rubber feeding tube (available in various sizes at drug stores) that is attached to a syringe. The lubricated rubber tube is inserted into the snake's throat, and the liquid food, fortified with vitamins A, B, C, D, and E, is passed painlessly into the snake's body—but give only small amounts at one time even with this method. If the force-fed snake digests the food properly and gains weight, it will in most cases start eating again of its own volition. Newborn snakes must never be force-fed before their first molt. If they do not start eating on their own after that they should be offered a piece of heart or fish or a newborn pink mouse.

BREEDING AND RAISING SNAKES

Most common aquarium fishes are bred regularly and without difficulty. This is not always the case with snakes and other reptiles. Sometimes the problem is finding a proper mate, but most breeding fiascos are the result of long-term incorrect care and conditions. Snakes that are too fat practically never reproduce; higher than necessary temperatures all year round inevitably lead to infertility; and temperate climate snakes that have not been allowed to hibernate show little or no interest in mating in the spring. Even disregarding the annual microclimatic fluctuations of a snake's natural habitat can affect the animal's reproductive behavior negatively.

DETERMINING A SNAKE'S SEX

It is not always easy to determine a snake's sex. In males the distance between the tip of the tail and the cloaca is proportionately longer than in females. But this difference in many cases is not so obvious that one can always unequivocally deduce the sex of a snake. A fairly reliable method of telling a snake's sex is possible with the help of a metal probe that is inserted into the paired openings at the posterior end of the cloaca. Probes of non-rusting metal used for this purpose are sold in stores specializing in medical supplies. These probes have blunt, rounded tips, and before they are inserted they must be lubricated with glycerine. This examination should be undertaken only with the greatest of care and gentleness in order not to hurt the snake. One person holds the snake and stretches its lower end so that it cannot move. A second person introduces the probe into one of the paired openings. In males the probe will penetrate a

couple to several inches and reach deep into the pocket of the hemipenes. In females it will not go deeper than 1/4 to 3/8 inch (1/2-1 cm). This method of sexing snakes is quite foolproof, but it should be attempted only by experts.

In many snake species there are distinct external sex differences with the males often having different coloration from the females. In some species the males are consistently larger than the females, and in some species the opposite is the case. Male pythons and boas have elongated anal spurs on both sides of the cloaca.

MATING

Snakes that are kept singly under proper conditions for an extended period of time show an increased eagerness to mate when they are placed with a partner of the opposite sex at the right time of year. Quite often the desired mating will take place within hours or days. I have seen two cases when a pair of Gray-banded Kingsnakes (*Lampropeltis mexicana*) began to mate five minutes after they were introduced to each other. Prospects are especially favorable if the pair is brought together shortly before the female is due to molt. Copulation then usually takes place shortly after the female has shed her old skin.

Healthy snakes that are kept in accordance with their natural needs are capable of producing offspring every year. A few weeks after mating you will usually notice that the females stop eating. This generally indicates that they are pregnant. It is often advisable to remove the gravid female to a separate container that is especially set up for this purpose. Of course, the environmental conditions in these new quarters have to be as optimal as possible.

The gestation period varies, depending on the species, from several weeks to several months.

If the segregated snake is of a live-bearing species, it is best to catch the mother after the young have been born and move her back to her regular terrarium. The young snakes molt either immediately after birth or a few days later, depending on the species. They usually eat for the first time soon after. They should be given only small prey animals suitable for the snake in question.

INCUBATION

In the case of an egg-laying female, some day you will discover a clump of eggs all stuck together, usually in a damp spot in the terrarium. Loosen this clutch of eggs very gently and move it to a special container. Be very careful in handling the eggs. Never turn the eggs but place them in the new substrate in the same position you found them in. Otherwise the relative position of the blastodisk to the yolk and the egg shell may be changed, which may harm or kill the embryo. Clay flower pots or glass containers are used as incubation chambers with largely constant temperature and humidity. Fill the pot or container with a moderately damp substrate made up of vermiculite, a mixture of peat and sand, composted leaves, or sterile foam material. Then place the eggs in this substrate, but do not cover them completely. Cover the top with a sheet of plastic screening and put a pane of glass on top of that. The narrow crack caused by the plastic between the pot and the glass allows sufficient entry of oxygen, and the air can circulate without a drop in humidity. The container is then placed on a brick in an aquarium. About three fourths of the brick should be submerged in the aquarium water, which is kept at an even temperature with the aid of an aquarium heater and a thermostat. The aquarium should be covered with a glass lid but has to have vents on the sides so that fresh air can enter.

A simple and safe method of incubation is to put the snake eggs in a transparent plastic container somewhat larger than the clutch with a cover into which you have punched many holes with a hot nail. I always pack the eggs in vermiculite since this material has proved ideal in every respect. It is almost completely sterile, and the individual particles are of varying size so that air can circulate and yet the moisture is retained. I never bury the eggs completely in the substrate so that I can check more easily on the clutch. I place a piece of clean blotting paper over the eggs. The blotting paper should be changed occasionally. The substrate should stay slightly damp, and I spray the blotting paper with lukewarm water (77°-86°F [25°-30°C]) whenever it dries out. Usually I place the plastic container with the snake eggs on top of a large terrarium or some other place where the temperature remains between 68° and 86°F (20°-30°C). I regard this method as the easiest and safest, and checking the eggs is simple. The perforated cover ensures sufficient air movement at constant temperatures.

Length of incubation depends primarily on the temperature and the dampness of the environment. The optimum incubation temperature for most snake species lies between 77° and 86°F (25°-30°C); in a few isolated cases it is between 68° and 77°F (20°-25°C).

Toward the end of the incubating period the eggs become wrinkled and unsightly. If the time passes when the eggs are expected to hatch and nothing happens it may be because the baby snakes are unable to push through the leathery egg skin from the inside. In that case you should score the skin for a few millimeters parallel with the longitudinal axis using a scalpel or a sterilized razor blade. Such a slit may save the baby snake from death by suffocation, and it facilitates the hatching in many cases. The first sign of a normal hatching is the appearance of one or several longitudinal tears in the egg's skin. Soon the baby snake will poke its head through one of these but will pull back immediately at the slightest activity nearby. The entire hatching may take from several hours to a few days.

CARE OF HATCHLINGS

To keep tabs on the newly hatched snakes, transfer them to a small terrarium set up especially for them and where optimum conditions should reign. The young snakes will independently eat for the first time after a few days or weeks, usually after their first molt. If the young snakes show no interest in food eventually they should be force-fed. Depending on the food habits of the species, give them newborn mice, small frogs, fish, pieces of fish, or strips of beef heart.

INFERTILE EGGS

Eggs that are infertile or contain an embryo that has died mold quickly and get hard. To keep the mold from spreading to the entire clutch, the bad eggs should be removed promptly. Although mold can form on eggs with live embryos this is never a good sign; the snakes hatching from such eggs often have malformations. Usually the spine is twisted or deformed. Less commonly, snakes are born with two heads. The author has seen this in a Sand Viper (*Vipera ammodytes*) and a Grass Snake (*Natrix natrix*). In his book *Snakes,* F. W. Fitzsimons tells of a double-headed African Red-Lipped Snake (*Crotaphopeltis hotamboeia*) that stayed alive for a full year in the Port Elisabeth Snake Park in South Africa and ate with both heads. The food from both mouths passed through a single stomach, and when one head got hold of a frog the other would try to grab and swallow the same prey. Usually such grotesque creatures do not live long, but a two-headed Kingsnake (*Lampropeltis getulus*) was kept at the San Diego zoo for many years.

Breeding snakes in captivity will become more and more crucial as time goes on because, due to the ever increasing changes in the environment, many species of snakes all over the world are getting scarcer.

DISEASES AND THEIR TREATMENT

An important chapter in the study of how to keep animals in a terrarium is an account of the various diseases that may attack our charges even under the best of care and in the most perfectly set up environment. In the past, veterinary medicine did not pay much attention to the ailments that afflict amphibians and reptiles, but this has changed in the last few years in response to the increasing interest in these cold-blooded creatures. More and more articles on the diseases of reptiles and on how to combat them have been appearing in specialized publications, and excellent treatments of the entire subject can be found. For this reason I will restrict myself to only the most common diseases.

It is a basic rule that any newly acquired snake, whether freshly caught or raised in captivity, should be placed by itself in a special container. The animal should be quarantined there as a precaution for three to six months. This gives you a chance to observe it carefully and make sure that it will not introduce any infections or parasites into your terrarium. It is a way to protect you against heavy losses and helps you keep your snake population healthy.

For a freshly caught snake adjustment to captivity is always very taxing. Often the newcomer is carrying some parasites that do not seriously affect the organism until the animal's general resistance is weakened.

Crowding too many snakes into one container is a poor habit that has dangerous consequences for the snakes. The animals are bothered by others crawling over them as well as by the greater amount of excrement. The more snakes are kept together, the greater the danger of disease-carrying organisms being transmitted. Ordinarily all snakes are solitary animals, and they thrive best if they are kept singly.

If a snake acts different from normal, this is usually a sign that the organism is in some way impaired. In many cases it is impossible to arrive at an exact diagnosis. Analysis of the stool can reveal the presence of disease-causing microorganisms, worms, or worm eggs. External signs that may indicate internal parasites are a snake lying all stretched out in its container; a sloughing off of old skin in pieces; general apathy; open mouth and labored breathing; loose skin folds on the sides of the body; improper eating; vomiting; and other abnormal behavior.

MITES AND TICKS

It is amazing how many different kinds of mites and ticks can be found on snakes. Luckily most of these parasites can be detected with the naked eye and are relatively easy to get rid of. Many insecticides are as harmful to snakes as they are to mites and kill both, even in minute doses. That is why only a few products can be used on snakes. The best one is Neguvon. It should be applied in a 0.2% water solution all over the snake in a fine spray. To make sure that all the mites are killed, the inside of the container has to be sprayed, too. If used in the concentration indicated, Neguvon kills mites and ticks without harming the snake. Another advantage of Neguvon is that it is chemically unstable and breaks down quickly. As a precaution any newly acquired snake should be sprayed with Neguvon while it is still in its cloth bag and before it is released into the terrarium. If this practice is followed, pests usually do not become a problem. Larger ticks can also be painted with salad oil, petroleum jelly or a cod-liver-oil salve. The oils plug up the breathing apparatus of the ticks, which then die and can be removed with tweezers. It is not advisable to rub the salve all over the snakes because it softens the skin and then the snakes usually do not molt well. The method of treating mite-infested snakes with camphor is no longer used. The mites are dead after about 80 minutes, to be sure, but the snake may also be harmed.

WORMS

Various kinds of worms that attack just about any organ are the most common endoparasites of snakes. They are especially common in the digestive tract, in the muscles, and in the lung; but they may also be found under the skin and inside the mouth. The presence of tapeworms is usually easy to detect because of the flat segments of the worm that are passed in the feces. These worms attach themselves with suckers on the wall of the intestines and cause localized inflammation. If bacteria enter the wound, abcesses may form. Tapeworms absorb food through their skin and thus deprive their host of valuable nutrients. The recommended treatment against tapeworms is "Yomesan," which is sold in drug stores in the form of white pills. This drug has no negative side effects and is effective against most kinds of tapeworms. Use 150 milligrams per kilogram of body weight (150 mg/kg BW). Usually one treatment is enough, though with snakes of the genus *Bothridium* a repeat treatment is sometimes necessary. The pill can be dissolved in water and passed into the stomach through a feeding tube, or it can be given as is, inside a dead prey animal.

Nematodes (roundworms) are especially common in snakes. They are found in the intestines, especially the small intestine, in the lung, in the circulatory system and in the lymph system, in the muscles, and under the skin. The kinds that live in the intestines are relatively easy to combat with various drugs. One of these is "Concurat," which is administered in food once in a dosage of 100 to 300 mg/kg BW. "Panacur" is effective against all nematodes, including *Ascarida*, *Oxyurida*, and *Spirurida*. Give a single dose of 30 to 50 mg/kg BW. (In severe cases the dosage can be raised by several multiples without danger.) *Oxyurida* and *Ascarida* also respond to "Tasnon," which uses piperazine monophosphate as the effective agent. Tasnon is given in a recommended dosage of 25 mg/kg BW. An effective drug against *Strongylida* is "Thibenzol," which is given twice with a one-week interval at a rate of 100 to 200 mg/kg BW.

Endoparasites that attack the muscles and internal organs other than the alimentary canal are harder to combat. "Citarin," which is administered subcutaneously, is especially helpful here. If given in the right amounts, Citarin destroys parasitic worms in the internal organs and the muscles. Never exceed a dosage of 50 mg/kg BW because otherwise the snake will probably die. But if the dosage is too low, the worms survive. Thirty to 50 mg/kg BW of "Panacur," given orally, kill both *Strongylida* and nematodes in the intestines.

INTESTINAL DISEASES

Stomach and intestinal disorders caused by bacteria and other microorganisms are very common in snakes. Vomiting of food and abnormal excreta are indicators of such disorders. But remember that snakes that have been disturbed while digesting or that are being kept too warm or too cool also frequently

TOP LEFT: Black-headed Python (*Aspidites melanocephalus*)
TOP RIGHT: Two-headed Python (*Calabaria reinhardtii*)
CENTER LEFT: Green Tree Python (*Chondropython viridis*)
CENTER RIGHT: Amethystine Python (*Morelia amethistina*)
BOTTOM LEFT: Mexican Python (*Loxocemus bicolor*)
BOTTOM RIGHT: Carpet Python (*Morelia spilota*)

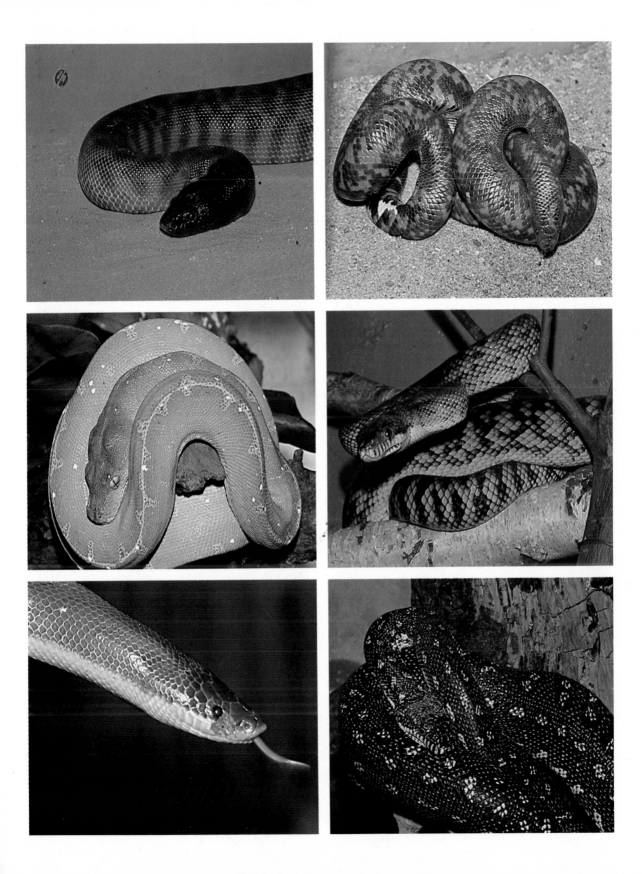

regurgitate what they have eaten. If disturbances and incorrect temperatures can be eliminated as possible causes for vomiting, you are probably dealing with some disease in the gastrointestinal tract. Send a sample of the stool to a veterinary laboratory for analysis. In response you will be told not only what organisms are causing the problem but also to which antibiotics they respond and to which ones they are resistant. You can then undertake the treatment of the sick snake yourself. About a week after you initiate treatment you should send in another stool sample to find out if the medication is having the desired effect. In the case of many intestinal diseases the excreta are loose, slimy, and mixed with blood, or runny and bad smelling. This means that the organism is getting dehydrated and the electrolyte balance is upset. The loss of water and salts can be compensated for with intramuscular injections of a 0.9% sodium chloride solution. Solutions with other body salts are also effective. The daily dose for a snake weighing about 2.2 pounds (1 kg) is 10 to 30 cubic centimeters of the fluid. Antibiotics are best dissolved in "Boviserin" and then given through a rubber tube that is inserted into the esophagus and down into the stomach. Boviserin contains valuable proteins that can be absorbed into the blood with almost no digestive action required.

Salmonella and *Klebsiella* bacteria cause many kinds of intestinal diseases. These pathogens respond to several antibiotics,

including chloramphenicol, neomycin, Chloromycetin, and Humatin. I generally use chloramphenicol at a rate of 50 to 100 mg/kg BW over four to six days. Avoid giving too large doses of antibiotics or sulfonamides and be sure to consult the directions. Reptiles usually survive a double or triple dose without obvious harm, but if the dosage is increased more than that, the antibacterial drugs and their by-products can have harmful side effects and even kill snakes. The side effects may be caused by the drug itself, or they may be the result of poisonous substances given off by the bacteria killed by the drug. In addition, treatment with antibiotics affects the normal intestinal flora and can hide secondary infections.

Inflammations of the stomach and intestines are also often caused by various species of *Psuedomonas* bacteria which destroy the upper layer of the intestinal mucous membrane. The drug to be used is Chloromycetin given orally or intramuscularly over seven days at a rate of about 50 mg/kg BW.

One of the worst intestinal diseases affecting snakes is amoebic dysentery. This disease inevitably leads to death within a few weeks unless it is treated immediately. It is caused by the protozoan *Entamoebae invadens*, and its symptoms are foul-smelling, runny stool that is mixed with a bloody mucous discharge. This causes the large intestine to get inflamed and turn into a curdlike and pussey consistency, the walls often thickening to several times their normal thickness and forming a hard, solid section just above the cloaca. In severe cases the inflamed intestine can grow together with the peritoneum. The amoebae first penetrate into the mucous membrane of the intestines and destroy them. From there they move through the bloodstream into the liver and other organs where they can cause serious infarcts. Since amebiasis is extremely contagious, the affected animals must always be quarantined singly. Excrement must be removed promptly, and the container cleaned every time with a disinfectant (e.g., Tego, Sagrotan). A drug specifically effective against amebiasis is "Humatin," which is available in capsules or as

TOP LEFT: Indian Python (*Python molurus molurus*)
TOP RIGHT: Rainbow Boa (*Epicrates cenchria*)
CENTER LEFT: Reticulate Python (*Python reticulatus*)
CENTER RIGHT: Timor Python (*Python timorensis*)
BOTTOM LEFT: Ball Python (*Python regius*)
BOTTOM RIGHT: Javelin Sand Boa (*Eryx jaculus*)

a syrup. The proper dosage is 200 to 500 mg/kg BW and should be given four times a week. Six to ten doses of Humatin will in all likelihood kill all the amoebae living in the intestines. But since Humatin is not absorbed by the intestines, it is ineffective against amoebae that have already spread to the liver. Another effective treatment against *Entamoeba invadens* is "Clont," of which 60 mg/kg BW should be given orally every other day for at least two weeks. Intramuscular injections of the malaria drug "Resochin" can be successfully used against amoebae both inside the intestines and outside, particularly those that have penetrated into the liver. The author has often used Resochin successfully to cure snakes affected with amebiasis. One ccm/kg BW is given every other day for at least two weeks.

A less common disease in snakes is coccidiosis. This disorder, too, leads to inflammation of the intestines and to diarrhea. The recommended drug for it is 2-sulfani-lamido-5-methoxy-pyrimidin, which is available commercially under the trade names "Bayrena" and "Durenat." It is given intramuscularly in an initial dose of 80 mg/kg BW on the first day and in successive doses of 40 mg/kg BW from the second through the fifth day.

RESPIRATORY INFECTIONS

Infections of the respiratory system are very prevalent in snakes, and they are hardly less serious than diseases of the digestive system. Only part of the respiratory system may be affected or all of it. Under good environmental conditions the infection along with its external symptoms, such as slimy discharge from the nose and mouth, gaping mouth because of shortness of breath, raising of the head and anterior body, and puffing up the lung and throat, eventually disappear without special treatment. The causes for this disorder are varied. Too high or too low temperatures may be the problem. Snakes that live continually in too warm an environment are especially prone

to these infections. Keeping a snake that needs moisture too dry or a desert snake too damp is likely to cause colds or pneumonia. Stale and smelly air in the terrarium also contributes to respiratory problems. This is another reason why excrement should always be removed promptly and completely. In the spring, outbreaks of pneumonia are common and quickly lead to death if nothing is done to treat them. Sick snakes should be removed from the terrarium promptly and placed in isolation. Respiratory infections have responded well to Terramycin, Chloromycetin, penicillin, and streptomycin, all of which can be given orally or by intramuscular injection. Continue treatment for five to seven days with daily doses of 50 mg/kg BW of Terramycin, 15 to 30 mg/kg BW of Chloromycetin, 50 mg/kg BW of penicillin, or 50 mg/kg BW of streptomycin.

MOUTH ROT

Infectious mouth rot is especially widespread in snakes. The causes for this inflammation of the mucous membranes in the mouth are poor hygiene, faulty environmental conditions, and, as a consequence of this, general lowered resistance against disease. The oral cavity is slimy and displays larger and smaller pussey areas. Bacteria, usually of the genus *Pseudomonas* (*P. fluorescens, aeruginosa, hydrophila*), attack the gums. If nothing is done to remedy the situation, the infection reaches into the deeper layers of the tissue, the teeth fall out, and the bones of the skull are affected and sometimes seriously damaged. Finally the infection spreads to the respiratory system and leads to death.

Mouth rot can be treated successfully with several drugs. If vitamins A and C are given with the proper medication this enhances the healing process. Often one to three treatments with a "Supronal" solution, a few drops of which are dripped into the snake's open mouth, take care of the problem. "Terramycin-Depot" (oxytetracyclin) also cures mouth rot.

Give the snake three intramuscular Terramycin injections at 24-hour intervals. The dosage per injection is 25 to 50 mg/kg BW. After a few days the snake will be well again.

ABNORMAL MOLTS

Any keeper of snakes may run into the problem of partial molts or failure to molt altogether. Such molts often indicate poor health. Quite frequently the animals are suffering from partial dehydration caused perhaps by untreated intestinal disorders or because they are kept too dry, in some cases even without any drinking water. A snake that is stuck in its old skin may be placed in a container of lukewarm water (77°-86°F [25°-30°C]) long enough for the old skin to peel off from the new one by itself. Quite often the old skin comes off completely except over the eyes. These last patches can then be removed with tweezers. (Proceed with great caution in order not to injure the eyes!) To do this, place the snake in a container with damp foam rubber and a temperature of 77° to 86°F (25°-30°C) until the skin over the cornea has become soft.

ABSCESSES

Abscesses of various sizes both on and under the skin and generally known as "pock marks" are almost always caused by bacteria. These, too, are treated with antibiotics such as penicillin or Terramycin in the dosages indicated above. Local application of an antibiotic salve often helps and speeds the healing. Surface wounds have to be carefully cleaned out and treated with an antibiotic salve or powder to prevent infections. While the wounds are healing the animals should be kept on a fairly sterile surface such as clean paper.

EYE INFECTION

Occasionally a snake's eyes get infected, and puss forms beneath the cornea. Make a tiny incision in the cornea, carefully press the puss out, and rinse the eye several times in some Ringer's solution to which an antibiotic such as neomycin has been added.

A FINAL WORD

Finally I should like to mention the beneficial use of activated charcoal. If an overdose of a deworming drug or of an antibiotic has been administered orally, dangerous side effects can quickly develop which manifest themselves in convulsions and end in death. At the first sign of such neurotoxic poisoning, activated charcoal, which comes in a very fine powder, should be mixed with water and immediately introduced into the snake's stomach through a rubber feeding tube. The activated charcoal will then quickly absorb the excess medication in the alimentary canal.

LIST OF DESCRIBED SPECIES

The following is a list of the species described in the last section of this book. Systems of classification are the subject of some dispute. The list and the descriptions that follow are arranged according to the classification system generally accepted by U.S. herpetologists. The zoogeographic region of origin of each species is also given.

Class Reptila—Reptiles
Order Squamata—Scaly Reptiles
Suborder Serpentes—Snakes

Infraorder Henophidia—Primitive Snakes

		Region of Origin
FAMILY PYTHONIDAE—PYTHONS		
Subfamily Pythoninae—True Pythons		
Genus *Aspidites*—Black-headed Pythons		
A. melanocephalus—Black-headed Python		Australian
Genus *Chondropython*—Tree Pythons		
C. viridis—Green Tree Python		Australian
Genus *Liasis*—Australian Rock Pythons		
L. fuscus—Brown Water Python		Australian
L. childreni—Children Python		Australian
Genus *Morelia*—Diamond Pythons		
M. amethistina—Amethystine Python		Australian
M. spilota—Carpet Python		Australian
Genus *Python*—Old World Pythons		
P. anchietae—Angola Python		Ethiopian
P. curtus—Blood Python		Oriental
P. molurus—Indian Python		Oriental
P. regius—Ball Python		Ethiopian
P. reticulatus—Reticulate Python		Oriental
P. sebae—African Rock Python		Ethiopian
P. timorensis—Timor Python		Indoaustralian
Subfamily Calabariinae—African Burrowing Pythons		
Genus *Calabaria*—African Burrowing Pythons		
C. reinhardtii—Two-headed Python		Ethiopian
Subfamily Loxoceminae—American Burrowing Pythons		
Genus *Loxocemus*—American Burrowing Pythons		
L. bicolor—Mexican Python		Neotropical

List of Described Species

FAMILY BOIDAE—BOAS AND SANDBOAS
Subfamily Boinae—True Boas

Region of
Origin

Genus	*Acranthophis*—Madagascan Boas	
	A. madagascariensis—Madagascan Boa	Madagascan
Genus	*Boa*—Boa Constrictors	
	B. constrictor—Boa Constrictor	Neotropical
Genus	*Candoia*—Pacific Boas	
	C. bibroni—Bibron's Boa	Australian
Genus	*Corallus*—American Tree Boas	
	C. enydris—Garden Tree Boa	Neotropical
	C. caninus—Emerald Tree Boa	Neotropical
Genus	*Epicrates*—Rock Boas	
	E. cenchria—Rainbow Boa	Neotropical
	E. striatus—Bahama Boa	Neotropical
Genus	*Eunectes*—Anacondas	
	E. murinus—Green Anaconda	Neotropical
	E. notaeus—Yellow Anaconda	Neotropical
Genus	*Sanzinia*—Madagascan Tree Boas	
	S. madagascariensis—Madagascan Tree Boa	Madagascan

Subfamily Erycinae—Sand Boas

Genus	*Eryx*—Old World Sandboas	
	E. colubrinus—Egyptian Sandboa	Palearctic
	E. jaculus—Javelin Sandboa	Palearctic
	E. johnii—Brown Sandboa	Palearctic
	E. miliaris—Mountain Sandboa	Palearctic
	E. tataricus—Giant Sandboa	Palearctic
Genus	*Lichanura*—Rosy Boas	
	L. trivirgata—Rosy Boa	Nearctic

FAMILY TROPIDOPHIIDAE—WOOD SNAKES AND RELATIVES

Genus	*Trachyboa*—Rough-scaled Snakes	
	T. boulengeri—Rough-scaled Snake	Neotropical
Genus	*Tropidophis*—Wood Snakes	
	T. melanurus—Cuban Woodsnake	Neotropical

Infraorder Caenophidia—Advanced Snakes

FAMILY COLUBRIDAE—HARMLESS SNAKES
Subfamily Lamprophiinae—African Wolfsnakes

Genus	*Lamprophis*—African Housesnakes	
	L. fulginosus—Brown Housesnake	Ethiopian
Genus	*Pseudaspis*—African Molesnakes	
	P. cana—African Molesnake	Ethiopian

List of Described Species

Subfamily Acrochordinae—Wart Snakes
    Genus   *Acrochordus*—Oriental Wartsnakes
           A. javanicus—Java Wartsnake   Oriental

FAMILY PYTHONIDAE—PYTHONS
Subfamily Homalopsinae—Rear-fanged Watersnakes

    Genus   *Cerberus*—Dogface Watersnake
           C. rhynchops—Dogface Watersnake   Oriental
    Genus   *Erpeton*—Tentacle Snakes
           E. tentaculatum—Tentacle Snake   Oriental
    Genus   *Homalopsis*—Puff-face Watersnakes
           H. buccata—Puff-face Watersnake   Oriental

Subfamily Xenodontinae—South American Snakes
    Genus   *Clelia*—Mussaranas
           C. clelia—Mussarana   Neotropical
    Genus   *Helicops*—South American Watersnakes
           H. carinicaudus—Roughtail Watersnake   Neotropical
    Genus   *Hydrodynastes*—False Watercobras
           H. gigas—Giant False Watercobra   Neotropical
    Genus   *Leimadophis*—Lined Snakes
           L. poecilogyrus—Angry Snake   Neotropical
    Genus   *Liophis*—South American Grass Snakes
           L. anomalus—Red-Tail Grass Snake   Neotropical
    Genus   *Philodryas*—South American Tree Snakes
           P. baroni—Baron's Tree Snake   Neotropical
           P. olfersii—Olfersi Tree Snake   Neotropical
    Genus   *Uromacer*—Hispaniola Bush Snakes
           U. oxyrhynchus—Sharp-nosed Bush Snake   Neotropical
    Genus   *Xenodon*—False Vipers
           X. merremi—Merrem's False Viper   Neotropical
    Genus   *Heterodon*—Hognose Snakes
           H. nasicus—Western Hognose Snake   Nearctic
           H. platyrhinos—Eastern Hognose Snake   Nearctic
    Genus   *Diadophis*—Ringneck Snakes
           D. punctatus—Ringneck Snake   Nearctic
    Genus   *Farancia*—Mud Snakes
           F. abacura—Mud Snake   Nearctic

Subfamily Dipsadinae—Middle American Snakes
    Genus   *Hypsiglena*—Night Snakes
           H. torquata—Night Snake   Nearctic
    Genus   *Leptodeira*—Cat-eye Snakes
           L. annulata—Banana Snake   Neotropical
           L. septentrionalis—Banded Cat-eye Snake   Neotropical

List of Described Species

	Region of Origin
Subfamily Psammophiinae—Sand Racers	
Genus *Malpolon*—Lizard Snakes	
M. monspessulanus—Montpellier Snake	Palearctic
Genus *Psammophis*—Sand Racers	
P. sibilans—Olive Sandracer	Ethiopian
Genus **Psammophylax*—Skaapstekers	
P. rhombeatus—Spotted Skaapsteker	Ethiopian
Subfamily Natricinae—Watersnakes and Allies	
Genus **Rhabdophis*—Rear-fanged Keelbacks	
R. tigrina—Tiger Keelback	Palearctic
Genus *Xenochrophis*—Fishing Keelbacks	
X. piscator—Checkered Keelback	Oriental
Genus *Amphisema*—Oriental Gartersnakes	
A. mairii—Moluccan Gartersnake	Indoaustralian
A. stolata—Striped Gartersnake	Oriental
Genus *Natriciteres*—African Marsh Snakes	
N. olivacea—Olive Marsh Snake	Ethiopian
Genus *Natrix*—European Watersnakes	
N. maura—Viperine Watersnake	Palearctic
N. natrix—Grass Snake	Palearctic
N. tessellata—Dice Snake	Palearctic
Genus *Nerodia*—American Watersnakes	
N. cyclopion—Green Watersnake	Nearctic
N. erythrogaster—Plainbelly Watersnake	Nearctic
N. fasciata—Southern Watersnake	Nearctic
N. rhombifera—Diamondback Watersnake	Nearctic
N. sipedon—Northern Watersnake	Nearctic
N. taxispilota—Brown Watersnake	Nearctic
Genus *Regina*—Crayfish Snakes	
R. septemvittata—Queen Snake	
Genus *Thamnophis*—American Gartersnakes	
T. butleri—Butler's Gartersnake	Nearctic
T. cyrtopsis—Blackneck Gartersnake	Nearctic
T. elegans—Elegant Gartersnake	Nearctic
T. sauritus—Eastern Ribbonsnake	Nearctic
T. sirtalis—Common Gartersnake	Nearctic
Genus *Storeria*—Brown Snakes	
S. dekayi—Brown Snake	Nearctic
S. occipitomaculata—Red-bellied Snake	Nearctic
Subfamily Colubrinae—Ratsnakes, Racers, and Allies **Ratsnakes**	
Genus *Coronella*—Smooth Snakes	
C. austraca—European Smooth Snake	Palearctic
C. girondica—Southern Smooth Snake	Palearctic

* Members of this genus are dangerously venomous.

List of Described Species

			Region of Origin
Genus	*Lampropeltis*—King Snakes		Nearctic
	L. getulus—Common King Snake		Nearctic
	L. mexicana—Gray-banded King Snake		Nearctic
	L. pyromelana—Sonora Mountain King Snake		Nearctic
	L. triangulum—Milk Snake		Nearctic-Neotropical
	L. zonata—California Mountain King Snake		Nearctic
Genus	*Rhinocheilus*—Longnose Snakes		
	R. lecontei—Longnose Snake		Nearctic
Genus	*Cemophora*—Scarlet Snakes		
	C. coccinea—Scarlet Snake		Nearctic
Genus	*Elaphe*—Rat Snakes		
	E. carinata—Stinking Goddess		Palearctic
	E. dione—Dione's Ratsnake		Palearctic
	E. guttata—Corn Snake		Nearctic
	E. hohenackeri—Transcaucasian Ratsnake		Palearctic
	E. longissima—Aesculapian Ratsnake		Palearctic
	E. mandarina—Jade-pattern Ratsnake		Palearctic
	E. moellendorffi—Red-headed Ratsnake		Oriental
	E. obsoleta—American Ratsnake		Nearctic
	E. quatuorlineata—Four-lined Ratsnake		Palearctic
	E. scalaris—Ladder Ratsnake		Palearctic
	E. schrencki—Amur Ratsnake		Palearctic
	E. situla—Leopard Ratsnake		Palearctic
	E. subocularis—Transpecos Ratsnake		Nearctic
	E. vulpina—Fox Snake		Nearctic
Genus	*Pituophis*—Bull Snakes		
	P. melanoleucus—Pine Snake		Nearctic
Genus	*Arizona*—Glossy Snakes		
	A. elegans—Glossy Snake		Nearctic

Sand Snakes

Genus	*Chionactis*—Shovelnose Snakes		
	C. occipitalis—Western Shovelnose Snake		Nearctic
Genus	*Eirenis*—Dwarf Snakes		
	E. modestus—Asia Minor Dwarfsnake		Palearctic
Genus	*Phyllorhynchus*—Leafnose Snakes		
	P. decurtatus—Spotted Leafnose Snake		Nearctic

Racers

Genus	*Masticophis*—American Whipsnakes		
	M. flagellum—Coachwhip		Nearctic
Genus	*Coluber*—Racers		
	C. constrictor—American Racer		Nearctic
	C. hippocrepis—Horseshoe Whipsnake		Palearctic
	C. jugularis—Caspian Whipsnake		Palearctic
	C. najadum—Dahl's Whipsnake		Palearctic
	C. ravergieri—Desert Whipsnake		Palearctic
	C. viridiflavus—European Whipsnake		Palearctic

		Region of Origin
Genus	*Spalerosophis*—Desert Racers	
	S. diadema—Diadem Snake	Palearctic
Genus	*Dasypeltis*—African Egg-eating Snakes	
	D. scabra—Common Egg-eater	Ethiopian
Genus	*Salvadora*—Patchnose Snakes	
	S. grahamiae—Mountain Patchnose Snake	Nearctic
Genus	*Opheodrys*—Green Snakes	
	O. aestivus—Rough Greensnake	Nearctic
	O. vernalis—Smooth Greensnake	Nearctic
Genus	*Drymarchon*—Indigo Snakes	
	D. corais—Indigo Snake	Neotropical-Nearctic
Genus	*Leptophis*—American Tree Racers	
	L. ahaetulla—Parrot Snake	Neotropical
Genus	*Drymobius*—Speckled Racers	
	D. margaritiferus—Speckled Racer	Neotropical-Nearctic
Genus	*Spilotes*—Tiger Ratsnakes	
	S. pullatus—Tiger Ratsnake	Neotropical
Genus	*Ptyas*—Oriental Ratsnakes	
	P. mucosus—Dhaman	Oriental
Genus	*Gonyosoma*—Oriental Tree Racers	
	G. oxycephalum—Red-tail Tree Racer	Oriental

Tree Snakes

Genus	*Ahaetulla*—Oriental Vinesnakes	
	A. nasuta—Longnose Vinesnake	Oriental
Genus	*Chrysopelea*—Flying Snakes	
	C. ornata—Ornate Flyingsnake	Oriental
Genus	*Oxybelis*—American Vinesnakes	
	O. aeneus—Mexican Vinesnake	Neotropical-Nearctic
	O. fulgidus—Green Vinesnake	Neotropical
Genus	*Philothamnus*—African Greensnakes	
	P. irregularis—West African Greensnake	Ethiopian

Cat Snakes

Genus	*Boiga*—Cat Snakes	
	B. dendrophila—Mangrove Snake	Oriental
Genus	*Crotaphopeltis*—African Herald Snakes	
	C. hotamboeia—Red-lip Snake	Ethiopian
Genus	*Dispholidus*—Boomslangs	
	D. typus—Boomslang	Ethiopian
Genus	*Thelotornis*—African Bird Snakes	
	T. kirtlandii—Bird Snake	Ethiopian
Genus	*Telescopus*—Tiger Snakes	
	T. fallax—European Tigersnake	Palearctic
	T. semiannulatus—Banded Tigersnake	Ethiopian
Genus	*Trimorphodon*—Lyre Snakes	
	T. biscutatus—Lyre Snake	Nearctic

* Members of this genus are dangerously venomous.

DESCRIPTIONS OF SPECIES

Family Pythonidae
Subfamily Pythoninae—True Pythons

Genus *Aspidites*
Black-headed Pythons
2 species

Aspidites melanocephalus
Black-headed Python
(photo, page 49)

PHYSICAL CHARACTERISTICS: The head is not set off from the powerful body. Both head and neck are a glossy brown-black to coal-black. The body is light brown with irregular cross-bands of reddish-brown and dark brown to blackish encircling the entire body and merging in places. The underside is grayish white to porcelain colored. The earlier form, considered a subspecies, *A. m. ramsayi*, is now regarded as a separate species.

LENGTH: 5 feet (1.5 m); in exceptional cases up to 9 feet (2.8 m).

DISTRIBUTION AND BEHAVIOR: *A. melanocephalus* is found in the northern third of Australia where it lives in dry areas where rocky terrain is interspersed with brush and open woods. The Black-headed Python is a ground-dweller that likes to move around among rocks and climbs trees only rarely; sometimes it likes to hide in rabbit warrens. It is not very aggressive and hardly ever bites when caught. If it feels threatened it arches up the anterior part of the body, flattens the throat, and emits a hollow hissing sound. The Black-headed Python is quite omnivorous, eating not only mammals and birds but also relishing snakes and lizards; of lizards it especially favors the bearded dragon (*Amphibolurus barbatus*). It seems to be largely immune to the bites of poisonous snakes. Very little is known about its reproductive habits except that it lays 10-to-20 eggs.

CAPTIVITY AND BREEDING: The Black-headed Python needs a dry terrarium of generous size with a refuge. Coming from a dry habitat, it abhors water in the terrarium as well. If water is splashed on it, it immediately assumes its typical defense posture. It will seek out water only if infested with mites to try to get rid of them. In order to thrive this snake needs daytime temperatures between 77° and 86°F (25°-30°C), and at night it should be about 9°F (5°C) cooler. In captivity it proves to be a voracious eater of mice and rats which it grabs hold of in any manner it can and squeezes to death. This rare giant python has thus far reproduced in captivity only in the Taronga Zoo in Sydney, Australia. Two live snakes hatched from ten fertile eggs.

Genus *Chondropython*
Tree Pythons
1 species

Chondropython viridis
Green Tree Python
(photo, page 49)

PHYSICAL CHARACTERISTICS: The short, impressive head is clearly set off from the slender neck. There is a surprising similarity between the Green Tree Python and the South American Emerald Tree Boa, and the two snakes are often confused with each other. The Green Tree Python, which we are dealing with here, has very small scales on the top of the head, whereas the Emerald Tree Boa has considerably larger ones that are developed into plates. The pupils of the Green Tree Python are vertical slits, and its front fangs are much elongated. These snakes have coiling, prehensile tails, which they use to hold onto tree branches. Grown snakes are a bright emerald green with a more or less continuous band of white dots running down the spine. In some individuals this band may show blue blotches. The underside is light yellow. In addition to this normal green coloration a light blue variant is occasionally found. The young of this species are brick red or golden yellow; the color on the upper side of their bodies changes to green when they are about three years old.

LENGTH: 5 to 6 feet (1.5-1.8 m).

DISTRIBUTION AND BEHAVIOR: The Green Tree Python occurs on New Guinea and the small nearby islands, the Schouten Islands, the Aru Islands, and in northern Australia (Cape York Peninsula). Soldiers discovered this species during World War II in the Cape York Peninsula, where it is said to be quite common. The Green Tree Python lives in tropical rain forests. Its green color and its pehensile tail suggest its arboreal habits. This python lunges at its prey rapidly and then kills it by wrapping it in several coils. With its long upper and lower teeth it can get a secure hold of birds, tree-dwelling frogs, and even small marsupials. This snake is largely nocturnal. It spends most of its time in the thicket of branches and descends to the ground only rarely. The female lays eggs and broods them.

CAPTIVITY AND BREEDING: A terrarium for this snake should be spacious, with plenty of plants and a climbing tree because the Green Tree Python almost always lies curled up on a branch during the day. In the evening and at night it becomes active and crawls around. The bottom material can consist of a mixture of sand and forest soil, which also works well for growing plants. The Green Tree Python prefers high humidity and should therefore be liberally sprayed with warm water (about 77°F [25°C]) every day. Because of this snake's great need for moisture, a sufficiently large water container is a must. There is no need for a bot-

tom heater because the snake spends almost all its time in the branches. The snake does best with 12 to 14 hours of lighting. Optimal temperatures during the day are 77° to 90°F (25°-32°C); at night the temperature can drop down to 72° to 74°F (22°-23°C). Feed the snake mice, medium sized rats, and birds. These are best offered dead with tongs. Dead as well as live prey is snatched as quick as lightning and enveloped. The snakes seem to be especially fond of sparrows. Some individuals eat a great deal and quickly become quite fat. Such animals should be given only one prey animal every week or every two or three weeks. Other individuals are fussy and unpredictable in their eating habits and may accept food only if kept singly or may reject all but one kind of prey.

Keepers of snakes have succeeded in breeding this snake in captivity several times. Mating takes place between May and July. The female incubates the eggs by curling herself around and over them and twitching her body. These twitching motions raise her body temperature to a level that is conducive to the development of the embryos. The baby snakes hatch after about 50 days. At this point they are about 1 foot (30 cm) long and of a beautiful reddish-brown color. A line of white triangular marks runs down their backs. The first molt occurs when the snakes are 2-to-3 weeks old. Not all of the young snakes eat baby mice after their first molt. Those that show no interest in food are best force-fed with newborn mice until they eat on their own.

Genus *Liasis*
Australian Rock Pythons
5 species

Liasis fuscus
Brown Water Python
2 subspecies
(cover photo)

PHYSICAL CHARACTERISTICS: The head is long and clearly set off from the neck. The plates on the head are arranged symmetrically. In the subspecies *L. f. fuscus* the top of the head is brown; in the subspecies *L. f. albertisii* it is black. The throat area is whitish, sometimes with a suggestion of pink. The upper and lower labial plates have a black and white stripe pattern. The body is medium to dark brown, and the belly side, a uniform light gray. In the light the colors glisten brilliantly.

LENGTH: 6 1/2 feet (2 m); in some cases up to 10 feet (3 m).

DISTRIBUTION AND BEHAVIOR: *L. fuscus* is found on Timor and New Guinea, and in northern Australia. It lives along forested river beds in grassy and bushy terrain, often close by, or directly in the water in which it often spends hours at a time during the day. Young snakes are sometimes found in trees. In its natural habitat *L. fuscus* lives on small mammals, birds, and reptiles. From October to December it hunts young Australian crocodiles (*Crocodylus johnsoni*), which hatch at this time of year. It hunts primarily at night. The name Brown Water Python is misleading because this snake cannot be said to dwell in the water even though it does like to spend some time there. This species, like other pythons, lays eggs, which are brooded by the female.

CAPTIVITY AND BREEDING: This snake needs a large terrarium for giant snakes with a tree limb for climbing and a large water basin. It should be kept very warm, 82° to 86°F (28°-30°C) during the day and down to 74° to 77°F (23°-25°C) at night. Since this snake likes to stay out of sight during the day, a refuge is important. The specimens kept by the author spend their days lying on decorative cork tubes or on the bottom heater. Although they visit the water basin only occasionally they like to be showered with lukewarm water. *L. fuscus* does not start moving about until evening or night but then climbs around actively. In captivity it will eat mice, rats, and baby chicks. It lunges forward up to half its body length with a mighty thrust, snatches hold of the prey, coils around it, and kills it by constriction. It waits for the prey to become completely motionless before eating it. *L. fuscus* is short-tempered and responds to any intrusion with a short hiss and immediate biting.

Only in recent times has *L. fuscus* been kept in captivity in any numbers, but it has already reproduced in a terrarium. In the Taronga Zoo in Sydney two Brown Water Pythons mated on August 11 and 14, 1972, and two months later, on October 6, the female laid eleven eggs, which she immediately began to brood. Sometimes she left the eggs for periods of 30 to 60 minutes. The humidity in the terrarium was kept high through spraying lukewarm water. The young snakes hatched between December 6 and 9, 1972. The newly hatched snakes measured an average of 16 inches (40 cm) and weighed 1 1/2 ounces (45 g). The young snakes shed their first skin within 5 days and started eating their first nestling mice a few days after that.

A female of the subspecies *L. f. albertisii* (regarded by some as a separate species) laid a clutch of 16 eggs on August 13, 1976. The eggs, which were about 2 1/2 inches (6 cm) long and weighed 1 3/4 ounces (50 g), were placed in a covered styrofoam container where an even temperature of 86°F (30°C) was maintained. A dish filled with water helped maintain the humidity in the container. On October 19, 2 snakes hatched, and 7 more emerged from eggs into which small openings were slit. The newborn snakes measured 18 inches (45 cm) and shed their first skins after 3 to 4 weeks. Since the young snakes did not eat on their own they were at first force-fed newborn mice. After a year they had grown to about 2 feet (60 cm).

Liasis childreni
Children Python

PHYSICAL CHARACTERISTICS: The longish head is somewhat set off from the neck. The top and the sides of the body are grayish brown. Dark brown crossbands and blotches on the back and sides are arranged in rows.

The top of the head is a uniform brown; in a few individuals it is mottled. On the sides of the head, a dark brown band runs from the corners of the mouth across the eyes to the nostrils. In young snakes the markings are almost black, and in snakes from the northern areas of distribution they are less distinct. In some rare cases these northern snakes are dark brown all over.

LENGTH: 2¹/₂ to 5 feet (75-150 cm); only rarely up to 6 feet (180 cm).

DISTRIBUTION AND BEHAVIOR: *L. childreni* occurs in western, northern, central, and eastern Australia as well as on the Torres Strait Islands. Though primarily terrestrial, this snake is quite often found in trees. Its range includes both the rain forests of the eastern coast and the deserts of central Australia. It favors rocky terrain where it hides under stones and in rock fissures. Sometimes it also uses termite hills as retreats. During the day it usually rests tucked away somewhere and becomes active only in the evening and at night. Then it wanders around in search of prey. Children python feeds on lizards, geckoes, birds, and small mammals. Like other members of the *Liasis* genus it lays eggs that it broods.

CAPTIVITY AND BREEDING: Small-to-medium sized terrariums are adequate for this species. Since the snake spends most of the daytime in hiding, 2 to 4 hours of artificial lighting in addition to the natural daylight suffice. A fair-sized water basin is important because some snakes of this species like to spend days on end in the water. The air should be about 77° to 86°F (25°-30°C) during the day and about 68° to 72°F (20°-22°C) at night. *L. childreni* will eat mice, rats, and baby chicks but only after the prey is dead.

This species is rarly offered for sale and is found in few terrariums of snake fanciers, but it has been successfully bred in captivity. The males go through a courtship display. Matings have occurred from late September to late March. One female deposited 9 eggs in mid-April and proceeded promptly to brood them. A second female laid 11 eggs and also did brooding duty in the characteristic python manner. A constant, high humidity was maintained in the terrarium. The snakes hatched after 65 to 66 days and shed their first skins a week later.

Genus *Morelia*
Diamond Pythons
5 species

Morelia amethistina
Amethystine Python
(photo, page 49)

PHYSICAL CHARACTERISTICS: The powerful head, which is clearly set off from the neck, is covered on the upper side with large, symmetrical plates. The eyes are large, and the pupils narrow to oval vertical slits. There are clearly visible sensory pits in the upper and lower labial plates. The ground color of the top and sides of the body is yellowish to reddish-brown with sharply delineated markings. These markings form a zigzag or "carpet pattern" on the back and sides. The underside is whitish gray. Solid-colored individuals are rare. *M. amethistina* differs from *M. argus variegata*, which it resembles in color and markings, by having large plates that form a regular pattern on the top of the head. In *M. a. variegata* the scales of the head are smaller and more irregular in shape.

LENGTH: About 16 feet (5 m); in exceptional cases sometimes over 26 feet (8 m).

DISTRIBUTION AND BEHAVIOR: The area of distribution of *M. amethistina* covers New Guinea, the Molucca Islands, the Philippines, the Bismarck Archipelago, Timor, the southern part of Mindanao, the islands Kei, Aru, Semao, Salawatti, Jobi, Tenimber, Trobriand, the Torres Strait Islands, and Queensland (Australia). The form occurring on the mainland in Queensland was in the past considered a separate subspecies and given the name *M.*

a. kinghorni. The Amethystine Python is found in tropical forests where it hides in trees and rock fissures, underneath rocks, in hollows, and in mangrove thickets. Occasionally it penetrates to human settlements. Although not especially lively by temperament this snake can present a threat because it is so large and strong. It can cut deep wounds with its long teeth. In nature it preys on small kangaroos, rabbits, rats, and other mammals. It also eats birds. Near farms it lies in wait for poultry.

CAPTIVITY AND BREEDING: A large snake like the Amethystine Python requires a large terrarium for giant snakes with solid tree limbs for climbing and a large water basin. Artificial lights should be on 12 to 14 hours a day. Air temperature should be 77° to 90°F (25°-32°C) during the day and may drop to 72° to 77°F (22°-25°C) at night. Mice, rats, rabbits, guinea pigs, and chickens may be offered as food. The snake grabs them with a powerful forward lunge and then kills them with a few tight coils of the body. The Amethystine Python is able to throw itself forward for about half the length of its body, and it is wise not to get too close to the animals while doing cleaning chores in the terrarium.

This species is quite rare and therefore seldom kept in captivity. Some attempts at breeding the snake in captivity have been successful. The female lays 7 to 15 eggs that it broods in typical python manner. Contractions of the body create favorable warmth for the eggs. The baby snakes, which are brown and about 26 inches (65 cm) long, hatch after about 80 days. The characteristic zigzag markings show up only after several molts.

Morelia spilota
Carpet Python
2 subspecies
(photo, page 49)

PHYSICAL CHARACTERISTICS: The head is broad with a short protruding snout. On the black to bluish-black ground color, which in the subspecies *M. a. argus* may be more olive colored, there are cream-colored to yellow spots that may combine to form lozenge-shaped patterns. These light spots may be more sparse in some individuals. The markings extend to the head where they form a pattern of yellow and black dots. The belly is yellowish and shows dark crossbands.

LENGTH: 10 to 13 feet (3-4 m).

DISTRIBUTION AND BEHAVIOR: This gorgeous python is found in the coastal areas of Australia from New South Wales to eastern Victoria, in central Australia, in New Guinea, and on the Tokelau Islands. It lives preferably in the bush or in wet, sometimes thickly wooded areas. It is quite often found in hollow trees and has a long, prehensile tail. This accounts for its excellent climbing ability. *M. argus* often hides under rocks, in crevices, and in rabbit warrens, and does not become active until dark. Sometimes it suns itself on a large rock in the early morning. It likes moisture and often spends long hours in the water. The Carpet Python is less aggressive by nature than other pythons, defending itself with strong bites only when seriously disturbed. Its long teeth, which are curved backward, can inflict deep wounds. It feeds on birds, small marsupials, rabbits, rats, and mice, and farmers often like to see them on their land and even close to their farms. The Carpet Python lays up to 35 eggs, which are deposited in one sticky clutch. The female coils herself around the eggs to help create temperatures conducive to the development of the embryonic snakes. The newborn snakes measure about 12 to 15 inches (30-37 cm) at birth.

CAPTIVITY AND BREEDING: Like all larger pythons used to warm temperatures, the Carpet Python needs a generous terrarium with high walls, a large water basin, climbing branches, a retreat, localized bottom heat, and artificial lighting that is on 12 to 14 hours a day. It adjusts quickly to captivity and happily eats small mammals like rats, mice, golden hamsters, and rabbits. Despite easy initial adjustment, this snake is quite delicate and needs attentive care, or else it will not live long in captivity. During the day it should be kept at 76° to 90°F (25°-32° C), and at night it should be a few degrees cooler. The bottom of the terrarium should be covered with flagstones set in cement; this way the excreta can be cleaned up completely and the meticulous hygienic conditions that are so crucial for this species maintained. Thus far there have been no reports of this snake reproducing in captivity.

Genus *Python*
Old World Pythons
7 species

Python anchietae
Angola Python

PHYSICAL CHARACTERISTICS: The head is clearly set off from the neck. In contrast to the African Rock Python, this species has only small scales on top of the head. There, there are triangular reddish-brown markings surrounded by a light and a dark band. At the center of this marking there is a white spot with a black line around it. The ground color of the body is a pale reddish-brown interspersed with many white blotches and bands that are also rimmed in black. On the yellowish underside only a few brown blotches are found.

LENGTH: 52 inches (130 cm); rarely more.

DISTRIBUTION AND BEHAVIOR: This rare species is found in the south of Angola and in some northern parts of Southwest Africa. *P. anchietae* is considerably smaller than *P. sebae* and is a close relative of *P. regius* (both are other Old World pythons). Thus far only a very few specimens of this species have been captured, and not much is known about its behavior in the wild. About the only thing we can say with certainty is that this snake occurs in rocky terrain.

CAPTIVITY AND BREEDING: There are very few imports of this snake. In contrast to other pythons, this species exhibits a calm temperament in captivity. It seems comfortable and is active when it is warm (84° to 90°F [29°-32°C]). An unproblematic eater, it has a tendency to get fat.

Tommy Logan, Assistant for Reptiles at the Houston Zoo, told me of his unsuccessful attempts to breed four Angola Pythons (two males and two females) at the zoo. An unusually long female (6 feet [183 cm]) was observed mating several times. Two months later it was obvious from the thickening of her body and swelling of the sides caused by eggs that the animal had conceived. But she stopped eating, and her behavior indicated that something was going wrong internally and that an operation was necessary. It turned out that the oviduct was torn. The eggs had passed into the abdominal cavity, were unfertilized, and some of them shriveled and were not fully developed. the largest of them measured $2^{1}/_{2}$ × $1^{1}/_{2}$ inches (63.5 x 38 mm). The exact length of the gestation period is not known; it appears to be about 3 months.

Python curtus
Blood Python
3 subspecies

PHYSICAL CHARACTERISTICS: The conically pointed head is clearly set off from the neck. The body is sturdy and squat, the prehensile tail, short. The ground color is brick to carmine red, gray, brown, or blackish. On the back and sides of the body there are yellowish-gray blotches and stripes of irregular shape that form more or less band-like patterns. The ventral plates have gray centers and are lighter at the sides. The head is brown to black. A thin dark or light line runs down the middle of the head, and another light line extends from the eyes to the corners of the mouth.

LENGTH: About 5 feet (150 cm); in exceptional cases up to 10 feet (3 m).

DISTRIBUTION AND BEHAVIOR: The Blood Python is native to the Malaysian Peninsula and to Sumatra and Borneo. It lives in the jungle and along the edges and in the clearings of thick tropical rain forests. Usually it is found near swamps, lakes, and large and small bodies of moving water. It is irascible, and if it is disturbed it lunges at the enemy like a released spring. Its diet consists of various kinds of birds and rodents. The Blood Python wraps itself around its eggs to brood them.

CAPTIVITY AND BREEDING: Blood Pythons often fail to thrive in captivity. The reason for this is usually faulty care. The bottom of the terrarium should be covered with a layer of peat or woody forest soil, and it should always be watered in a few places. Since this snake likes to lie in the water for hours, it should always have a large water basin. The artificial lighting should be on 12 to 14 hours during the day. Optimal temperatures are between 82° and 90°F (28°-32°C) during the day and 77° to 82°F (25°-28°C) at night. The Blood Python is active mostly at dusk and at night. It moves around during the day only rarely. The best time to feed it is in the evening. It can be given mice, rats, guinea pigs, doves, and small chickens. The prey is eaten both live and dead. Blood Pythons vary a great deal in their reactions to their caretakers. Some keep their nasty tempers and their propensity for biting during captivity and hiss angrily at the slightest disturbance. Others become tame quickly.

Blood Pythons have reproduced a number of times in terrariums kept at temperatures between 77° and 90°F (25°-32°C). The female curls herself around the eggs, periodically contracting the muscles in her body to raise the temperature inside the coil for the benefit of the developing embryos. The baby snakes hatch after 70 to 75 days, measuring 13 to 18 inches (33-45 cm) and weighing 1 1/2 to 2 1/2 ounces (37-69 g). Occasionally a female will not show any interest in her eggs. In such a case the eggs are incubated in a mixture of damp moss, sand, and peat at a constant temperature of 86° to 90°F (30°-32°C).

Python molurus
Indian Python
2 subspecies
(photo, page 50)

PHYSICAL CHARACTERISTICS: The head is somewhat set off from the neck. The body is powerful and very muscular. The ground color of both body and head varies from cream color to nut brown. The belly side is whitish to gray. A brown stripe starts at the nostrils, runs across the eyes, and extends to the corners of the mouth. There is a Y-shaped marking on the top of the head. The back is covered with largish brown blotches and the sides with smaller ones, forming a more or less regular pattern. In the subspecies *P. m. molurus,* these spots are of a lighter shade than in the Burmese python, *P. m. bivittatus.*

LENGTH: The lighter subspecies reaches a length of 16 feet (5 m); the darker one, 19 to 26 feet (6-8 m).

DISTRIBUTION AND BEHAVIOR: The Indian Python is distributed over large parts of southern Asia. The lighter subspecies is found in western Pakistan, in Nepal, India, and Sri Lanka, and the darker form is native to Burma, southern China, Indochina, Hainan, Borneo, Celebes, Java, and Sumbawa. The Indian Python is fonder than the Reticulate Python of wet habitats at higher altitudes. In the northern parts of its range it even hibernates. But it also occurs in flat and hilly terrain, and as a creature of the humid jungle it is more or less restricted to areas with lakes, swamps, and rivers. This snake climbs and swims equally well. Quite often it spends hours in the water with only the nostrils protruding from the surface. In the north, these

TOP: Bahama Boa (*Epicrates striatus*)
BOTTOM: Southern Watersnake (*Nerodia fasciata*)

pythons mate during or shortly after hibernation. The 8 to 30 eggs measure about 5 × 2¹/₂ inches (12 × 6 cm) and take about 3 months to mature. The mother snake protects the eggs in typical python manner but raises her body temperature only slightly. The Indian Python is basically rather lethargic but can rear up and bite in a minute if annoyed. According to herpetologist M. Vanderhaege, this snake hunts primarily water fowl in Pakistan, but it will eat any warm-blooded animal it can subdue. There are even tales of Indian Pythons attacking and swallowing leopards whole. Stories that *P. molurus* attacks and eats human beings probably belong in the realm of myth; however, there is one report that a small child was supposedly eaten by one of these snakes in China.

CAPTIVITY AND BREEDING: The Indian Python does well in a spacious terrarium. A large water basin is essential. The Indian Pythons under the author's care often spend whole days in the water. A tree limb for climbing is not absolutely necessary, but there should always be a retreat of solidly mortared rocks. Lights should be on 12 to 14 hours a day, and a bottom heater should gently heat one area of the bottom for 12 hours. Indian Pythons like daytime temperatures between 82° and 90°F (28°-32°C), and it can get 9° to 15°F (5°-8°C) cooler at night. They rest during the day, coming to life toward evening or at night when they spend hours crawling and climbing around in the terrarium. They accept food readily and present no problems to their keepers. They consume rabbits, guinea pigs, rats, mice, and poultry with equal enjoyment. My Indian Pythons seem to enjoy rats and chickens and eat two of the latter at one meal. They do not start ingesting their prey until they have killed it by constriction. Since Indian Pythons become active at dusk it makes sense to feed them in the evening.

P. molurus has been bred in captivity a number of times. The lighter subspecies requires 2 to 2¹/₂ months of hibernation from early December until February during which time the temperature has to be reduced to 64° to 68°F (18°-20°C) and the artificial lighting left off. These winter temperatures apply only to snakes from the northern part of their area of distribution. The eggs are deposited about 3 months after mating has occurred, and they take about 2 to 3 months to develop. The mother snake coils herself around the clutch of sticky eggs and broods them this way. Shortly before the eggs are due one should see to it that they will be deposited in some peat or forest soil with high humus content where they will retain the necessary moisture if sprayed with lukewarm water every day. During brooding, muscle spasms keep running down through the mother snake's body, creating some warmth that is beneficial to the development of the embryonic snakes. The temperature in the terrarium should stay fairly steady at 82° to 90°F (28°-32°C) during the incubation of the eggs. The baby snakes shed their first skins a few days after hatching, and soon after that they start eating mice of medium size. The further rearing presents no problems.

TOP LEFT: Green Anaconda (*Eunectes murinus*)
TOP RIGHT: Yellow Anaconda (*Eunectes notaeus*)
CENTER LEFT: Rough-scaled Snake (*Trachyboa boulengeri*)
CENTER RIGHT: Viperine Snake (*Natrix maura*)
BOTTOM LEFT: Grass Snake (*Natrix natrix*)
BOTTOM RIGHT: Diamondback Watersnake (*Nerodia rhombifera*)

Python regius
Ball Python
(photo, page 50)

PHYSICAL CHARACTERISTICS: The conical head is clearly set off from the neck. The body is thick, the tail surprisingly short and carrot-shaped. The ground color on the back of the body is a chocolate brown, and there are yellowish to grayish-white blotches of irregular shape all over it and the sides. The blotches can be unicolored or have one or several brown dots at the center. A narrow, yellow stripe runs across the temples from the tip of the nose to the neck region. Below this yellow stripe there is a dark band, which ends at the corners of the mouth. The top of the head looks dark brown to black, and the belly is procelain white.

LENGTH: 3 to 4 feet (90-120 cm); in exceptional cases over 5 feet (150 cm).

DISTRIBUTION AND BEHAVIOR: The Ball Python is native to western Africa, where it is distributed from Senegal to Sierra Leone and the Ivory Coast and in large areas of central Africa. It lives in open forests, in the savanna, and in the bush and is often found near water. It is not at all aggressive toward humans and bites only in rare cases. This snake is known as the Ball Python because, if it feels threatened, it rolls itself up into a ball, a peculiarity found in no other pythons. Although the Ball Python occasionally likes to sun itself, it is active primarily at dusk and at night. In keeping with its nocturnal nature, it hunts primarily gerbils and gerboas of the genus *Gerbillus*, which are also nocturnal. In nature, *P. regius* is largely specialized to this one prey, which is why it is so hard to make it accept food in captivity. Mating and the laying of eggs take place in the spring.

CAPTIVITY AND BREEDING: Since this species of python does not grow very large, a fairly small terrarium of approximately 40 × 24 × 24 inches (100 × 60 × 60 cm) is adequate. The Ball Python likes to climb and should not lack for a sturdy climbing branch. Pure sand or a mixture of sand, peat, and forest soil can be used as bottom material, and a bottom heater that provides gentle heat in one area for 12 hours a day is important. A basin with water is also required. Because of its moderate size and light weight, this snake can coexist with some vegetation, and a fairly sturdy plant can be placed, preferably in a plastic pot, in the terrarium. *P. regius* requires an even temperature between 79° and 90°F (26°-32°C) that should not drop more than 4° to 9°F (2°-5°C) at night. Ball Pythons are often finicky about accepting food in captivity and can fast for months without suffering. In an English zoo, two specimens of this snake did not eat anything for the first 22 months.

Successful reproduction has taken place several times in captivity. Mating time is in February and March, and the eggs are deposited from March to May. The 6 to 8 eggs, which are usually laid at night, stick together and are remarkably large (2³/₄-3 × 1³/₄-2³/₈ inches [7-8 × 4.5-6.1 cm]). The period between the laying of the eggs and the hatching of the young snakes is about 90 to 105 days. In the Tarango Zoo in Sydney it took only from November 30th until December 30th, 1972. This remarkably short incubation of only slightly over 4 weeks should probably be ascribed to the long period that elapsed between the mating and the laying of the eggs (from February to June). Ball Pythons engage in brood care. The young snakes are from 9 to 17 inches (23-43 cm) long at birth, and they molt after a few days. Soon therafter they start eating nestling mice. Under good care, young Ball Pythons grow to 3 feet (90 cm).

Python reticulatus
Reticulate Python
(photo, page 50)

PHYSICAL CHARACTERISTICS: The long head is somewhat set off from the neck. The body is more slender than that of other pythons but it is very powerful. The ground color varies from pale yellow to dark or olive brown. The back is covered with roundish, oval, or rhombic blotches that form a kind of lattice pattern. The blotches are yellowish to brown with yellow and shiny black borders. A black line runs down the center of the head from the tip of the snout to the nape, and there is a black band running from the eye to the neck on both sides. The yellowish underside is sparsely sprinkled with black. The body surface has a wonderful metallic sheen to it, especially under a bright light or after the old skin has been shed.

LENGTH: 16 to 19 feet (5-6 m); in exceptional cases over 26 feet (8 m).

DISTRIBUTION AND BEHAVIOR: The Reticulate Python is distributed over wide parts of Southeast Asia. On the mainland it is found in Burma, Thailand, Laos, Vietnam, Cambodia, and on the Malay peninsula, and it occurs on Sumatra, the Philippines, Borneo, Celebes, the Moluccas, Java, Lombok, Sumbawa, Sumba, Flores, Timor, and a number of smaller islands. It likes the dense, hot, humid jungle. Sometimes it penetrates to inhabited areas and is, in fact, encountered there quite frequently. Even today it is still found in suburbs of Bangkok and even in the city proper. It hides there under all kinds of trash, in living quarters and storage buildings as well as along the banks of the klongs (waterways) where there is much activity and innumerable small boats move back and forth. *P. reticulatus* is primarily crepuscular. It feeds on various mammals and birds that may be as large as ducks or dogs. The prey is crushed to death before it is swallowed. In their behavior toward humans, Reticulate Pythons vary. Some become almost tame, but most remain unpredictable and are capable of ferocious attack if disturbed.

The following story was told to me by a Vietnamese French teacher who had spent many years teaching in Vietnam during the colonial period. Almost everybody in Vietnam is acquainted with Reticulate Pythons and hardly anyone is afraid ot them. One day several men teased a large Reticulate Python. They were not aware that the snake had gotten hold of one of their party and had wrapped itself around him so tightly that the man was helpless. His companions did not realize his plight, standing around aimlessly laughing out loud at the weird sounds and gestures made by their friend, who was completely enveloped by now. When it finally occurred to

them to release him from the snake's embrace, he was dead. Such instances are of course extremely rare. There is a report that a 14-year-old boy was swallowed by a *P. reticulatus* in the Netherlands Indies; and the small size and slight build of the people there lends some credence to the story. Reticulate Pythons are oviparous and look after their eggs. Mature specimens lay up to 100 eggs, which mature within 60 to 80 days.

CAPTIVITY AND BREEDING: These snakes need a sizable terrarium, a large water basin, and a very sturdy tree limb for climbing. Hygienic considerations make a floor of flagstones more desirable than a layer of peat, sand, or comparable material. One part of the floor should be slightly warmed with a bottom heater for over 12 hours a day. During the day the air should be 77° to 90°F (25°-32°C); at night it can be 8° to 10°F (4°-6°C) cooler. This impressive looking snake usually spends its days sleeping in one place and moving very little. Often it lies in the water basin. Toward evening it comes alive and spends hours moving around the terrarium. The Reticulate Python is easy to keep. It is not fussy about food, eating anything from chickens and ducks to mice, rats, guinea pigs, rabbits, cats, dogs, and piglets. It passes the remains of a meal after 3 to 10 days, quite often in the water basin.

P. reticulatus has been bred successfully in captivity a number of times. A 16-foot (5 m) female owned by the author was observed mating with an 11-foot (3.5 m) male for several hours in the evening of December 2, 1976. On April 23, 1977, she laid 45 eggs on forest soil rich in humus and immediately coiled herself around them to brood them. The mother snake and the clutch were then sprayed with several quarts of lukewarm water every 2 to 3 days. The air in the terrarium was kept at 82° to 90°F (28°-32°C) during the entire incubation period. I measured 90°F (32°C) between the coils of the snake's body although I observed none of the muscle activity characteristic of other brooding pythons. On June 25, 1977, I moved the eggs to a container with humus and leaves and covered them with damp blotting paper. The temperature was kept at 82° to 86°F (28°-30°C), and the clutch sprayed with lukewarm water every day. Between June 16 and 19, 37 baby snakes hatched, and they first molted between July 31 and August 3. On August 11, the young snakes ate their first, medium-sized mice. The baby pythons measured 29 to 31 inches (75-79 cm) and weighed 5.6 to 6 ounces (160-170 g) at birth. Raising them presented no problems, and they had reached a length of $4^{1}/_{4}$ feet (130 cm) by the time they were 3 months old.

Python sebae
African Rock Python

PHYSICAL CHARACTERISTICS: The conical head is set off from the neck only slightly, and the body is sturdy. The ground color varies from light brown to grayish-brown. The markings on the back consist of blackish-brown or reddish-brown blotches. More or less distinct crescent-shaped spots that are light at the center and darker to black toward the edges dot the sides at fairly even spacings. The top of the head carries a dark triangular mark, which is flanked on both sides by a light band. There is also a dark stripe running from the nostril to the eye and beyond the eye to the corner of the mouth. The belly is pale gray sprinkled with dark dots.

LENGTH: 13 feet (4 m), occasionally up to 19 feet (6 m).

DISTRIBUTION AND BEHAVIOR: The African Rock Python is found in large parts of Africa south of the Sahara, but it is rare in tropical rain forests because it favors the open savannas. It usually lives near bodies of water and likes to lie in the water. That is why these snakes sometimes get caught in the nets of fishermen and are pulled out of the water along with the fish. African Rock Pythons climb as well as they swim. They often lie on tree limbs, and if a prey animal passes underneath they scoop it up. Thanks to their strong, prehensile tails they have no trouble keeping their balance in the tree. African Rock Pythons live primarily off warm-blooded prey like birds, rats, rabbits, wild boars, small antelopes, and monkeys. The prey is seized with a mighty lunge, strangled, and then swallowed, usually head first. African Rock Pythons are generally calmer than Reticulate Pythons, but some individuals bite readily. They move about during the day, but usually they hunt at night when they track their warm-blooded prey with the aid of pit-shaped, heat-sensitive organs in the upper and lower labials. In South Africa, *P. sebae* hibernates for 2 to 4 months. This species lays 30 to 50 and in rare cases up to 100 eggs which the female broods, resting her head on the clutch. The eggs are covered with a tough, leathery skin and measure about $3^{1}/_{2} \times 2^{1}/_{4}$ inches (90 × 60 mm). The eggs usually take about 3 months to hatch. The newborn snakes are about as thick as a finger and measure 24 to 28 inches (60-70 cm). They grow quickly and, if fed well, can reach 8 feet (2.5 m) within 5 years.

CAPTIVITY AND BREEDING: In size and arrangement the terrarium should be like that used for a Reticulate Python. A climbing tree is essential because African Rock Pythons often rest on branches. Sometimes they also spend hours or even days lying in the water with only the nose sticking out. Lights and heater should be on 12 to 14 hours a day. The air temperature should be kept at 77° to 90°F (25°-32°C) during the day, but it can drop to 65° to 72°F (18°-22°C) at night. The African Rock Python is quite unproblematic in captivity. Unlike the Ball and the Blood Pythons it readily accepts food and hardly shows any preferences, eating mice, rats, hamsters, guinea pigs, rabbits, cats, and dogs, as well as all kinds of poultry. The specimen I have will eat any kind of warm-blooded animal, but it seems to have a special fondness for cats, eating 2 to 3 full-grown ones at a meal. The huge snake waits until a cat has stopped moving and then devours it head first.

In July 1975, this snake of mine laid 56 eggs

which were infertile because there was no male present. She immediately coiled herself around the eggs, and while brooding she was unusually aggressive and always ready to attack. She did not stop eating while brooding. There have been some cases of *P. sebae* reproducing in captivity. In one of these the eggs took 52 days to mature at temperatures between 72° and 86°F (22°-30°C).

Python timorensis
Timor Python
(photo, page 50)

PHYSICAL CHARACTERISTICS: The head is an elongated oval but clearly set off from the neck. The body is slender like that of a colubrid. The pit-shaped, heat-sensitive organs in the upper labials are particularly pronounced in this species. The ground color of the back and sides is yellow to reddish-brown with darker blotches throughout. These blotches merge into a net-like pattern which becomes less distinct toward the tail and finally disappears altogether. The belly is a uniform yellowish color.

LENGTH: Slightly over 10 feet (3 m).

DISTRIBUTION AND BEHAVIOR: This rare snake is found only on Timor and Flores. It lives in the bush and in dry forests. Practically nothing is known about its life in the wild.

CAPTIVITY AND BREEDING: *P. anchietae* and *P. timorensis* are the two rarest species of pythons. *P. timorensis* needs a good-sized terrarium with quite a few climbing branches as well as a water basin. A bottom heater and artificial lighting should be on 12 to 14 hours a day. *P. timorensis* is comfortable at a temperature of 77° to 90°F (25°-32°C) during the day. At night it should be 5° to 9°F (3°-5°C) cooler. The specimens kept by the author spend their days lying in a corner of the terrarium or hiding in hollow pieces of cork bark. Occasionally they crawl up onto the climbing tree, which is bathed in the light of the heat lamp. They do not really come to life until dark when they start crawling around. *P. timorensis* eats mice, rats, and baby chicks, which it kills by strangling. Thus far there have been no reports of this snake reproducing in captivity.

Subfamily Calabariinae—African Burrowing Pythons

Genus *Calabaria*
African Burrowing Pythons
1 species

Calabaria reinhardtii
Two-headed Python
(photo, page 49)

PHYSICAL CHARACTERISTICS: The markedly flattened head is not set off from the body. The body is of the same thickness for almost the full length. The plates on the head are large, and the scales on the body smooth and glossy. The tail is short. The ground color of the back and sides is blackish-brown, brown, or reddish-brown and has irregular blotches of brick red, pale yellow, or porcelain color. The tip of the head and the tail are almost black. In some specimens the tip of the tail is set off by a white crossband. The pupil is a vertical slit. The underside can be brown or gray and also with yellow or brown blotches.

LENGTH: Up to 40 inches (1 m).

DISTRIBUTION AND BEHAVIOR: The Two-headed Python occurs on Fernando Po and in the western part of the African continent from Liberia to Cameroon and from Gabon to the Congo. It inhabits humid tropical forests where it is found crawling or burrowing in decaying leaves and in the soil as well as in the burrows of small rodents. It feeds on small mice and earthworms, an unusual diet for such a large snake. It kills the mice not by catching hold of them and then squeezing them to death but by squashing them against the walls of their burrows. The Two-headed

Python is nocturnal. If it is discovered in its hiding place it tries to get away by quickly burrowing into the ground. The characteristic pose of this species is to keep the head pointing down almost vertically while the tail is held erect. If escape is impossible this snake acts like *Python regius* or *Lichanura trivirgata*. It rolls up in a ball and hides the head, which points down, in the middle of the ball. It never tries to bite. Two-headed Pythons lay eggs, but the clutch is small.

CAPTIVITY AND BREEDING: The Two-headed Python is imported only rarely, and consequently little is known about its behavior in captivity. It does not need much space or special lighting; ordinary daylight is sufficient. For this burrowing snake the bottom of the terrarium should have a layer of forest soil or a mixture of peat and sand, which should be dampened in some places. A water dish where the snake can drink and where it will occasionally bathe is essential. For hiding it should have a large piece of bark or a flat rock to serve as a retreat during the day. Very young mice and earthworms should be offered as food, but most of these snakes respond to feeding reluctantly or not at all. Some individuals will eat if they are locked into a small box with the prey overnight. During the day *C. reinhardtii* needs temperatures between 82° and 90°F (28°-32°C). At night it should be 8°-10°F (4°-6°C) cooler. This species has never been bred in captivity.

Subfamily Loxoceminae—American Burrowing Pythons

Genus *Loxocemus*
American Burrowing Pythons
1 species

Loxocemus bicolor
Mexican Python
(photo, page 49)

PHYSICAL CHARACTERISTICS: The Mexican Python is probably the only python of the New World. This presents some difficulties to the scientists who try to fit it into the classification of snakes. It cannot be clearly classed with the subfamily Pythoninae or the family Xenopeltidae. Problems arise in either case because of anatomical inconsistencies, and it is placed here in its own subfamily.

The snout of this snake is flattened into a wedge-shaped tip. The sturdy body is dark brown and takes on a beautiful purple sheen in bright light. There are a few white blotches scattered along the sides.

LENGTH: 4 to 5 feet (120-150 cm).

DISTRIBUTION AND BEHAVIOR: The Mexican Python is found from Nayarit (Mexico) to Costa Rica. We do not know much about its habits in the wild. It burrows among leaves and in loose soil where its coloration makes it hard to see. It is usually caught in piles of leaves rather than in the soil. In nature it feeds primarily on small mammals, and it lays eggs. We do not know whether or not it looks after the eggs the way other pythons do.

CAPTIVITY AND BREEDING: The Mexican Python is easy to keep because it does not need a large terrarium. Soil from pine woods mixed with sphagnum and leaves is used as bottom material, into which the snake burrows. The bottom is kept damp by spraying a little lukewarm water over it every day. There is no need for bottom heating, but the air temperature should be kept between 75° and 82°F (24°-28°C). Artificial lighting is unnecessary because the animals stay in hiding during the day. There are reports that these snakes eat readily. They favor baby chicks and will more rarely consume mice.

Attempts to have this snake reproduce in captivity have not yet been successful, but some matings have been observed—occurring in the month of November.

Family Boidae—Boas and Sandboas
Subfamily Boinae—True Boas

Genus *Acranthophis*
Madagascan Boas
2 species

Acranthophis madagascariensis
Madagascan Boa

PHYSICAL CHARACTERISTICS: The Madagascan Boa looks very much like the South American Boa Constrictor. The head is clearly set off from the neck. The body is thick and strong. The large eyes have vertical slits as pupils. The back is brown. The sides are a lighter color with black or very dark oval blotches at regular intervals. Toward the belly, these oval blotches merge with large, round patches of a brownish color with light centers. The spaces between the brown blotches on the sides show an irregular pattern of black dots. Down the middle of the back, lighter or darker lines form a zigzag pattern that shows up more or less clearly. In the light, grown snakes of this species glisten with beautiful metallic colors ranging from blue to a golden green. A stripe runs from the eye to the corner of the mouth. The side of the head is a uniform brown, and the porcelain-colored underside has dark blotches.

LENGTH: Slightly over 10 feet (3 m).

DISTRIBUTION AND BEHAVIOR: This species is native to northern Madagascar, and we know very little about its life in nature. Unlike the closely related *A. dumerili*, which favors dry ground near water, *A. madagascariensis* lives in hot and humid jungles. It is gentle and seldom bites. It lives on birds and smallish mammals which it kills by constriction before swallowing them. The Madagascan boa bears young after a gestation period of about 6 months.

CAPTIVITY AND BREEDING: An opportunity to acquire this giant snake either from a dealer or a private fancier presents itself very rarely. The terrarium for such a snake should be large. Peat or forest soil is a good bottom material. *A. madagascariensis* likes moisture and needs a large water basin where it will take long and frequent baths. During the day the temperature should lie between 82° and 86°F (28°-30°C), and it should drop very little at night. The artificial lighting should be on 12 to 14 hours. The Madagascan boa moves very little during the day but starts crawling around at dusk. It adjusts well to captivity and readily eats pigeons, baby chicks, mice, rats, and rabbits. This species has reproduced in captivity. M. Vanderhaege lets his snakes hibernate from the end of May to July at 63°F (17°C). They mated early in July, and in October of the same year 4 baby snakes were born, measuring between $16^{1}/_{2}$ and 19 inches (42 and 48 cm). The raising of the young snakes presented no problems.

Genus *Boa*
Boa Constrictors
1 species

Boa constrictor
Boa constrictor
8 subspecies

PHYSICAL CHARACTERISTICS: The Boa Constrictor is the most generally known though by no means the largest of the boas. The head of the Boa Constrictor is arrowhead-shaped and set off from the neck. The body is thick and powerful. The coloration varies a great deal not only from subspecies to subspecies but also among individuals of the same geographical race. The ground color may be reddish-gray, yellowish-brown, or reddish-brown, or other dark brown shades. A pattern of alternating light and dark blotches runs down the back. Toward the tail these blotches take on a reddish or, in some animals, even a blood-red hue. On the top of the head there is a band that starts near the nose and ends at the nape, and a dark stripe runs across the temples from the nose to the sides of the neck. The belly is a grayish porcelain color sprinkled with dark dots.

LENGTH: Over 10 feet (3 m).

DISTRIBUTION AND BEHAVIOR: The Boa Constrictor is found from southern Mexico down to Argentina as well as on the Lesser Antilles. It is especially common in dry terrain with open forests or thick bushes. Usually it lives near rivers, lakes, and ponds. It is equally at home on the ground as in trees, where it hunts for birds and small mammals. In its natural habitat it is reported to kill and eat lizards and even small caimans occasionally. It spends most of the day resting in its retreat or some protected spot and does not become active until dusk. Individuals vary considerably in their behavior. Some bite at the slightest provocation while others are very docile and refrain from using their teeth even when seriously molested. In Brazil, many farmers have no objections to Boa Constrictors on their silos or under their roofs because they keep the rats under control. Boa Constrictors bear live young from May to August. There are often up to 60 fully developed young measuring from 14 to 20 inches (35-50 cm).

CAPTIVITY AND BREEDING: The Boa Constrictor is the most frequently kept giant snake. To thrive it needs a large terrarium with localized bottom heat, a climbing tree, and a large water basin. The bottom can be covered with pure sand or a mixture of sand and peat. The heat and the lighting should be on all day, and a temperature of 77° to 90°F (25°-32°C) should be maintained during the day. At night it may get as cool as 68° to 72°F (20°-22°C). This snake spends most of its days on the floor of the terrarium. Occasionally it may bask on a branch under the heat lamp. It is crepuscular and comes to life only in the evening. In nature it is said to stay away from water, but in captivity some of these snakes spend hours at a time in the water. Healthy specimens almost always show interest in the food offered them and make little distinction between mice, rats, guinea pigs, rabbits, baby chicks, and birds. As their name suggests, Boa Constrictors crush their prey before eating it. They generally do this in captivity, too.

It is not particularly hard to get these snakes to reproduce in captivity, and this has been accomplished a number of times. There have even been offspring from a crossing of a *B. C. constrictor* and a *B. C. occidentalis*. The mating usually occurs in February or March, and the gestation lasts from 5 to 7 months. Before copulation the male crawls over the back of the female. The baby snakes shed their first skins about 1 to 3 weeks after birth. After that they can be given small mice. Raising these snakes presents no problems, and, if well fed, they usually reach sexual maturity by the time they are 3 years old.

Genus *Candoia*
Pacific Boas
3 species

Candoia bibroni
Bibron's Boa
2 subspecies

PHYSICAL CHARACTERISTICS: The arrowhead-shaped head is very distinctly set off from the neck and the stout body. The ground color of the body can be almost any shade of brown and varies from individual to individual. The sides often have a reddish tinge. The back and flanks are marked with chocolate brown to black blotches. The top of the head and the sides behind the eyes also look chocolate brown to black and have a sprinkling of white dots. The belly plates are porcelain colored and have dark blotches toward the posterior part of the body. The underside of the tail has narrow light and dark cross stripes. Bibron's boa sometimes undergoes a change of color in the course of the day. This phenomenon, which is quite rare in snakes and which I have also observed in Reticulate Pythons (*Python reticulatus*), is brought about through external stimuli and light factors associated with the rhythm of daylight and dark. In the forenoon the snake's body is light colored, and in the afternoon and at night it clearly becomes darker.

LENGTH: Slightly over 6$^{1}/_{2}$ feet (2 m).

DISTRIBUTION AND BEHAVIOR: This species is native to Ceram, Melanesia, and Polynesia. It is common on many islands but only in wet tropical forests. In spite of this it is more ground-dwelling than arboreal. Very little is known about its life in the wild. It feeds on birds and small mammals.

CAPTIVITY AND BREEDING: This rare boa was first imported alive to Europe in the early 1960's by Mrs. Schetty and thus made available to snake fanciers. Bibron's Boa needs a large terrarium and a climbing tree on which it often rests during the day. The tree must have branches that offer a good hold. A water basin is also necessary even though this snake will not use it for bathing. Bibron's Boa likes a high air humidity of 75%. It should also be sprayed twice a week with lukewarm water. These snakes are not very tolerant of people and are quick to bite if disturbed. The lights should be on 12 to 14 hours. Snake fancier Hans Schweizer had two of these animals. In the summer he kept them at 74° to 84°F (23°-29°C) and in the fall at 66° to 75°F (19°-24°C). A box that served as a den was kept permanently at a higher temperature of 77° to 86°F (25°-30°C). The snakes lived on birds, baby chicks, mice, rats, and dace.
Thus far, Bibron's Boas have not been bred in captivity though babies of the species have been born in terrariums by newly imported females that were gravid when taken into captivity.

Genus *Corallus*
American Tree Boas
3 species

Corallus enydris
Garden Tree Boa
2 subspecies

PHYSICAL CHARACTERISTICS: The wedge-shaped head is clearly set off from the flattened body that is slender like that of a colubrid and comes to a ridge along the spine. This snake has a long, well-developed prehensile tail. The ground color of the body can be brown to gray to grayish-green. The back and sides of the body have irregular black blotches with the ones on the sides often being square or hexagonal and lighter at the center. The black rhomboid blotches often seem to have light borders which vary in brightness. This lighter color extends toward the back where it merges with a band of zigzag patterns or closely spaced blotches. These dorsal markings vary greatly in distinctness. Uniformly colored yellowish-gray specimens are not uncommon. The head has dark spots, and a black band runs from the eye to the corner of the mouth.

LENGTH: Rarely over 8 feet (2.5 m).

DISTRIBUTION AND BEHAVIOR: This snake occurs from southern Central America (Nicaragua) to northern South America (northern and western Brazil, Peru, Bolivia) and on the Windward Islands. It inhabits primarily wet tropical forests, where it lives mostly in trees, preferably sleeping in a network of branches and foliage. When it moves it uses a technique known as "concertina" locomotion, wrapping the forward third of its body around a branch, drawing the rear up to it, then raising its front end and scouting for the next higher place where it can safely anchor itself again. Climbing in this way it keeps gaining some altitude. The Garden Tree Boa lives primarily off birds and small mammals. Both the upper and the lower front teeth are long, extremely sharp, and arched backward. They can easily penetrate through the feathers and into the muscles of birds. Before striking, the snake bends its head back into an S-shape. Then it springs at its victim and strangles it. The Garden Tree Boa is wild and violent. If it is bothered at all, it immediately strikes at its intruder and inflicts deep wounds with its sharp teeth. Both *C. enydris* and *C. caninus* bear live young.

CAPTIVITY AND BREEDING: This arboreal snake, which descends to the ground only rarely, needs a tall terrarium which offers extensive opportunity for climbing. Before molting it often spends considerable time in the water. This is an essentially nocturnal snake that spends most of the evening and night crawling around in the branches. It thrives at daytime temperatures between 77° and 86°F (25°-30°C), which may drop at night to 68° to 75°F (20°-24°C). These snakes will stay healthy for years in captivity and are always willing to accept food, preferably mice, which they squeeze to death by looping their anterior body around them. They keep hold of a branch with their prehensile tail and swallow their prey while hanging upside down.
C.enydris has been repeatedly bred without complications in terrariums.

Corallus caninus
Emerald Tree Boa

PHYSICAL CHARACTERISTICS: In terms of coloration and body build, the South American Emerald Tree Boa is the exact counterpart of the Green Python (*Chondropython viridis*) of New Guinea and Australia. The two snakes are practically indistinguishable. The Emerald Tree Boa is one of the most beautiful members of the Boidae family. Its wedge-shaped head is clearly set off from the powerful body. The body is vertically compressed to form a ridge along the spine. The snake also has a clearly prehensile tail. The ground color of the body and sides is a bright leaf green. The labials and the belly are the color of egg yolk. A white line from which white or yellowish cross stripes emanate at regular intervals runs down the spine. In juveniles, the upper side is red. The pit-shaped, heat-sensitive organs in the upper and lower labials are clearly visible. The teeth of the upper and lower jaws are long and recurved.

LENGTH: 6½ to 10 feet (2-3 m).

DISTRIBUTION AND BEHAVIOR: The Emerald Tree Boa is native to Guyana, Brazil, eastern Peru, and northern Bolivia. It spends most of its time hidden in the thick foliage of trees where, thanks to its excellent adaptive coloration, it stays practically invisible. The snake coils itself up on a branch in such a way that the head rests more or less in the center of the loops formed by its body. *C. caninus* lives on birds and mammals which it usually grabs from above and kills by wrapping three coils of its body around the animal. The long teeth are clearly evident in this process of subduing the prey. The Emerald Tree Boa is active at dusk and at night. It descends from the tree branches only rarely. This snake is not only an expert climber but also a good swimmer. It has a calm temperament but will bite fiercely if pestered. The long teeth cause deep and painful wounds. This snake bears live young.

CAPTIVITY AND BREEDING: This snake requires a large, tall terrarium where conditions of a tropical rain forest are simulated with plenty of opportunity for climbing in a complex network of branches. The bottom may be covered with peat or forest soil with high humus content. The terrarium should be equipped with adequate heating both of the air and the bottom and always have an air humidity of over 70%. To achieve this, a large water basin is necessary and water should be sprayed several times a week. The snake can also live happily over a large surface of water. Suitable plants for such a terrarium are philodendron, hoya, and scindapsus. To feel comfortable the Emerald Tree Boa needs temperatures between 77° and 95°F (25°-35°C) during the day and between 68° and 77°F (20°-25°C) at night. But the snake does not do well in the atmosphere of a greenhouse. It is often a problematic animal to keep, and people's experiences with it vary. It also tends to suffer from mouth rot and is not always willing to take the food offered so that the keeper has to resort to force-feeding. With some individuals one has to wait for weeks or even months before they start eating on their own. Some Emerald Tree Boas refuse all but one kind of prey and will accept even that only if it is offered at night from below as from a small pail hanging from a branch. These snakes are passive animals that do not like to be disturbed during the day. Success in keeping them often depends on the animals' state of health when they were imported and on the proper conditions in the terrarium. Some individuals have survived in captivity over 6 years.

Thus far, *C. caninus* has been bred in terrariums only rarely. The young snakes (up to 6) measure about 18 inches (45 cm) and are rust brown with bright white markings. This initial coloration gives way after a few molts to a dirty brownish green, which later changes into the typical deep leaf green.

Genus *Epicrates*
Rock Boas
7 species

Epicrates cenchria
Rainbow Boa
10 subspecies
(photo, page 50)

PHYSICAL CHARACTERISTICS: The head is longish and hardly set off from the neck at all. The powerful body is equipped with a fully developed prehensile tail. There are no heat-sensitive pits in the upper labials. The ground color of the body can be any shade ranging from yellowish-brown to reddish brown. The back is covered with black rings that form chain-like rows and may fade into each other in places. In some specimens these dark rings are almost totally absent. On the sides of the body there are dark blotches with crescent-shaped lighter areas directly above them. A black stripe runs from the lower edge of the eye to the corner of the mouth. The color on the top of the head is divided by a dark line running down the center, and a dark line extends from above the eye to the back of the head. Specimens with only faint markings or of a uniform reddish-brown color are not infrequent.

LENGTH: Up to $6^{1}/_{2}$ feet (2 m).

DISTRIBUTION AND BEHAVIOR: The Rainbow Boa is distributed from Costa Rica to Argentina. It prefers rocky terrain and woods and is also found on plantations. Being an excellent climber, it is found in trees as often as on the ground. Its food consists mostly of birds and mammals, which it kills by wrapping its slender but extremely strong body around them. During the day it rests in some hidden place and becomes active toward evening. The species bears live young.

CAPTIVITY AND BREEDING: This snake requires a large terrarium with a climbing tree and a large water basin. A mixture of sand and peat or peat and forest soil is used in the bottom. The lights should be on 12 to 14 hours a day, and the temperature should range from 79° to 90°F (26°-32°C) during the day and 72° to 77°F (22°-25°C) at night. Although not as aggressive as other members of its family, the Rainbow Boa can tear deep wounds with its long, recurved teeth. Because it is easy to keep and remarkably beautiful, the Rainbow Boa is an ideal candidate for a terrarium. It accepts food readily and likes mice, rats, birds, and baby chicks.

The Rainbow Boa has been bred in captivity numerous times, and hybrids from the two subspecies *E. c. maurus* and *E. c. cenchria* have even been raised. The gestation period is about 5 months. The young snakes, which measure about 20 to 26 inches (50-65 cm) at birth, shed their first skins at about 10 to 20 days of age. Soon after that they will eat young, furred mice.

Epicrates striatus
Bahama Boa
5 subspecies
(photo, page 67)

PHYSICAL CHARACTERISTICS: The head is clearly set off from the slender but very muscular body. The snake has a well-developed prehensile tail. The ground color of the body is a lovely grayish to copper brown. The back is covered with light to dark gray, more or less irregularly notched blotches that merge into each other in places. Light crossbands run between these spots. The sides of the body also show irregular spots. The head is a uniform gray or brown, and the belly is gray with a sparse dark sprinkling.

LENGTH: Up to 10 feet (3 m).

DISTRIBUTION AND BEHAVIOR: The Bahama Boa comes from the island of Hispaniola and the Bahamas. The author has studied the habitat of the subspecies *E. s. fosteri* on Bimini Island. Bahama Boas are found especially in thick forests and mangrove thickets. They like to rest in tree branches as well as in piles of loose rock. They seem to be especially fond of hiding under rafters and old boards of dilapidated wooden houses, and they are found under the straw roofs of the huts of natives as well as in sugar cane fields, where they hunt primarily for birds, mice, and rats. During the day they are lethargic and come to life only in the evening, which is why the natives often refer to them as "sleeping snakes." When freshly captured, the Bahama Boa often bites ferociously, but after a while in the terrarium it soon becomes hand tame. If terrified and picked up by a person, this snake—like all giant serpents and many other snakes—emits a strong-smelling secretion from its anal glands. The species bears live young.

CAPTIVITY AND BREEDING: *E. striatus* needs a large and tall terrarium containing a solid climbing tree with many forked branches. A large bathing basin is also essential. The snake often spends days on end in the water before molting. Sand and rocks or a mixture of sand and peat can be used on the bottom. Bahama Boas climb a lot and sometimes bask on branches under a heat lamp for hours. But they also spend time on the ground. The lights should be on 12 to 14 hours, and gentle, local bottom heat is recommended. The animals are comfortable at 75° to 86°F (24°-30°C) during the day and 65° to 72°F (18°-22°C) at night. Bahama Boas usually hibernate in December and January in their natural habitat, and it is therefore appropriate to lower the temperature in the terrarium by 9° to 11°F (5°-6°C) at this time of year, too. Partially grown and adult snakes eat birds, baby chicks, mice, rats, and other small mammals.

A female Bahama Boa under the care of the author had 19 young in September 1975, which measured 16 to 20 inches (40-50 cm) at birth. They molted about 2 weeks after being born. Baby snakes of this species eat lizards, especially geckos, but refuse small mice during their first year and therefore have to be stuffed with one or two newborn mice a week. Mating takes place from December to March. On September 14, 1977, the female mentioned above gave birth to 1 live snake, 2 stillborn ones (measuring $16^5/8$ and 17 inches [42.7 and 43.6 cm]) and a number of infertile eggs. I then observed behavior that is probably quite uncommon: The mother snake ate most of the infertile eggs during and after birth. *E. striatus* has been bred in terrariums quite frequently, including successful crossings between *E. s. striatus* and *E. s. strigilatus*.

Genus *Eunectes*
Anacondas
4 species

Eunectes murinus
Green Anaconda
2 subspecies
(photo, page 68)

PHYSICAL CHARACTERISTICS: The head is longish and barely set off from the neck. The ground color of the back and sides is grayish to olive green. Young animals sometimes have a suggestion of rusty red on the sides. On the back there are dark round blotches that sometimes merge into each other. The sides also have dark blotches with yellow at the centers. The belly is grayish-white or yellowish with black blotches. A whitish-gray to yellowish band edged on both sides with black connects the eye and the corner of the mouth.

LENGTH: Over 30 feet (9 m).

DISTRIBUTION AND BEHAVIOR: The Anaconda is native to Brazil, Colombia, Peru, Ecuador, Venezuela, Guyana, and Trinidad. Being a superb swimmer, it is almost always found near water, and it can stay submerged for a very long time. On the shore it loves to bask on overhanging trees, on rocks, or in the hot sand. Fish form part of its diet, but it feeds primarily on various mammals such as capybaras and agoutis as well as on birds, and it also eats young caimans. At the height of summer this huge snake enters a kind of estivation by burying itself in the mud of swamps that are drying up. The Green Anaconda bears live young which measure about 28 inches (70 cm).

CAPTIVITY AND BREEDING: The Green Anaconda needs a large terrarium with a very solid climbing tree and a big water basin which it will often not leave for days if the water is at an ideal 79° to 84°F (26°-29°C). This snake is quite phlegmatic but moves more at dusk than during the day. Coming from the tropical parts of South America, it is used to constant high temperatures between 79° and 82°F (26°-32°C) both day and night with only minor fluctuations. If well cared for, Green Anacondas do well in captivity. There are individuals that will consume anything from rats, guinea pigs, rabbits, pigeons, and chickens to fish and other prey. But others have narrowed their interest down to one specific prey and will refuse everything else no matter how hungry they are. Most Anacondas are testy and

combative and should therefore be approached with caution. They bite hard and hang on with their long, recurved teeth, coiling themselves around the part of the victim's body they have got hold of. Anacondas should always be kept singly because they sometimes forget themselves and attack and even eat their companions in captivity.

E. murinus has been successfully bred in captivity a number of times, and females that were pregnant when captured have given birth to some young in terrariums. In preparation for mating the male crawls over the female's back. Copulation usually takes place in the water. The gestation period is about 230 days. The newborn snakes measure about 30 inches (75 cm) and weigh about 8¾ ounces (250 g). They shed their first skins after 5 to 8 days and soon after start eating mice, rats, and baby chicks at irregular intervals. The further rearing is unproblematic. Like their parents, the young snakes enjoy lying in water.

Eunectes notaeus
Yellow Anaconda
(photo, page 68)

PHYSICAL CHARACTERISTICS: The longish head is barely set off from the neck. The ground color is a lovely, light, yellowish-brown with large, dark blotches on the back. The blotches on the sides are much smaller, irregular in shape, and without the yellow centers characteristic of the *E. murinus*. A wide, dark band connects the eye to the corner of the mouth. The belly is yellowish to porcelain-colored and mottled with black.

LENGTH: Over 10 feet (3 m) and sometimes up to 16 feet (5 m).

DISTRIBUTION AND BEHAVIOR: The Yellow Anaconda comes from southern Brazil, Bolivia, Paraguay, and northern Argentina. Like its larger cousin it loves the water and is found near all kinds of bodies of water. It also inhabits less dense places in wet forests. Its swimming and diving are developed to perfecfection, and it can stay underwater for quite a long time. When on land it usually stays close to the ground and climbs trees only now and then. It is very resistant to the cold and hibernates in its native habitat. Its diet consists of mammals, birds, fish, and occasionally reptiles. It is viviparous, and the newborn snakes shed their first skins within a few hours after birth.

CAPTIVITY AND BREEDING: Although the Yellow Anaconda is not anywhere near as long and heavy as its northern relative it still needs a large terrarium designed for giant snakes with a big water basin in it. Often it spends whole days in the water with only the head protruding. The artificial lights should be on 12 to 14 hours, and the air temperature should be between 77° and 86°F (25°-30°C) during the day. A considerable drop at night down to 59°-68°F (15°-20°C) is beneficial. This snake is very resistant to the cold. It is more active at dusk than during the day. In the evening and at night it often crawls around for hours. The Yellow Anaconda varies a great deal in its response to humans. Some are vicious and aggressive, attacking wildly at the slightest provocation. Others are placid from the first day on, never try to bite, and become hand tame. This species readily accepts food it is offered, eating rabbits, rats, mice, guinea pigs, pigeons, and baby chicks. Some individuals also take fish. Sometimes this snake refuses food in the winter. This is probably connected with the fact that this species hibernates in its native habitat.

E. notaeus has been imported pregnant, and pairs have also mated and produced young in captivity. The gestation period is about 9 months, and there may be as many as 30 snakes or more in a litter, measuring between 22 and 28 inches (55-70 cm) at birth.

Genus *Sanzinia*
Madagascan Tree Boas
1 species

Sanzinia madagascariensis
Madagascan Tree Boa

PHYSICAL CHARACTERISTICS: The heart-shaped head is clearly set off from the neck. The body is sturdy and reminiscent in shape of the South American Emerald Tree Boa (*Corallus enydris*). The coloration of the back and sides of the body is grayish to olive green. The back is marked with regularly spaced cross-bands that extend down the sides where they flare out in diamond shapes. These lozenge-shaped blotches often have light-colored centers. The dark head is lightly sprinkled with black, and a black stripe runs from the eye to the corner of the mouth.

LENGTH: Up to 8 feet (2.5 m).

DISTRIBUTION AND BEHAVIOR: This species is found only on Madagascar. Although it likes dry ground it almost always lives near or immediately adjacent to water. It feeds on birds, mice, rats, and other small mammals and is mostly crepuscular. In rainy weather it is often found on roads in the evening and at night. In its natural habitat *S. madagascariensis* hibernates from late May to July or August. An interesting difference in behavior between animals coming from the eastern and the western parts of Madagascar deserves mentioning. The eastern snakes are wild and fierce, responding to any approach with attacks during which they flatten their heads in the style of vipers. Their western counterparts are just the opposite. They have a very calm temper and hardly ever resort to biting, even when they are interfered with. This species usually bears from 5 to 10 young which measure about 16 inches (40 cm) at birth and shed their first skin after 10 to 14 days.

CAPTIVITY AND BREEDING: A fair-sized terrarium is required with a floor area of at least 32

× 32 inches (80 × 80 cm) and a height of 40 to 60 inches (100-150 cm). A climbing tree with many forked branches is also necessary. The floor should be covered with a mixture of sand, forest soil, and peat and should be covered in places with clumps of moss. Localized bottom heat is required. The Madagascan Tree Boa feels comfortable at daytime temperatures of 82° to 86°F (28°-30°C) which should be lowered at night to 72° to 74°F (22°-23°C). *S. madagascariensis* does very well in a terrarium and is always interested in food, which can consist of day-old chicks, mice, and rats.

Offspring have been produced in captivity, though mostly from females that were pregnant when imported. The gestation period lasts about 150 days. Among the young snakes born in captivity there has been a large percentage of malformations. The cause may be hereditary. In imitation of the snake's natural conditions, the temperature in the terrarium should be lowered to 63° to 68°F (17°-20°C) from late May to late July. This dormancy period in dim light seems to constitute an important factor in successful breeding.

Subfamily Erycinae—Sand Boas

Genus *Eryx*
Old World Sandboas
10 species

Eryx colubrinus
Egyptian Sandboa
2 subspecies

PHYSICAL CHARACTERISTICS: The head is not set off from the neck. The tail is very short and carrot-shaped, the body very sturdy and muscular. Dark brown and orange blotches cover the back and sides of the body, the orange-colored ones forming a zigzag pattern along the spine. Greenish dots are sprinkled throughout the blotches. A dark stripe runs across the temple from the eye to the corner of the mouth. The eye is round with a vertical slit for a pupil. The belly is gray to yellowish-gray.

LENGTH: Slightly over 28 inches (70 cm).

DISTRIBUTION AND BEHAVIOR: This snake is native to northern and eastern Africa as well as Arabia. It lives in the steppes and other arid areas, where it spends the daytime hours in the ground, under rocks, and in the holes of small mammals. The snake is often turned up in the course of plowing or clearing. Its food consists partly of lizards and mostly of mammals, which it captures in a flash, kills by tightening the coils of its body around them, and swallows head first. It is active primarily at dusk and emerges from the ground in the evening and at night. Like other Boidae, it is viviparous.

CAPTIVITY AND BREEDING: A medium-sized terrarium with a floor area of 28 × 16 inches (70 × 40 cm) is sufficient for this snake. The bottom is covered with 3 to 4 inches (7-10 cm) of sand. Localized bottom heat is required, but no artificial lighting is needed to supplement natural daylight. A water container should be placed in such a way that the snakes can neither shove it aside nor upset it. Rocks should be firmly cemented in place. This boa is comfortable in sand that is warmed to between 86° and 95°F (30°-35°C). At night the temperature can be lowered by about 18°F (10°C). Mice are offered as food and almost always accepted without problems.

This snake has been bred in captivity numerous times. The mating takes place in summer, and the young (up to 15) are usually born in October. They measure an average of 7 3/4 inches (198 mm) and shed their first skins 8 to 10 days after birth. A few days later the young snakes are already strong enough to squeeze tiny mice to death and eat them. From that point on it is easy to raise them.

Eryx jaculus
Javelin Sand Boa
3 subspecies
(photo, page 50)

PHYSICAL CHARACTERISTICS: The head is hardly set off from the neck at all. The upper jaw clearly projects beyond the lower one, and the rostral plate at the tip of the snout is very strongly developed, reflecting its function for digging. The sides of the body are gray to brownish, and dark brown blotches form an irregular band of lozenge shapes down the back. There are regularly spaced dark blotches on the sides. A dark stripe runs from the eye to the corner of the mouth, and the belly is light gray to whitish, usually unicolored but in a few cases speckled.

LENGTH: 12 to 24 inches (30-60 cm); rarely up to 32 inches (80 cm).

DISTRIBUTION AND BEHAVIOR: This sand boa ranges from southeastern Europe to southwestern Asia and northern Africa. It inhabits steppe- or desert-like wastelands with sparse vegetation, and it is found on flatland as well as in hilly country. Here it lives primarily under rocks, in dry and sandy soil, and in various holes. The snake spends most of the time hiding under stones and in the ground and emerges only in the morning and early evening. It is extremely well adapted to its habitat and is very quick and adept at burrowing into the loose earth when threatened. It never approaches water of its own free will. It is quite unhostile toward people and does not use its teeth when attacked. Mating occurs in April or May, and like other members of the genus *Eryx*, this snake gives birth to live young, usually 5 to 12 in number and in rare cases up to 15. The Javelin Sand Boa lives primarily on lizards and mice that it pounces on quickly and strangles. When the prey is dead it is swallowed head first. In some regions it is mistakenly thought to be poisonous.

CAPTIVITY AND BREEDING: This snake needs only a small terrarium with some clayey sand on the bottom and some rocks for hiding under. Although it loves a dry environment, it should have a small water dish, which must be solidly anchored in the terrarium. In order to thrive these snakes also need a bottom heater that warms one spot gently. During the day a bottom temperature between 68° and 82°F (20°-28°C) is adequate, and at night it should drop as much as 18°F (10°C). During the day the Javelin Sand Boa always burrows into the ground so that only the nose and the eyes are visible. It is a voracious eater and darts out of the sand like a flash, grabbing its prey and strangling it by wrapping itself around it in 2 or 3 loops. Many Javelin Sand Boas eat both lizards and mice while some individuals accept only one of these two prey animals. Some of them are also very greedy, leaving a prey they have just captured to try to steal a prey just killed by another snake. This often results in a wild tangle of snakes pushing and pulling each other around, and keeping them singly is therefore the better part of wisdom.
Some females that were pregnant when imported have given birth in captivity, and the young they produced measured about 4³/4 inches (12 cm). Within a year they grew to 10 or 11 inches (25-28 cm). As far as I know, no Javelin Sand Boas have yet been successfully bred in a terrarium.

Eryx johnii
Brown Sand Boa
2 subspecies

PHYSICAL CHARACTERISTICS: The head is not set off from the neck at all, and the short and

TOP: Eastern Ribbonsnake (*Thamnophis sauritus*)
BOTTOM: Common Gartersnake (*Thamnophis sirtalis*)

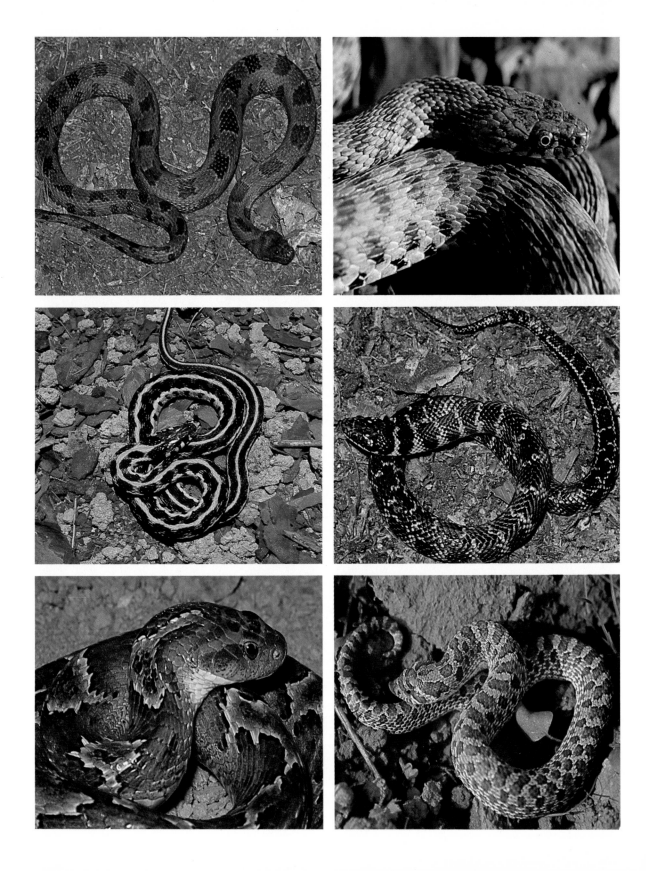

stubby tail is so similar in shape to the head that it is sometimes hard to tell which is which. The upper jaw clearly protrudes beyond the lower one, and the eyes are very small. In the center of the back there is a groove that keeps the sand from sliding off the animal's back when it moves in the sand but close to the surface. The coloration is yellow to dark brown.

LENGTH: Up to 3 feet (1 m).

DISTRIBUTION AND BEHAVIOR: The Brown Sand Boa comes from Iran, western Pakistan, and India, where it lives in all different kinds of dry terrain and occasionally in wetter areas. During the day it usually stays burrowed in loose desert ground and goes hunting at night and the very early morning. Its prey are birds and small rodents which it kills by constriction. The species is viviparous.

CAPTIVITY AND BREEDING: All that is needed for keeping a Brown Sand Boa is a medium-sized container with a layer of about 8 to 10 inches (20-25 cm) of sand. Rocks supplied to provide hiding places should be solidly attached (cemented) to the floor. A bottom heater that creates local temperatures of 86° to 95°F (30°-35°C) is absolutely essential, as is a small water container. During the day, air and general bottom temperatures should be 82° to 86°F (28°-30°C) if the snake is to be comfortable. At night the temperature may drop to 68°F (20°C). The Brown Sand Boa is not aggressive toward humans, but when it is hungry it may mistake your finger for the mouse and then be reluctant to let go again. Otherwise this snake bites only rarely. It consumes mice, rats, and hamsters with equal appetite but will not take lizards.

Before mating, the male burrows his head into the sand to expose the partially or entirely buried female in order to be able to court her better. Finally he shoves the female's tail end out of the sand completely and crawls over her back before copulating. Gestation takes approximately 4 months, and the young snakes measure about 11 inches (27-28 cm) and weigh about .7 ounces (20-22 g) at birth. An umbilical cord about ³/₄ inches (2 cm) long attached to the newborn snake drops off after 10 to 12 days. The first molt occurs after about 2 weeks. The young snakes are sometimes reluctant to take food and may or may not accept furred baby mice.

Eryx miliaris
Mountain Sandboa

PHYSICAL CHARACTERISTICS: The head is not set off from the neck. The eyes are on the upper slant of the head, and the upper jaw protrudes beyond the lower one. The body looks very muscular, and the tail ends in a carrot shape. The upper side of the body is an olive sand to grayish-brown color, and the back is covered with irregular, cinnamon-colored blotches that are arranged symmetrically on the anterior body. Toward the tail end this symmetrical pattern is lost more and more. The lighter belly is speckled with dark brown. The females are lighter in color than the males.

LENGTH: 20 inches (50 cm); occasionally up to 38 inches (95 cm).

DISTRIBUTION AND BEHAVIOR: *E. miliaris* occurs from the northern shore of the Caspian Sea to east of Kasakstan, west central Mongo-

TOP LEFT: Brown Watersnake (*Nerodia taxispilota*)
TOP RIGHT: Dice Snake (*Natrix tessellata*)
CENTER LEFT: Blackneck Snake (*Thamnophis cyrtopsis*)
CENTER RIGHT: *Liophis anomalus*
BOTTOM LEFT: Merrem's False Viper (*Xenoden merremi*)
BOTTOM RIGHT: Western Hognose Snake (*Heterodon nasicus*)

lia, and south as far as Turkmenistan and Afghanistan. It inhabits desertlike terrain. During the day it stays buried about 4 inches (10 cm) underground; it emerges from its hiding place at night. The Mountain Sandboa is quick to bite if it feels threatened. It moves rapidly and can manage to disappear into loose sand with amazing alacrity. Its diet consists of beetles, all sorts of insects, lizards, birds, and mammals. The larger prey are strangled before they are swallowed. The Mountain Sandboa hibernates in the burrows of rodents, and it bears up to 10 live young in June or July. The newborn snakes measure 5 to 5¼ inches (13-13.5 cm).

CAPTIVITY AND BREEDING: Being so small in size, the Mountain Sandboa requires only a small terrarium. The bottom should have at least 4 inches (10 cm) of fine sand. The water dish has to be placed somewhere where it cannot be knocked over or pushed around. Because of the amount of burrowing this snake does, it is advisable to cement rocks in place. A heating cable and artificial lights are necessary. The snake's wellbeing is greatly enhanced by major fluctuations between daytime and nighttime temperatures. During the day both the air and the bottom material should be between 77° and 95°F (25°-35°C). At night it should be considerably cooler, but not below 41°F (5°C). In captivity, the Mountain Sandboa will eat mice which it catches by shooting out of the sand like lightning but which it consumes only after crushing them to death. Like *E. jaculus*, *E. miliaris* should be wintered-over for 3 to 4 months in dry sand at temperatures between 43° and 50°F (6°-10°C), especially if it is your ambition to breed the snake. In behavior, the Mountain Sandboa is considerably feistier than other members of the *Eryx* genus. If it is disturbed it will sink its teeth into you and refuse to let go. Often the mouth has to be pried open by force, and sometimes a tooth will be left sticking in the wound.

A number of pregnant females of this species have been imported and have born their young in captivity. The snakes have also mated in captivity, and a female *E. tataricus tataricus* and a male *E. miliaris* have produced hybrid offspring.

Eryx tataricus
Giant Sandboa
3 subspecies

PHYSICAL CHARACTERISTICS: The head is not set off from the neck. The body looks muscular, and the tail gradually tapers to a blunt end. The eyes are small and pointed more sideways than in other snakes of the *Eryx* genus. The whitish-gray to yellowish-brown back has slate gray or blackish-brown to pure black transverse blotches across it and smaller spots on the sides.

LENGTH: Up to 38½ inches (98 cm).

DISTRIBUTION AND BEHAVIOR: The Giant Sandboa occurs in Kazakstan, central Asia, western China, Iran, Afghanistan, and northern West Pakistan. It is found primarily in steppes, desert-like terrain, and dry forests where it lives mostly in the burrows of rodents. It also burrows into the ground and climbs onto low branches. It feeds mostly on lizards (especially of the *Eremias* and *Phrynocephalus* genera) but also hunts birds, mice, rats, and ground squirrels, generally in the evening and during the night. In late August or early September the female gives birth to 10 to 20 young, which measure 5 to 8 inches (12-20 cm).

CAPTIVITY AND BREEDING: The terrarium should have a layer of mixed sand and loam at the bottom. *E. tataricus* is even less fond of the wet than *E. johnii*. Still it should be given a water dish because it does drink water and even likes to lie in it for a few hours when it is too hot. A climbing branch should also be provided. The bottom temperature can be as high as 95°F (35°C) in one place but should cool down to 64° to 68°F (18°-20°C) at night. The snake can be fed mice, young rats, and baby chicks. It is advisable to give these snakes one mouse, or whatever, at a time with tongs, especially if several snakes live in one terrarium. This way it is easier to keep track of how much each snake has eaten. Sometimes a Giant Sandboa will hold onto one mouse with the coils of its body and simultaneously snatch and kill another one. If offspring are desired, 3 to 4 months of hibernation are necessary.

This species has been bred in captivity a number of times. The first food to be offered the young snakes is nestling mice.

Genus *Lichanura*
Rosy Boas
1 species

Lichanura trivirgata
Rosy Boa
3 subspecies

PHYSICAL CHARACTERISTICS: The oval head with its small eyes is not set off from the neck. The body looks compact and very muscular, and the tail is short. The body is brown to bluish-gray. Irregularly toothed, brown to rose-colored markings form 3 bands running down the spine and the sides. The belly is porcelain-colored sprinkled with gray.

LENGTH: Up to 3 feet (90 cm).

DISTRIBUTION AND BEHAVIOR: *L. trivirgata* is native to northern Baja California, southern California, southwestern Arizona, and northwestern Mexico. It lives primarily in flat deserts and rocky country dotted with bush-like vegetation. It is found up to an altitude of 5000 feet (1500 m) and especially at the foot of mountains and near rivers. Peaceful by nature it does not bite when it is captured. If it is picked up, it rolls itself up into a ball like the Ball Python (*Python regius*), tucking its head inside the coils of its body. It is active during the day, but more so at dusk and in the night. It emerges from its hiding places especially when it rains and on cloudy days. Its movements are slow, and it stays on the ground most of the time but does occasionally climb onto low bushes and trees. Depending on the weather, it hibernates 3 to 6 months. Its diet consists mostly of mice and birds.

CAPTIVITY AND BREEDING: The Rosy Boa needs a medium-sized terrarium. A mixture of sand and forest soil has proved to make a good bottom material for this snake, and a few flat rocks and some pieces of cork bark will provide necessary retreats. Some climbing branches are important because this snake likes to take long siestas there. A small water dish is also essential. One area of the bottom should be moderately heated. To stay healthy, the Rosy Boa needs a daytime temperature of 68° to 79°F (20°-26°C) with a slight drop at night. The light requirements can be met with a weak flourescent tube or simply daylight. This snake feeds on nestling birds and mice, which it kills by constriction. Unfortunately it is sometimes difficult to induce this snake to eat, but otherwise this small boa makes a good terrarium pet that has been known to live up to 12 years in captivity.

A hibernating period of 3 to 4 months at 50° to 59°F (10°-15°C) is especially important if you have any intention of breeding this snake. Rosy Boas have been bred at the San Diego Zoo. They measured about 12 inches (30 cm) at birth. Under good conditions such baby snakes can grow to 29 inches (74 cm) within one year and reach sexual maturity by the time they are 2 years old. But then the growth rate generally slows down to no more than 3/4 to 1 1/2 inches (2-4 cm) a year.

Family Tropidophiidae—Wood Snakes And Relatives

Genus *Trachyboa*
Rough-scaled Snakes
2 species

Trachyboa boulengeri
Rough-scaled Snake
(photo, page 68)

PHYSICAL CHARACTERISTICS: The Rough-scaled Snake is one of the smallest boas. The head is covered with small scales and clearly set off from the neck. The rostral shield is lacking or much reduced. Hornlike scales over the eyes and at the tip of the nose are a characteristic feature of this snake. Its compact body and the prominently set off head give this small boa a viperlike look. The scales of the body have pronounced keels. The entire length of the body is a coffee brown with two parallel rows of black blotches interrupted by reddish-brown blotches running down both sides. The reddish-brown belly has black spots.

LENGTH: Up to 17 inches (43 cm).

DISTRIBUTION AND BEHAVIOR: This snake is found in the Choco region of Ecuador, in Colombia, and in Panama. Very little is known about its way of life in the wild. It lives well concealed in wet areas. Sometimes it is found in the tops of trees. It feeds primarily on frogs, toads, and fish, which it does not stalk and pursue but pounces on and strangles when they pass near its head. *T. boulengeri* is not aggressive toward humans. It does not bite when it is picked up but instead emits a foul-smelling secretion from its anal glands. When it is touched it stretches out full length and goes rigid. It is viviparous.

CAPTIVITY AND BREEDING: Because of its diminutive size this snake needs only a small terrarium whose bottom should be covered with peat or forest soil and dry leaves and moss, reflecting the animal's natural environment. Some pieces of bark can provide cover. A small water basin is required so that the snake can bathe frequently. Since the Rough-scaled Snake normally lives in a wet environment, the bottom of the terrarium always has to be kept damp. This species is completely nocturnal and comes out of hiding only at night. It needs daytime temperatures between 68° and 77°F (20°-25°C) to thrive and will eat frogs, toads, and fish. It has thus far not been productively mated in captivity, but pregnant females have been imported. The newborn snakes measure about 5 inches (12-13cm). Gestation takes about 10 months.

Genus *Tropidophis*
Wood Snakes
15 species

Tropidophis melanurus
Cuban Woodsnake
4 subspecies

PHYSICAL CHARACTERISTICS: The head is clearly set off from the neck, and the body is thick-set and strong. The scales are keeled. The top of the body is grayish-brown with a suggestion of red. Two symmetrical rows of gray blotches run down the spine. The belly is yellowish. The upper labials are yellow, and there is a dark brown band behind the eye. In young specimens the tip of the tail is yellowish, but in grown animals it is black above and green below.

LENGTH: Up to 3 feet (1 m).

DISTRIBUTION AND BEHAVIOR: This snake occurs in Cuba, on Navassa Island, and some of the other Greater Antilles. It lives under heaps of leaves, in rock piles, cracks in stone walls, and piles of old, rotting wood, always close to water. Not much is known about its life in nature except that it eats frogs, lizards, and birds. It gives birth to as many as 21 live young which measure about 6 to 7 inches (15-17 cm). Gestation takes about 70 days.

CAPTIVITY AND BREEDING: A medium-sized terrarium with a floor area of 28 × 16 inches (70 × 40 cm) will do for a Cuban Woodsnake, and a mixture of sand, peat, and leaf mold is used as bottom material. This should always be kept slightly moist in one area. A water container is an important item for this snake. Some flat rocks and pieces of cork oak bark should be provided for the snake to retreat under. The Cuban Woodsnake is nocturnal and stays in its hiding place during the day. It crawls around only at dark. In captivity these snakes will eat frogs, salamanders, and lizards, which they often swallow while they are still alive. Only rare individuals are brave enough to attack mice, which they suffocate by coiling themselves around them. This snake has a very unusual fright reaction that deserves to be mentioned: When it is frightened and picked up, blood sometimes drips from its mouth, or sometimes it tries to defend itself by curling up in a ball in a way similar to that of the Ball Python (*Python regius*). This snake has been successfully bred in the Basel Zoo, Switzerland.

Infraorder Caenophidia — Advanced Snakes

Family Colubridae — Harmless Snakes
Subfamily Lamprophiinae — African Wolfsnakes

Genus *Lamprophis*
African Housesnakes
5 species

Lamprophis fuliginosus
Brown Housesnake
2 subspecies

PHYSICAL CHARACTERISTICS: The flat head is barely set off from the neck, and the large eyes have vertical slits for pupils. The body is sturdy and the tail relatively short. The scales are smooth, and the anal plate undivided. Head, back, and sides are light to dark brown or yel-lowish-to-reddish-brown and in some cases almost black. On both sides of the head a beige band runs from the tip of the snout across the neck and on to the anterior body, forming a V shape. Sometimes there are small reddish spots on the sides of the body, which may be quite prominent in young specimens. The belly is whitish to yellowish with an iridescent sheen.

LENGTH: 48 to 52 inches (120-130 cm).

DISTRIBUTION AND BEHAVIOR: *B. fuliginosus* is one of the most widely distributed snakes in Africa, ranging from southern Morocco and the upper Nile to South Africa. This snake avoids dense forests and instead favors savannas. In settled areas where mice and rats abound it is quite common. Since small rodents are some of its favorite prey, farmers are glad to see it around. It also eats shrews, birds and their eggs, reptiles, and frogs. The prey is struck in a flash, killed in the coils of the body, and then swallowed. *B. fuliginosus* is largely nocturnal, which is why one rarely encounters it during the day. It bites ferociously when captured, but its bite is completely harmless. In late spring or early summer it lays 8 to 10 and, in exceptional cases, up to 16 longish eggs in some rotting leaves, a termite hill, under rocks, or in some other suitable spot. The young snakes, which usually hatch in late summer, are 8¾ to 10 inches (22-25 cm) long.

CAPTIVITY AND BREEDING: The Brown Housesnake is a hardy and interesting snake for the terrarium that soon gets so tame that it will eventually take mice from the keeper's hand. Since it is nocturnal one rarely sees it during the day. The individual I have hides all day in a hollow piece of cork and comes out into the open only rarely even at night. A small to medium-sized terrarium with a layer of coarse sand on the bottom will do for the Housesnake. A few rocks or a piece or ornamental cork for hiding under are necessary as well as a small water dish. Artificial lights are not required if the terrarium gets any daylight. Mild bottom heat is recommended. During the day the air should measure 72° to 81°F (22°- 27°C), and the temperature should drop a little at night. This snake is not fussy about food. Digestion takes about 3 to 4 days. There is no need for cool wintering over. There are no reports of this snake having been bred in captivity.

Genus *Pseudaspis*
African Molesnakes
1 species

Pseudaspis cana
African Molesnake
2 subspecies
(photo, page 122)

PHYSICAL CHARACTERISTICS: The head of this fairly stout and muscular snake is relatively narrow and hardly set off from the neck. The small eyes have round pupils. In bright light the smooth scales shine. The coloration can be anything from light gray, brown, or reddish-brown to ink black. Young animals differ markedly in coloration and markings from adult ones. Whereas adult snakes are usually unicolored, juveniles have dark brown to black blotches on the back and the sides. These blotches are arranged more or less symmetrically in four longitudinal rows, but sometimes an irregular zigzag pattern is formed down along the spine. The blotches often have either light centers or white rims. The belly is yellowish with a light sprinkling of spots.

LENGTH: 5 feet (1.5 m); occasionally over 6½ feet (2 m).

DISTRIBUTION AND BEHAVIOR: *P. cana* is distributed and well known from Angola and Kenya down to South Africa. It is frequently found in dry bush country with sandy soil, but one sometimes meets it in deserts and on mountains as well. It is active in the day as well as in the night. It spends most of its time underground in the holes and burrows of small mammals. With its wedge-shaped tail, narrow head, strong neck muscles, and smooth scales it has no trouble making its way through the loose sand. The Molesnake feeds on small mammals, i.e., rats, mice, jerboas, and—as its name implies—moles, which it hunts underground. but it also consumes bird eggs, digesting them, shells and all; and it is said to eat even the eggs of the Cape Cobra (*Naja nivea*). If the Molesnake is threatened, young animals in particular will often fight, striking at their attacker wildly with open mouths. Adult individuals are generally less ferocious. Matings take place in October, and in March or April, 30 to 50 live young are born. These measure about 8 inches (20 cm) and start out eating lizards.

CAPTIVITY AND BREEDING: The Molesnake adjusts to captivity quickly and becomes an interesting and tame pet. It needs a medium-sized terrarium with a sandy bottom into which it will often burrow. The set-up also includes some large stones, a built-in water container that cannot be knocked over, and a bottom heater that is cemented in. The terrarium should get 8 to 10 hours of artificial light or be exposed to the morning and afternoon sun. The temperature should be kept between 68° and 86°F (20°-30°C) during the day and 64° to 72°F (18°-22°C) at night for the snake to feel comfortable. *P. cana* takes mice and rats readily, both alive and dead; and, if kept dry, survives well. Hibernation is not necessary, but it is recommended that the temperature be lowered a little from June to August in imitation of natural conditions.

This snake has produced offspring in captivity. In the Port Elisabeth Snake Park a female measuring about 83 inches (210 cm) had 84 young, and this record was surpassed by the London Zoo, where there was a litter of 95.

Subfamily Acrochordinae—Wart Snakes

Genus *Acrochordus*
Oriental Wartsnakes
1 species

Acrochordus javanicus
Java Wartsnake

PHYSICAL CHARACTERISTICS: The Java Wartsnake has a muscular body with a short, very mobile, prehensile tail and a flat, broad-snouted head that is hardly set off from the neck. The nostrils are located on the upper side of the snout. The scales are small, horn-like, and have knobby, triangular keels. The body of this snake always looks somewhat baggy because it does not bulge after a meal and the skin always stays slack. The top of the body is an even brown that changes into a light yellow on the sides and the belly. Young animals have irregular, longitudinal blotches on the brown ground color which become less distinct with time and eventually disappear altogether. The females are always somewhat longer and more powerfully built than the males.

LENGTH: Up to 8 feet (2.5 m).

DISTRIBUTION AND BEHAVIOR: *A. javanicus* is native to India, the Malay Archipelago, Southeast Asia, and the Indonesian islands west of Australia. This rough-scaled snake, which some authorities class with the colubrids and others elevate to the status of a separate family, lives primarily in brackish water. It penetrates from coastal waters to estuaries and brackish lakes and swamps. One of its preferred habitats is washed-out banks. It lives exclusively in the water which it is said never to leave on its own accord. And indeed, the Java Wartsnake moves with great ease and agility in the water while it is quite helpless on the ground. It is able to stay underwater for a long time—over 40 minutes—without coming up for air, and when it does surface, it generally takes only 15 to 50 seconds to breathe before it dives again. The Java Wartsnake is quite irascible toward humans, and with its sharp, recurved teeth that sometimes break off and stay in the flesh it is capable of inflicting unpleasant wounds. This snake lives almost exclusively on fish, although it does occasionally eat frogs. It usually gives birth to between 20 and 30 young.

CAPTIVITY AND BREEDING: This species requires a fair-sized aquarium that should be at least 32 to 40 inches (80-100 cm) deep. If the water is not deep enough, these snakes approach their food unenthusiastically or not at all so that they have to be force-fed. Pebbles are used for the bottom, and some solidly cemented rocks provide necessary hiding places. The aquarium has to be tightly covered so that the snake cannot escape. The aquarium heater should be mounted in such a way that the snake cannot damage it. The water should be kept at 77° to 82°F (25°-28°C) day and night. *A. javanicus* stays hidden during the day, coming alive and crawling around the bottom only at night. In captivity it eats only fish, which it seizes with lightning speed, quickly envelops, and immediately swallows, often while they are still alive. This remarkable snake has become quite a rarity and is seldom offered for sale. This may have something to do with the fact that this species used to be captured in large numbers primarily because of its skin, which is turned into fancy leather. This snake has not yet been successfully bred in captivity.

Subfamily Homalopsinae—Rear-fanged Watersnakes

Genus *Cerberus*
Dogface Watersnakes
2 species

Cerberus rhynchops
Dogface Watersnake
2 subspecies

PHYSICAL CHARACTERISTICS: The small, short head is hardly set off from the neck, and the small eyes have vertical slits as pupils. The body, which is round in cross-section, has strongly keeled scales. The tail is somewhat compressed on the sides. The gray, brownish, or olive-colored top of the body is covered with dark crossbands or blotches. A dark stripe runs from the tip of the snout across the eyes and on to the sides of the neck. The belly is whitish, mottled with black, striped with black, or solid black.

LENGTH: 32 to 40 inches (80-100 cm).

DISTRIBUTION AND BEHAVIOR: *C. rhynchops* occurs on Ceylon, in India, on the Malay Peninsula, the Malay Archipelago, the Andamans, the Nicobars, the Philippines, and in northern Australia. It is particularly common in Burma and in the Gulf of Siam. This snake lives primarily in brackish water near estuaries and has been found as far as 90 miles (150 km) from the coast. Sometimes it wraps its tail around a submerged branch and stays immobile. When out of the water it likes to rest on mangroves and branches overhanging the water. When danger lurks it immediately drops back into the water. It is also good at moving through the muddy bottom and catching fishes called mud skippers of the genera *Periophthalmus* and *Boleophthalmus*. *C. rhynchops* lives primarily on fish but sometimes also eats crustaceans. It is not an aggressive snake, but when it is seized it flattens its body, bites, and emits an unpleasant smelling secretion from its anal glands. It also wraps itself around one's hand and squeezes hard.

Females give birth to between 8 and 26 fully developed young that measure 7 to 8 inches (18-20 cm).

CAPTIVITY AND BREEDING: The Dogfaced Watersnake adjusts quickly to captivity and becomes completely tame. It can be kept either in an aquarium or an aqua-terrarium with more water area than land area. A few rocks sticking out of the water and some climbing branches should be included. The temperature should be between 77° and 86°F (25°-30°C), and the lights should be on all day. This snake, which is more active at night than during the day spends most of its time lying in the water with the head below the surface. Live and dead fish are used as food. The snake will kill newts and frogs but does not eat them. It has a very good nose for live fish, and its bite is deadly for fish. The snake takes them by the head when they are dead and swallows them, often underwater. *C. rhynchops* has not yet reproduced in captivity, but females that were pregnant when imported have given birth to young in aquariums and raised them.

Genus *Erpeton*
Tentacle Snakes
1 species

Erpeton tentaculatum
Tentacle Snake

PHYSICAL CHARACTERISTICS: This species is one of the most remarkable snakes. It has feelerlike appendages, one pointing straight forward on each side of the snout. Their function is unknown. The head is longish and rectangular. The small eyes with their slit pupils are always level no matter how the snake tilts its head. The body of this snake looks relatively slender, and the scales are strongly keeled. The Tentacle Snake is reddish-brown or yellowish on the top with two dark stripes running down the back on each side of the spine. On the side of the body there is a dark band starting near the eyes, and on the center of the back there are numerous dark blotches.

The belly is yellowish to brownish with irregular dark mottling. In addition to these longitudinally striped snakes there are also others with transverse blotches. The Tentacled Snake is often covered with algae that grow on it.

LENGTH: 28 to 36 inches (70-90 cm).

DISTRIBUTION AND BEHAVIOR: This exclusively aquatic snake occurs in Thailand, Cambodia, and South Vietnam, where it is sometimes found in large numbers in puddles, swamps, and muddy, slow water. On land it moves only with great effort. If it is picked up it tries to bite or get away. In water it wraps its tail around aquatic plants or submerged branches and remains stiff and immobile. Because of this habit the Siamese call it "Ngu kradan" or "board snake." Nothing convincing has yet been written about the function of the tentacles on the snake's head. Perhaps these are supposed to lure fish, which make up the sole food of the Tentacle Snake. *E. tentaculatum* bears 9 to 13 fully developed young.

CAPTIVITY AND BREEDING: In recent years this snake has occasionally been imported in fairly large numbers. It is kept in a well planted aquarium for tropical fish with a sandy bottom and a water temperature of 77° to 81°F (25°-27°C). A fitted frame covered with nylon netting or a glass cover is necessary to keep the snake from escaping. The Tentacle Snake is more active at dusk than during the day, and it often spends the night moving about the aquarium without pause. It is fed nothing but fish, which it does not pursue but usually grabs by the head and quickly swallows when they swim past. Although matings have been observed in aquariums, this snake has not yet reproduced in captivity.

Genus *Homalopsis*
Puff-face Watersnakes

Homalopsis buccata
Puff-face Watersnake
2 subspecies

PHYSICAL CHARACTERISTICS: The Puff-face Watersnake has a sturdy body, a short, pug-faced head that is clearly set off from the neck, and small eyes with vertical slits as pupils. The scales are keeled, and the dark gray, brown, or reddish-brown body is covered with wide and narrow transverse bands that may be yellowish, ochre, or whitish-gray. The head is grayish-white to yellowish, and there is a triangular mark pointing backward on the snout. Another triangular mark pointing forward lies farther back on the head, and there is a dark, oval spot under each eye. A dark line runs across the eyes and ends at the corners of the mouth. The white belly is mottled with black, gray, or brown on the sides, and there are dark brown or black blotches under the tail.

LENGTH: 40 inches (1 m).

DISTRIBUTION AND BEHAVIOR: *H. buccata* is found in Burma, Thailand, Laos, Cambodia, Vietnam, on the Malay Peninsula, and the Malay Archipelago. It lives in small rivers, puddles, ponds, klongs, flooded rice paddies, and swamps, and is quite numerous in some places. Fishermen often catch it in their nets. This species spends more time on land than other Homalopsinae but never roams far from its native waters. Clumsy and slow-moving on the ground, this snake turns into an agile swimmer when in the water. Its diet consists of fish, frogs, and occasionally crustaceans. *H. buccata* is gentle and practically never bites when picked up. It bears 9 to 21 fully developed young.

CAPTIVITY AND BREEDING: The Puff-face Watersnake does well in captivity. It becomes hand tame within a few days and adjusts to the keeper. This adaptable snake is kept in an aqua-terrarium similar to the one described in the section on *Cerberus rhynchops* and under similar temperature and light conditions. *H. buccata* often spends hours in the land area of the aqua-terrarium and digs in the damp earth. It is fed fish and frogs. Thus far this species has not reproduced in captivity.

Subfamily Xenodontinae—South American Snakes

Genus *Clelia*
Mussuranas
6 species

Clelia clelia
Mussurana
2 subspecies

PHYSICAL CHARACTERISTICS: The short head is hardly set off from the neck, and the small eyes have round pupils. The body appears slender but is very muscular. The scales are smooth. The top of the body is a shiny bluish-black, and the belly is white. The subspecies *C. c. plumbea* has a brown back with a light transverse on the nape of the neck. The Mussurana undergoes a color change at a certain age. Juveniles have a brownish to black head and a brownish-red to salmon pink back with a white ring around the neck that gradually disappears with age.

LENGTH: Over 6^1/$_2$ feet (2 m).

DISTRIBUTION AND BEHAVIOR: *C. clelia* occurs from Guatemala and Honduras to as far south as Uruguay and Argentina. It is not very common and is not restricted to any one kind of habitat. During the day it stays hidden and does not appear on the open ground until night. In its native regions *C. clelia* is said to hibernate from May to October and to go without food during this period. In Brazil the Mussurana is well known and much appreciated because it feeds almost entirely on snakes and is not even daunted by venomous ones. It pounces on its prey with lightning speed, coils its entire body around it, and squeezes it. The victim is also paralyzed with the venom from the fangs way back in the mouth. Then the dead snake is swallowed head first. Mussuranas are immune to snake venom. In his publications, Vital Brasil, the Brazilian expert on snakes and snake serum, depicts the Mussurana as a valuable ally to humans in fighting poisonous snakes and had a stone image of the Mussurana set over the portal of his institute. *C. clelia* behaves unaggressively toward humans and hardly ever bites. It reproduces by means of eggs.

CAPTIVITY AND BREEDING: This snake is not frequently seen in terrariums. Although it lasts well in captivity and soon becomes friendly it cannot be recommended for private individuals because in the long run it can be kept alive only by being fed snakes. Depending on its size it will consume 1 to 4 snakes per month that can be given alive or dead. Since Mussuranas will eat other members of their own species, these snakes have to be kept singly. As a temporary measure one can give the Mussurana strips of beef or pork heart instead of snakes. *C. clelia* needs a large terrarium with a suitable hiding place, a big water basin, and air temperatures between 77° and 86°F (25°-30°C). Bottom heat is also required. This snake spends most of the day in hiding. Since it likes to bathe, the water basin has to be cleaned frequently. A mixture of peat and forest soil makes a good litter for the bottom, absorbing the smelly excreta well. Still, the litter has to be changed from time to time. Thus far the Mussurana has not reproduced in captivity.

Genus *Helicops*
South American Watersnakes
13 species

Helicops carinicaudus
Roughtail Watersnake
2 subspecies

PHYSICAL CHARACTERISTICS: *H. carinicaudus* is distinguished by an undivided internasal plate, a broad, flattened head, and small, round-pupiled eyes that are far up and forward on the head near the nostrils, which also point upward. The body is short and sturdy, and the tail portion is much reduced in length. The scales are keeled and lack end pores. The ground color is a dirty gray to ochre, and there are three darker longitudinal stripes. The belly has rows of regular black, checker-board markings on a yellow ground. The coloration of the belly varies a great deal with different ages. Some individuals have very few black markings on the belly and tail plates, and in others these areas are almost totally black. Apart from the black markings there are sometimes some contrasting white blotches.

LENGTH: About 3 feet (1 m).

DISTRIBUTION AND BEHAVIOR: *H. carinicaudus* comes from southern Brazil, Uruguay, and Argentina. It is commonly found in any flat area with sufficient water accumulations where there are enough food animals for it. A truly aquatic snake, the Roughtail Watersnake rarely moves on dry ground. It prefers lying among water plants in rivers and in the shallow water of quiet bays. It is largely diurnal, and its way of life is similar to that of other water snakes. Fish make up the bulk of its diet and to a lesser extent frogs. Though it has neither poison fangs nor specialized poison glands, its bite nevertheless has an almost toxic effect on its prey. The Roughtail Watersnake is shy by nature and immediately makes for the bottom of the water when danger threatens, and it never tries to find safety on land. The female bears fully developed young.

CAPTIVITY AND BREEDING: This snake requires an aqua-terrarium with a large water section. A climbing tree is also necessary because this snake likes to rest in the sun on a branch. Localized bottom heat and 12 to 14 hours of artificial light are recommended. *H. carinicaudus* does not need a lot of heat; daytime temperatures between 68° and 86°F (20°-30°C) are adequate. If the water is cool, the snake becomes quite pale but still eats even at 54°F (12°C). It eats fish, around which it sometimes coils itself. The Roughtail Watersnake reacts in an unusual way when it is grasped. It sets its ribs at a right angle to the spine and sucks in its belly to form a concave surface. Nothing is known about breeding this snake in captivity.

Genus *Hydrodynastes*
False Watercobras
1 species

Hydrodynastes gigas
Giant False Watercobra

PHYSICAL CHARACTERISTICS: This strong and stout snake has a longish head that is barely set off from the neck. The black eyes are not very large. The scales are smooth on the anterior and middle parts of the body and slightly keeled farther back. The coloration of the two sexes differs. Males are yellowish with black or dark brown irregular transverse stripes and blotches. Females are light brown with indistinct, dark transverse blotches, which are lacking in some animals, however. Both males and females have similar markings on the head. A broad, dark stripe runs from the eyes back to the sides of the neck. The anterior body is lighter than the posterior half and the tail, and the yellowish belly is mottled with black.

LENGTH: Over 6½ feet (2 m).

DISTRIBUTION AND BEHAVIOR: *H. gigas* comes from southern Brazil, eastern Bolivia, Paraguay, and northern Argentina. Not much is known about its life in nature. In Brazil this snake often occurs in the caatingas, or thorn forests—namely, in impenetrable thickets of mimosa bushes, cacti, and barriduga trees. It spends most of its time in the scrub growth and, as a ground-dwelling snake, lives a well hidden life. Its diet consists of small mammals, birds, frogs, toads, and fish. Its reaction to humans is not aggressive. If it is startled, it spreads its cervical ribs horizontally and raises its anterior body somewhat off the ground. Because of this habit it is sometimes called False Water Cobra. In Brazil it also goes under the name Surucucu do Pantanal. *H. gigas* reproduces by means of eggs.

CAPTIVITY AND BREEDING: This snake is very seldom imported. If kept in a generous terrarium with a large water section and at temperatures between 68° and 82°F (20°-28°C) it can live for years. Artificial lights have to be on 10 to 12 hours a day, and since these snakes like to lie in dark corners, they have to be supplied with hiding places. The Brazilian Smooth Snake does not climb much but instead likes to spend whole days on and in the water when the weather is particularly hot. In captivity it is offered rats, mice, guinea pigs, hamsters, chicks, and pigeons for food. The snake strangles its prey and eats it while it is dazed but not yet dead.

H. gigas has been successfully bred a number of times in captivity. Some specimens owned by Vogel mated repeatedly in August, and the females laid their eggs—in one case 36 of them—in October. Unfortunately they did not hatch.

Genus *Leimadophis*
Lined Snakes
40 species

Leimadophis poecilogyrus
Angry Snake
12 subspecies

PHYSICAL CHARACTERISTICS: The head of this lovely snake is an elongated oval and is set off from the neck only slightly. The body looks relatively slender. Coloration can vary considerably. The yellowish-green to grayish-blue of the body is shot through with black, and on the flanks dark red semicircles alternate between the right and left side. These markings may not be present in juveniles. Some-

times this snake flattens its body so much that the scales spread and the bright red skin underneath becomes visible. The belly is grayish-blue or brick red. Some melanistic specimens occur.

LENGTH: 40 to 48 inches (100-120 cm).

DISTRIBUTION AND BEHAVIOR: *L. poecilogyrus* occurs in Argentina, Uruguay, Brazil, and Ecuador. In behavior and environmental needs it resembles the North American water snakes. It lives in wet areas in and along different bodies of water. Its diet consists primarily of amphibians, fish, lizards, and occasionally of small mammals. The Angry Snake reproduces by means of eggs.

CAPTIVITY AND BREEDING: This species requires about the same care in a terrarium as the water snakes of the *Natrix* genus. A large water container is essential to this snake's wellbeing because the Angry Snake often spends hours at a time or even days in the water. It also climbs a lot and should therefore have some climbing branches. Plain sand or sand mixed with gravel makes a suitable bottom material, and some rocks, pieces of bark, and moss clumps serve to provide cover. The moss should be replaced periodically. *L. poecilogyrus* prefers daytime temperatures between 77° and 86°F (25°-30°C). At night it should be a few degrees cooler. This snake is active during the day as well as at dusk. It readily accepts food offered to it and eats fish, frogs, toads, and occasionally even mice. It is very good at catching fish in the water. In time this snake becomes quite tame and learns to take food from tongs. It sheds its skin 3 to 4 times a year. Hibernation is not necessary.

L. poecilogyrus has mated a number of times in captivity, and in at least one case the eggs hatched. Snake expert Schweizer placed seven eggs in some damp peat moss and kept them at 82° to 84°F (28°-29°C). The eggs hatched after 43 days.

Genus *Liophis*
26 species

Liophis anomalus
(photo, page 86)

PHYSICAL CHARACTERISTICS: The head is barely set off from the neck, and the large eyes have round pupils. The body is slender, and the scales are not keeled. The top of the head is olive green to blackish-gray, the nape, black. The back and sides of the body are olive green to yellowish with many black blotches that may form lateral ribbons near the middle of the body and on the tail. Coloration and markings vary widely. In some specimens the dark blotches on the back are saddle-shaped and evenly spaced. The spaces between them are yellowish-green, and the belly is mottled black and yellow.

LENGTH: About 30 inches (75 cm).

DISTRIBUTION AND BEHAVIOR: *L. anomalus* is native to southern Brazil, northern Argentina, Uruguay, and Paraguay. It lives along streams, rivers, puddles, ponds, and lakes. In behavior it resembles the European water snakes, but hardly anything is known about its life in nature. It lays eggs.

CAPTIVITY AND BREEDING: This snake is hardly ever sold. The author introduced this pretty water snake into West Germany twice. These specimens came from the vicinity of Buenos Aires. *L. anomalus* needs an aqua-terrarium with a few dry spots on the land area and some flat rocks and pieces of bark under which it can hide. During the day the terrarium should be kept between 77° and 81°F (25°-27°C). At night 65° to 68°F (18°-20°C) is warm enough. Lights should be on 12 to 14 hours. The snakes spend a lot of their time in the water. They show interest in food and eat live as well as dead frogs and strips of fish. This snake has not thus far been bred in captivity, but *L. miliaris,* which is a very close relative of it and has the same requirements in terms of terrarium set-up, temperature, light, and diet, has been mated repeatedly in captivity and has laid eggs, three of which produced young snakes. These grew at a rapid rate and were as big as their parents at 7 months of age.

Genus *Philodryas*
15 species
Philodryas baroni

PHYSICAL CHARACTERISTICS: The longish head is barely set off from the neck. In no other *Phylodryas* species is the snout turned up as much as in this snake where it ends in a short, pointed extension. The large eyes have round pupils, and the scales are smooth. *P. baroni* occurs in a brown and a green color variant. In the green variant the back and sides of the body are dark green with the color lightening on the underside. A black stripe starts at either side of the snout, runs down the sides of the neck, and disappears somewhere along the sides of the upper body. Another dark stripe runs down the spine, and a whitish-yellow band starting on the upper and lower labials continues along the sides of the neck and changes to yellowish-green or plain green on the upper third of the body.

LENGTH: 6½ feet (2 m).

DISTRIBUTION AND BEHAVIOR: This snake comes from Argentina, Bolivia, and Paraguay. We know very little about the life of this primarily diurnal snake that lives on trees as well as on the ground. A snake catcher from Argentina told me that this species is found mostly in forests near water. *P. baroni* feeds on mammals, birds, frogs, and fish, and reproduces by laying eggs.

CAPTIVITY AND BREEDING: This lovely snake is kept by only a few fanciers. It should be housed in a rain forest terrarium with an air humidity between 60 and 95% and daytime temperatures between 79° and 81°F (26°-27°C). At night the temperature should drop to about 74° to 76°F (23°-24°C). Lights should be turned on 12 to 14 hours a day. This snake will prowl around on the ground as well as on the branches and will sometimes spend several hours at a time in the water basin. With attentive care it soon grows tame. It is given mice to eat, which it swallows alive. The venom of this snake is not very potent.

P. baroni has been bred in captivity. A female laid 12 whitish eggs that were cylindrical in shape on November 22. After 83 days during which the eggs were kept at 72° to 77°F (22°-25°C) the baby snakes hatched. They measured an average of 15 inches (37.5 cm) and there were both green and brown color variants among them.

Philodryas olfersii
(photo, page 158)

PHYSICAL CHARACTERISTICS: The short head is hardly set off from the neck, and the large eyes have round pupils. *P. olfersii* has a slender but muscular body and smooth scales. Head and body are the same shade of light green. A thin black line starts just behind the nostril and ends near the corner of the mouth. There are a few specimens with a yellow or red dorsal stripe. The upper and lower labials as well as the throat are whitish, and the belly is yellowish-green or bluish-green.

LENGTH: 40 inches (1 m).

DISTRIBUTION AND BEHAVIOR: *P. olfersii* is native to western Brazil, eastern Peru, Bolivia, Paraguay, Uruguay, and Argentina. It is found mostly along the edges of rain forests and of more or less dense secondary forests near water and lives both on the ground and in trees and bushes. Its prime period of activity is during the day. It does not behave aggressively toward humans, but its bite can in some cases give rise to symptoms of mild poisoning. *P. olfersii* lives mostly on small mammals and occasionally also eats birds and frogs. We know very little about its life in the wild. *P. olfersii* lays eggs.

CAPTIVITY AND BREEDING: In keeping with the abundant vegetation of its natural habitat this snake should be housed in a rain forest terrarium filled with plants. The bottom should be covered with forest soil or peat, and a largish water basin and numerous climbing branches should be supplied. Artificial lights should be on 12 to 14 hours during the day, and the temperature should range between 73° and 80°F (23°-28°C). At night it should be 5° to 7°F (3°-4°C) cooler. Under these conditions and with a high air humidity of 70 to 90% this snake can thrive in captivity. Mice and frogs are offered as food. The prey is not strangled but held between the jaws until it is swallowed either alive or dead. *P. olfersii* grows tame quickly in captivity and practically never tries to bite. F. Golder has successfully bred this snake. Eight barrel-shaped eggs measuring an average of $1^1/2 \times {}^5/8$ inches (39×17 mm) were laid on October 18 and placed in an incubator that was kept at 72° to 77°F (22°-25°C). The young snakes hatched after 89 days on January 15, 1973, measuring an average length of 11 inches (28 cm).

Genus *Uromacer*
Hispaniola Bush Snakes
3 species

Uromacer oxyrhynchus
Sharp-nosed Bush Snake
2 subspecies

PHYSICAL CHARACTERISTICS: The long, very pointed head is hardly set off from the neck, and moderately large eyes have round pupils. The body and tail are extremely thin, and the scales are smooth. The snake is grass green with a yellow and a white stripe between the top of the body and the underside. The belly may be yellowish-green or reddish-brown.

LENGTH: Just short of $6^1/2$ feet (2 m).

DISTRIBUTION AND BEHAVIOR: *U. oxyrhynchus* is widely distributed on Hispaniola (Haiti) and the West Indian island Gonave. It lives mostly in light, bushy forests but also occurs in different kinds of habitat. Usually it stays in bushes about 6 to 10 feet (2-3 m) above the ground and descends to the ground from time to time. When it is captured it does not bite but opens its mouth in a threatening gesture, spreading its lower jaw very far to make itself look more dangerous than it actually is. The diet of this diurnal snake consists primarily of lizards of the genus *Anolis*, but it also eats small frogs. The bite of *U. oxyrynchus* is fatal to lizards but harmless to humans. This specieis reproduces by means of eggs that stick together in a clutch.

CAPTIVITY AND BREEDING: This snake requires a large terrarium for arboreal snakes with many climbing branches, plenty of growing plants, and a big water basin. Daytime temperatures should range between 77° and 82°F (25°-28°C), and lights should be provided 12 to 14 hours a day. The temperature should not drop below 64°F (18°C) at night. If kept under the proper conditions, *U. oxyrynchus* does well in captivity and soon loses its initial shyness. The movements of this thin snake are incredibly fast, and when cleaning up the terrarium or doing other chores in it one has to be extremely careful because this snake will take advantage of any oportunity to make a dash for freedom. *U. oxyrynchus* is fed small lizards, which it seizes with lightning speed and kills with its venom rather than by constriction with continuing chewing motions. This rear-fanged snake digs its teeth into the prey animal which soon hangs lifeless and is then swallowed head first. A snake will eat one lizard every 2 or 3 days. Digestion is very rapid.

Thus far, *U. oxyrynchus* has not been successfully bred in captivity. The closely related *U. catesbyi* is about 50 inches (130 cm) long, also occurs in Haiti, and is found in the same habitats as *U. oxyrynchus*. The two snakes require the same care. The emerald green, diurnally active *U. catesbyi* is even more exclusively arboreal in its habitats than its cousin. It feeds on small frogs and lizards. In a terrarium it is not as long-lived as its larger relative.

Genus *Xenodon*
False Vipers
7 species

Xenodon merremi
Merrem's False Viper
(photo, page 86)

PHYSICAL CHARACTERISTICS: The quite short and broad head is clearly set off from the neck, and the large eyes with their round pupils are high up on the head, lending this plump-bodied colubrid a look reminiscent of venomous snakes. The scales are not keeled. *X. merremi* has an unusual set of teeth. The upper jaw, which is shorter than the lower one and thicker toward the back, has 8 to 9 teeth. The seven front ones of these are short, but the last one is much elongated. This fang is not hollow as in the case of the viper or equipped with a groove like the teeth of the poisonous elapids. But through a rotation of the movable upper jaw these long teeth can be pointed far forward. Some snake keepers speak of this snake as poisonous although its bite is harmless for humans, as this author can assert from his own experience. In frogs and toads, however, a poisonous reaction is clearly evident.

The coloration of this snake varies widely. Several years ago I had Merrem's False Viper shipped to me several times from Argentina. The animals, which all came from the same area, had, in some cases, bold markings in different colors whereas others were unicolored. The ground color of the upper side of the body can be any shade of gray or brown. Light and dark crossbands, sometimes edged in black, can be of various widths, may be broken up, or may fuse together to form a zig-zag band on the back. The markings are reminiscent of the poisonous lance-head snakes of the *Bothrops* genus or of the rattlesnakes of the *Crotalus* genus, and the natives in fact consider it venomous, calling it a "fake rattlesnake." The head and temples of the snake are mottled light and dark or are solid colored. The belly, too, can be unicolored or mottled. There are also solid brown or black individuals.

LENGTH: Up to 6¹/₂ feet (2 m).

DISTRIBUTION AND BEHAVIOR: *X. merremi* is native to Guyana, Brazil, Bolivia, Paraguay, and central and northern Argentina. It seems to be common in its range and lives primarily in forests and clearings near water. Not much is known about its life in the wild. It moves slowly and feeds on frogs and toads. If it is threatened or excited it puts on an impressive show. It inflates its body, dramatically flattening the throat and anterior body. At the same time it presses its body to the ground and quivers excitedly with the tail. If it is pestered too much, however, it will then sink its teeth into its enemy. Merrem's False Viper reproduces through eggs. The hatchlings measure about 6¹/₂ to 8 inches (12-20 cm).

CAPTIVITY AND BREEDING: *X. merremi* proves an interesting and enduring terrarium occupant. Unfortunately this snake is only rarely imported. To keep this species you need a terrarium with a large water section. Although this snake hardly spends any time in the water it needs very high humidity, up to 100%. As bottom material sand can be used or, even better, forest soil which holds moisture best. Rocks have to be cemented in place because the powerful snake will otherwise shove them aside. There is no need for a climbing tree because this snake always stays on the ground. During the day consistently high temperatures between 77° and 86°F (25°-30°C) are necessary. Artificial lights should be on 12 to 14 hours. Localized bottom heat is recommended. In its native habitat this snake is often found basking in the sun. At night the temperature should drop only insignificantly. *X. merremi* is a voracious eater but will unfortunately accept nothing but frogs and toads. There seems to be no way to change its tastes to fish. If you run out of frogs and toads you have to force-feed it fish, which it digests perfectly well. You can also resort to tying a fish to a dead frog, and the snake will swallow both. *X. merremi* has not thus far reproduced in captivity, although gravid females have laid fertile eggs, which took 110 days to hatch.

Genus *Heterodon*
Hognose Snakes
3 species

Heterodon nasicus
Western Hognose Snake
3 subspecies
(photo, page 86)

PHYSICAL CHARACTERISTICS: The broad and very short head of this chunky snake is clearly set off from the neck. The snout is turned up like a pig's nose and has a shovel-like rim. The scales on the body are strongly keeled. The top of the body is light gray. The back is covered with a row of broad, dark blotches, and the sides have double rows of staggered spots. Two parallel dark lines run across the forehead from one eye to the other, and a dark band connects the eye with the corner of the mouth. On the nape there are 2 broad spots that come to a sharp point at the back of the head. Between these spots there is a thin, longish band. The belly is black.

LENGTH: Up to 35 inches (89 cm).

DISTRIBUTION AND BEHAVIOR: *H. nasicus* is found from central southern Canada through the central United States and as far south as northeastern Mexico. It lives primarily in dry prairies where it favors sandy ground. With its turned up snout and strong neck muscles this snake is capable of burrowing in the ground and can vanish amazingly fast into the loose sand. It lives in the plains but is also found in mountains as high up as 7000 feet (2600 m). Its diet consists primarily of amphibians, especially frogs and toads, but it also consumes mice and lizards. When the Western Hognose Snake is taken by surprise and has no

TOP: Rough Greensnake (*Opheodrys aestivus*)
BOTTOM: Western Coachwhip (*Mastocophis flagellum testaceus*)

chance to make an escape it goes through a curious performance. It spreads its head and neck, hisses loudly, and strikes out with sham bites. If it is further provoked, it turns its belly up, opens its mouth, lets its tongue loll out, and plays dead. If it is then picked up it feels limp and completely lifeless. The Western Hognose Snake is completely harmless to humans. It hibernates for 5 to 6 months. Mating takes place toward the end of March or in April or May, and in June or July, 7 to 39 eggs are laid that take about 2 to 3 months to develop. The hatchlings measure about 6½ inches (17 cm).

CAPTIVITY AND BREEDING: The Western Hognose Snake is easy to keep in captivity. Because of its modest size it needs only a small to medium terrarium. The bottom is covered with a mixture of sand and loam. A few flat rocks or some pieces of bark will do for hiding places. The only other item needed is a small water dish made of glass, china, or plastic. There is no need for bottom heat. I have two of these snakes in a box measuring 21 × 18 inches (53 × 45 cm) in which I successfully use a 25-watt light to supply light and heat. During the day the temperature in the box is between 73° and 81°F (23°-27°C). The snakes often bask in this light for long periods. At night the temperature drops to 64° to 68°F (18°-20°). *H. nasicus* burrows a great deal and digs regular tunnels. Since frogs and toads are protected they should not be used as snake food. West-

ern Hognose Snakes will eagerly devour both naked mice and ones with the fur just growing in. The snakes grab hold of the mice any way they can and swallow them either head or tail first. Four to 5 months of winter rest is recommended. As far as I know, Kansas is the only place where this snake was bred in captivity. The young snakes become sexually mature at 2 years of age.

Heterodon platyrhinos
Eastern Hognose Snake
(photo, page 104)

PHYSICAL CHARACTERISTICS: This snake is much like a viper in body structure and in behavior. Its broad head is clearly set off from the neck. The body is thick, the tail short. The rostral plate is flattened, and the snout much turned up. The body color is variable. The upper side can be green, gray, brown, or reddish, and the back and sides are covered with many black, gray, brown, and reddish blotches. A dark band extends from the eyes to the corners of the mouth. A lyre-shaped mark covers the back of the head and the neck. The belly is blotched. There are also solid red and solid black populations, but albinos are extremely rare.

LENGTH: 32 to 36 inches (80-90 cm); rarely up to 3 feet (120 cm).

DISTRIBUTION AND BEHAVIOR: This snake is distributed from southern Canada across the central United States to southern Florida. It prefers dry ground on sandy knolls and is found in open woods, the edges of fields and meadows, and at heights up to 2600 feet (800 m). I have observed this species a number of times in the sun-drenched pine forests of South Carolina. The snakes were lying in the open, quite unprotected on the forest ground but always near a hole of a cotton rat den into which they would vanish at the approach of danger. If an Eastern Hognose Snake finds itself cornered it behaves just like its cousin, *H. nasicus,* but in an even more exaggerated way. Matings take place in the spring after a

TOP LEFT: Eastern Hognose Snake (*Heterodon platyrhinos*)
TOP RIGHT: European Smooth Snake (*Coronella austraca*)
CENTER LEFT: Southern Smooth Snake (*Coronella girondica*)
CENTER RIGHT: Asia Minor Dwarfsnake (*Eirenis modestus*)
BOTTOM LEFT: Ringneck Snake (*Diadophis punctatus*)
BOTTOM RIGHT: Glossy Snake (*Arizona elegans*)

winter rest of 4 to 6 months. The 6 to 42 eggs are longish and are usually deposited in June and occasionally in July or August. The young snakes hatch after 39 to 60 days. They have a length of 6 to 8 inches (15-20 cm). *H. platyrhinos* feeds primarily on toads, frogs, and salamanders and more rarely on fish, snakes, lizards, insects, and worms.

CAPTIVITY AND BREEDING: This snake has the same demands in captivity as the species described above. The only difference is that *H. platyrhinos* refuses to eat mice. It accepts nothing but frogs and toads, both dead and alive. The best solution is to collect amphibians that were killed on the road. These will keep for years in a freezer. One way to stretch one's supplies is to tie a piece of frog to a fish or some meat. This method helps stretch your supply of frogs and toads but also satisfies the snake's voracious appetite. There has been no record of this snake reproducing in captivity.

Genus *Diadophis*
Ringneck Snakes

Diadophis punctatus
Ringneck Snake
12 subspecies
(photo, page 104)

PHYSICAL CHARACTERISTICS: The head is barely set off from the neck, and the large eyes have round pupils. The body is slender, and the scales are smooth. The back and sides of the body are grayish-green or gray to black. The ring around the neck is whitish, yellow, or orange. Sometimes it is broken at the center by a row of dark scales. The belly is yellow or orange, and toward the tail the yellow often changes into a salmon pink. The belly plates may have irregular blotches which sometimes combine into distinct lines. Entirely black individuals and albinos are rare.

LENGTH: Up to 25 inches (63 cm).

DISTRIBUTION AND BEHAVIOR: *D. punctatus* is found almost throughout the United States from southeastern Canada to northern Mexico. The small snake seeks out moist places near swamps, rivers, streams, in wet forests, in quarries, and along fields and the edges of woods. I have often come across Ringneck Snakes under rotting logs or hidden under bark or stones. They never reacted aggresively. Most of them would curl up and hide their heads in the coils of their bodies. Even the tails were curled up, and the snakes would twist themselves in such a way that the red warning color of the belly was in clear evidence. The Ringneck Snake is quite common but usually stays well hidden. It lives on earthworms, insects, small frogs, salamanders, and occasionally on reptiles. Often large numbers of these snakes hibernate together under a tree stump or in a hole in the ground. In June or July, 1 to 8 eggs are laid in a moist spot that is often chosen so that it will get some sun warmth. The young, which hatch after 50 to 60 days, measure 4 to 5½ inches (10-14 cm) at hatching. Matings take place both in the spring and the fall, but most females lay only one clutch during one active season, though a few do lay two.

CAPTIVITY AND BREEDING: The Ringneck Snake is not commonly kept in terrariums. It needs only a small container with some forest soil on the bottom to which pieces of decaying wood and bark are added. Some of these serve as hiding places. A fair-sized water dish is necessary. *D. punctatus* seldom makes an appearance during the day and does not become active until evening or night. It should not be kept with other small snakes because it may eat them. It requires high air humidity and soil moisture and a daytime temperature between 72° and 79°F (22°-26°C). As food it can be offered earthworms, tadpoles, and small frogs. It goes after its prey on land. The Ringneck Snake should be wintered over for 3 or 4 months at low temperatures between 43° and 50°F (6°-10°C) in moist soil that is rich in humus. Although females that were gravid when caught have often deposited eggs in terrariums there are no reports of reproduction initiated in captivity.

Genus *Farancia*
Mud Snakes
2 species

Farancia abacura
Mud Snake
2 subspecies
(photo, page 158)

PHYSICAL CHARACTERISTICS: The short, oval head is not set off from the neck, and the body looks squat and strong. The short tail ends in a horny spine, which is why the snake is sometimes called the "horn snake." The scales are smooth everywhere except above the anal region. The anal plate is generally divided, though in some specimens undivided. The scales have a metallic sheen especially in bright light. The eyes are rather small. The top of the body is a shiny gray to black, and the belly is red mottled with black. Albinos are sometimes found, but they are rare.

LENGTH: 40 to 52 inches (100-130 cm); in rare cases up to 81 inches (206 cm).

DISTRIBUTION AND BEHAVIOR: *F. a. abacura* occurs in Virginia, North and South Carolina, Georgia, Florida, and Alabama, and *F. a. reinwardti* is found in Illinois, Indiana, Kentucky, Arkansas, Mississippi, Missouri, Oklahoma, Tennessee, Alabama, Louisiana, and Texas. The Mud Snake inhabits plains up to an altitude of 650 feet (200 m). It spends most of its time in the water. Its favorite haunts are cypress swamps, wet lowlands, and small and large ponds surrounded by dense vegetation. Often it lies under logs, hidden in sphagnum moss, or under piles of leaves. Young snakes are often found on water hyacinth roots (*Eichhornia crassipes*) sticking out of the shallow water. *F. abacura* is largely nocturnal. It leaves its lair at dusk, shortly after rainfalls, and during the mating season in spring. In some places this snake is very common. North of Orlando, Florida, I once saw hundreds of them in one evening. They came crawling out of a large cypress swamp near a highway, and

many of them were run over by cars. We filled several large flour bags with snakes mostly of this species in an hour. *F. abacura* feeds on salamanders (mostly *Amphiuma means* and *Siren lacertina*), newts, frogs, fish, and worms. It is not aggressive toward humans. When it is picked up it does not bite but rolls itself up in a ball, displaying the red and black warning colors on its belly. Mud snakes usually hibernate from October to March. Matings take place in the water as well as on the ground, and the eggs are deposited between April and June. *F. abacura* is very prolific, and as many as 104 eggs have been counted in one clutch. The female broods the eggs by coiling herself around them. The baby snakes, about 6¼ inches long (16 cm), hatch between August and October and undergo their first molt after about one week.

CAPTIVITY AND BREEDING: This snake is best kept in an aqua-terrarium with a water section that is larger than the land area. The land area is covered with a mixture of sand, forest soil, and peat. A fair-sized tree stump, a few peat bricks, some large pieces of bark, and a few rocks are added to provide refuges. There is no need for bottom heat if the temperature in the terrarium ranges between 75° and 86°F (24°-30°C) during the day and between 64° and 72°F (18°-22°C) at night. In the wintertime a rest period of 2 to 3 months at cooler temperatures of 50° to 59°F (10°-15°C) is necessary. The Mud Snake survives well in captivity if the proper kind of food can be provided. The zoo in Philadelphia, for instance, has a snake of this species that has been there for 18 years. Some Mud Snakes will eat nothing but *Amphiuma* and *Siren* while others will get used to frogs, newts, and fish. During the day *F. abacura* usually rests in its hiding place or in the water basin, or it burrows into the loose soil. It comes to life and appears in the open only toward evening. At least one snake keeper has bred this species in captivity. The snakes mated on July 11; the female deposited eggs on September 5; and the young snakes hatched on October 30.

Subfamily Dipsadinae—Middle American Snakes

Genus *Hypsiglena*
Night Snakes
4 species

Hypsiglena torquata
Night Snake
7 subspecies

PHYSICAL CHARACTERISTICS: The flat head is hardly set off from the neck, and the large eyes have vertically elliptical pupils. The body is slender, and the scales are smooth. The ground color of the body varies from cream to gray and brown. On each side of the neck there is a large brown mark. These two marks may extend to the middle of the nape and merge there, or they may not be present at all. A dark line runs from the tip of the snout to the sides of the neck. The back and sides of the body are covered with dark, blotches. The belly is yellowish to grayish-white.

LENGTH: 12 to 16 inches (30-40 cm); rarely up to or slightly over 20 inches (50 cm).

DISTRIBUTION AND BEHAVIOR: *H. torquata* is found in the western United States, in Mexico, and as far south as Costa Rica. This small snake inhabits different biotopes both in plains and in mountains up to 9500 feet (2900 m). It is found in the desert, in loose rocks at the foot of mountains, and especially often on rocky mountainsides with patches of shrubbery and open woods. During the day *H. torquata* stays hidden under rocks, old wood, etc., but at dusk or at night it starts prowling and is then often run over on roads. Its diet is made up of small lizards and frogs, which it paralyses with its weak venom. *H. torquata* often hibernates in great numbers in the tunnels dug in the ground by gopher tortoises (*Gopherus agassizi*). Hibernation usually lasts from October to April. Matings take place in the spring. Between April and July the female lays 4 to 6 eggs which take 50 to 60 days to mature.

CAPTIVITY AND BREEDING: This snake is rarely offered for sale by dealers. Because of its diminutive size this snake can be kept in a small container with dry sand and loam at the bottom. To provide cover a few flat rocks and pieces of bark are added under which the snake burrows during the day. A small water container is sufficient. *H. torquata* requires strong bottom heat, and a bottom heater warming one area of the floor is thus essential. Since this snake does not come out in the open until dark no special lighting is required. Temperatures should range between 72° and 82°F (22°-28°C) during the day to be lowered to about 64° to 68°F (18°-20°C) at night. Small lizards and frogs—which constitute the snake's diet in nature—are offered for food. The snake seizes its prey by whatever part of the body it can and either paralyzes it with its venom or swallows it alive. Apparently nobody has yet succeeded in breeding this snake in captivity, but eggs deposited by females that were gravid when captured have been incubated and have hatched.

Genus *Leptodeira*
Cat-eye Snakes
9 species

Leptodeira annulata
Banana Snake
7 subspecies

PHYSICAL CHARACTERISTICS: The short, broad head is clearly set off from the neck, and the large eyes have vertically elliptical pupils. The body looks short and somewhat compressed on the sides. Its coloration varies from yellowish to reddish-brown. The head is solid brown with a dark stripe behind the eyes. The markings on the back consist of large, dark blotches that have light borders and sometimes merge together in a zigzag pattern. Dark patches on the sides are arranged in a staggered pattern to those on the back. On the tail the patches grow indistinct. The light gray belly has faint gray dots.

LENGTH: 20 to 28 inches (50-70 cm).

DISTRIBUTION AND BEHAVIOR: The Banana Snake is common from Mexico to Argentina. Sometimes it finds its way to Europe in a shipment of bananas or fancy wood. In its native regions it occurs primarily in wet areas with rich vegetation. It is especially frequent along the edges of swamps. Its diet consists of frogs, toads, lizards, and insects. Occasionally it also eats snakes. Juveniles live almost exclusively on trees, but the fully grown dwell on the ground. *L. annulata* hides in dark places during the day and starts prowling around at night. It is often found near human habitations and sometimes climbs up on straw roofs. In tropical South America, the mating season of this snake extends practically throughout the year. Females lay clutches of up to 10 eggs. The newly hatched snakes are $6^{1}/_{4}$ to $7^{1}/_{2}$ inches (16-19 cm) long.

CAPTIVITY AND BREEDING: *L. annulata* is not often found in the terrariums of snake fanciers although it is quite long-lived in captivity and adjusts quickly. It requires a medium-sized terrarium with a large water basin, a piece of bark or tree stump to hide under, and a few climbing branches. Forest soil or a mixture of sand and peat are used for the bottom. Ordinary daylight is adequate. The air temperature should be between 77° and 86°F (25°-30°C) during the day and be lowered a little at night. Frogs and lizards are offered as food. It is a good idea to keep this snake singly because some individuals eat other snakes.
A number of female snakes that were gravid when captured have laid several clutches of eggs in captivity. One report states that a female, after 5 years in captivity, laid a clutch of 11 eggs, 6 of which were fertile. Previous to this the snake had laid 2 other clutches although she had had no contact with males in captivity.

Leptodeira septentrionalis
Banded Cat-eye Snake
3 subspecies

PHYSICAL CHARACTERISTICS: The short, broad head is clearly set off from the neck, and the eyes have vertically elliptical pupils. The body looks sturdy and has smooth scales. Its ground color is greenish-yellow to reddish-brown, and there are broad, dark brown to black saddle-shaped blotches across the back and sides at regular intervals. A dark stripe runs from the eyes to the corners of the mouth, and the top of the head has dark spots. The belly is solid yellow.

LENGTH: 20 to 30 inches (50-75 cm).

DISTRIBUTION AND BEHAVIOR: The Banded Cat-eye Snake is found from southern Texas to Costa Rica. Like *L. annulata* it is nocturnally active. It lives both in the plains and in mountains up to 3300 feet (1000 m) and likes to be near various bodies of water. It spends more time on trees than on the ground. Its food consists almost entirely of frogs, but it will also consume lizards, mice, and snakes. Little is known about its habits of reproduction except that it lays eggs and that the hatchling snakes are about 7 inches (18 cm) long.

CAPTIVITY AND BREEDING: *L. septentrionalis* requires the same care as *L. annulata* and, if kept under the proper conditions is long-lived in captivity. The Lincoln Park Zoo in Chicago has a Banded Cat-eye Snake that has lived there for over 11 years. But since these snakes sometimes eat other members of their own species they had better be kept singly. The most likely choice of food for *L. septentrionalis* is frogs, which are, however, becoming less abundant. Occasionally one can substitute fish, and since Cat-eye Snakes also do eat mice an effort should be made to accustom them to this prey. Healthy individuals accept food regularly and eagerly and only stop eating for a few weeks in the summer. Banded Cat-eye Snakes sometimes like to soak in the water basin for days before molting. This species has not yet been bred in captivity, but a female owned by herpetologist Ditmar that had been gravid when captured deposited 12 eggs under a rock.

Subfamily Psammophiinae—Sand Racers

Genus *Malpolon*
Lizard Snakes
2 species

Malpolon monspessulanus
Montpellier Snake
2 subspecies

PHYSICAL CHARACTERISTICS: The long head is hardly set off from the neck. The forehead is furrowed between and in front of the eyes, and the supraocular plates stick out a little beyond the strikingly large eyes with their round pupils. The body is moderately slender, and the scales are smooth. The Montpellier Snake comes in all kinds of shades ranging from pale yellow to grayish-green and black. The back and sides are covered with small, blackish spots that are partially or totally rimmed with yellow or white. These spots usually form 5 to 7 rows and are arranged in such a pattern that they alternate from row to row. The belly is a uniform yellowish-gray or shows 4 rows of dots. The head has markings made up of dark spots and lines with light borders; and, in the *M. m. monspessulanus*, these markings grow fainter with age.

LENGTH: Sometimes over 6½ feet (2 m).

DISTRIBUTION AND BEHAVIOR: *M. monspessulanus* is native to southern Europe, northern Africa, and Asia Minor where it inhabits arid regions that are sunny and warm and are covered with low scrub and thorny bushes. Some of its favorite haunts are the edges of fields, rock piles, stone walls, slopes of loose rock, and old walls. It is more active during the day than during warm nights and moves very fast and impetuously. When it is captured it produces a long and loud hiss. Since its poison fangs are located far in the rear and rarely make contact the Montpellier Snake's bite is usually harmless. But if the venom does penetrate into the flesh it can cause pain, swelling,

nausea, and symptoms of poisoning of the nervous system. *M. monspessulanus* feeds on small mammals, birds, lizards, and snakes, which it strangles and kills with its venom. Smaller prey is swallowed alive. The Montpellier Snake often does not retire to its hibernating quarters until November and reappears as early as March. Matings take place in April or May, and in July or August, 4 to 18 eggs are laid, from which baby snakes hatch after 2 to 3 months.

CAPTIVITY AND BREEDING: This big rear-fanged snake requires a large dry terrarium with a layer of sand and loam on the bottom. Several large, flat, limestone rocks, preferably cemented in place, serve as a retreat. A small water container is also required. To feel comfortable the Montpellier Snake requires daytime temperatures between 77° and 90°F (25°-32°C). Localized bottom heat is essential because this snake visits the water frequently during the day. A bright location with morning and afternoon sun is ideal; otherwise artificial light should be provided 12 to 14 hours a day. At first the Montpellier Snake is shy and violent, and when it feels watched it immediately disappears under a rock or a piece of hollow cork, hissing fiercely. It curls up tightly and hides its head in the coils of the body. Some individuals refuse to eat at first and start eating the mice they are given only after some time. But his initial timidity soon diminishes and some individuals become hand tame. Mice as well as rats, golden hamsters, small rabbits, sparrows, and chicks can be offered as food. If kept in a dry and warm environment Montpellier Snakes show good appetite and survive well. They should be wintered over from November to late February at 50° to 59°F (10°-15°C). This snake has not yet been bred in captivity.

Genus *Psammophis*
Sand Racers
16 species

Psammophis sibilans
Olive Sandracer
4 subspecies

PHYSICAL CHARACTERISTICS: The longish head is clearly set off from the neck, and the large eyes have round pupils. The neck and body are very slender, and the scales are smooth. Coloration is quite varied. The head is gray or brown, either all one color or mottled. The back and sides of the body are solid gray, olive colored, or yellowish to dark brown, or there may be a yellow stripe on the back and a stripe on each side. The belly is a solid porcelain color, yellowish, or greenish, or is striped.

LENGTH: 4 to 5 feet (120-150 cm).

DISTRIBUTION AND BEHAVIOR: *P. sibilans* is distributed all over Africa except the northwestern parts, tropical forests, and desert areas. Despite its genus name *P. sibilans* is not restricted to regions with sandy ground but is especially frequent in dry savannas with bush growth. It dwells almost exclusively on the ground and only rarely climbs on low bushes to sun itself. *P. sibilans* is very shy and moves with great speed. At the slightest suggestion of danger it vanishes into some bushes, a mouse hole, or a pile of stones and is then practically impossible to find. If it is captured it bites without hesitation. The bite can cause pain, swelling, and nausea but is not, as far as we know, fatal. The Olive Sandracer eats small mammals, birds, lizards, and frogs, and it in turn is pursued by cobras, boomslangs, and predator birds. It is particularly vulnerable to the latter when it suns itself on bushes, and it is therefore far from surprising that a large percentage of these snakes have lost their tails. The eggs—up to 30—are usually laid in December or January. The baby snakes measure 11 to 12 inches (28-30 cm) at birth.

CAPTIVITY AND BREEDING: This Sand Racer reacts with great violence when captured, but it adjusts relatively quickly to captivity and soon becomes hand tame. Still, caution is in order when handling it. *P. sibilans* is easier to keep than its close relative, *P. schokari*. There are some individuals that have survived in captivity over 10 years. *P. sibilans* eagerly consumes mice both dead and alive. Some individuals specialize in one kind of prey animal and refuse any other food they are offered. This snake holds its prey in its jaws until the poison takes effect. It may also crush the prey animal to the ground. A large, dry terrarium with sand and loam at the bottom is required for *P. sibilans*. A few flat rocks have to be provided to serve as a retreat. The terrarium also needs a small water basin and—most important—a well functioning bottom heater. The lights should be on 12 to 14 hours. This diurnal snake appreciates the morning and afternoon sun and thrives at daytime temperatures between 77° and 86°F (25°-30°C). At night it should be 9° to 18°F (5°-10°C) cooler. There are no reports of this snake having been bred in captivity as yet.

Genus *Psammophylax**
Skaapstekers

Psammophylax rhombeatus
Spotted Skaapsteker
(photo, page 176)

PHYSICAL CHARACTERISTICS: The head is moderately set off from the neck with the upper jaw protruding beyond the lower one. The large eyes have vertical slits for pupils. The coloration of the back varies from grayish-brown to yellowish-brown and a pale olive brown. The markings of the back and sides consist of a row of dark, roundish or lozenge-shaped blotches that sometimes combine in a zigzag or irregularly undulating band. On the tail the blotches merge into 3 longitudinal stripes that are separated from each other by

*This genus is dangerously venomous

111

light lines. The head is a uniform brown or black, and the whitish-yellow belly has gray to black blotches.

LENGTH: Up to 4 feet (120 cm).

DISTRIBUTION AND BEHAVIOR: The area of distribution of *P. rhombeatus* reaches from western Cape Province eastward and northward across Orange Free State and Natal as far as Transvaal. This terrestrial snake occurs in dry savannas and grasslands where it is encountered sometimes in considerable numbers from the coast to high up in the mountains. It is quick but still falls prey to predatory birds and cobras quite often. *P. rhombeatus* is a peaceful snake that hardly ever bites, and its Afrikaans name "shaapsteker" is quite misleading. This snake does not represent a threat to sheep or any other fair-sized animal, let alone humans, because its fangs are set too far in the rear of the mouth. Although its neurotoxic venom is similar to that of poisonous elapids and has even more drastic effects, thus far no serious cases of poisoning have been reported. The "shaapsteker" feeds on lizards and mice and occasionally frogs. Sometime between October and December it lays up to 30 eggs in some rotting leaves or another suitable spot. The female engages in brooding behavior, curling herself around the eggs until the 7- to 8-inch-long baby snakes hatch after 5 to 6 weeks.

CAPTIVITY AND BREEDING: *P. rhombeatus* does well in a medium-sized dry terrarium with sand and loam at the bottom, some flat rocks as a refuge, and a small water basin. A potted Christ's-thorn lends the set-up a more natural look. Bottom heat is a requirement, and artificial lights should be on all day. Five members of this species I temporarily looked after were especially fond of lying in the morning sun. *P. rhombeatus* becomes tame quickly and feels comfortable during the day at 77° to 86°F (25°-30°C). At night the temperature should drop a few degrees. If kept at these temperatures *P. rhombeatus* eats regularly.

Mice are the prey that is offered in captivity. Thus far this snake has not been bred in captivity. Two of my snakes that were later owned by N. Wittmann laid 5 and 6 eggs on October 25 and 26, respectively. The young snakes hatched on December 8 and 10, and they underwent their first molt after 2 to 3 weeks. Since the young snakes refused to eat on their own they were force-fed some heart, which they digested well. The young snakes grew rapidly.

Subfamily Natricinae—Watersnakes and Allies

Genus *Rhabdophis**
Rear-fanged Keelbacks

Rhabdophis tigrina
Tiger Keelback
3 subspecies

PHYSICAL CHARACTERISTICS: The head is barely set off from the neck, and the large eyes have round pupils. The body is slender, and the tail long and tapered. The keeled scales are considerably widened in the male near the cloaca. The ground color is greenish to pale gray, and the back is covered with black and orange blotches. The sides of the neck are pale red with black dots. A black crossband runs across the nape of the neck, and the top of the head is greenish. A dark stripe connects the eye and the corner of the mouth. The slate-colored belly shows dark blotches toward the head and becomes solid black toward the tail.

LENGTH: 24 to 28 inches (60-70 cm); only rarely over 3 feet (1 m).

DISTRIBUTION AND BEHAVIOR: *R. tigrina* occurs in Manchuria, Korea, Japan, and China. It lives in the lowlands but quite frequently also in mountains up to an altitude of of 7800 feet (2000 m). This snake is found in

*Members of this genus are dangerously venomous.

water as well as on dry land. In dry areas it seeks out the proximity of water, and in wetter regions it lives in grass-covered hilly country far away from bodies of water. The Tiger Keelback lives primarily on frogs, toads, and fish but will also eat mice, rats, birds, and even grasshoppers. Its movements are very rapid. Toward people it is not aggressive. When faced with danger it flattens its body and especially the throat, assuming a cobra-like look. *R. tigrina* lays about 14 eggs measuring about $1^1/2 \times {}^3/4$ inches (36×20 mm) in July or August.

CAPTIVITY AND BREEDING: This snake has been imported rarely thus far. As for other watersnakes, the container for a Tiger Keelback should be an aqua-terrarium that is half watersnakes, the container for a Tiger Keelbottom heat is recommended. Daytime temperatures should range between 68° and 86°F (20°-30°C). Artificial lighting is not necessary if the terrarium gets several hours of sunlight. *R. tigrina* does well in captivity, is not sensitive to the cold, and eats well. The climate conditions of its natural habitat can be simulated by allowing it to hibernate from November to March.

No planned breeding of this snake in captivity has been reported thus far, but there is a report of the laying of eggs in the terrarium. The incubation took 46 to 47 days, and the newborn snakes measured between 6 and 7 inches (15-17 cm).

Genus *Xenochrophis*
Fishing Keelbacks

Xenochrophis piscator
Checkered Keelback
4 subspecies

PHYSICAL CHARACTERISTICS: The head is barely set off from the the neck, and the body is slender. The scales on the back are strongly keeled, those on the sides less so or not at all. The large eyes have round pupils. The back and the sides of the body are yellow, olive, brown, or reddish with black blotches. The black blotches are arranged in 5 parallel rows. There are also solidly colored specimens without spots. The head is olive-colored to brown on top. Two lines run to the corner of the mouth, one from above the eye and the other from below it. The belly is a uniform yellowish-white.

LENGTH: Up to 4 feet (120 cm).

DISTRIBUTION AND BEHAVIOR: *X. piscator* has a huge area of distribution reaching from Pakistan to China and Southeast Asia and including the Malaysian islands. As its Latin name indicates, this snake is always found near water, and sometimes it occurs in great numbers. It inhabits both lowlands and hilly country, and it is one of the most common snakes in the rice paddies of Thailand. The Checkered Keelback wanders a great deal and sometimes travels far from its home waters. It is both diurnal and nocturnal. It is quick and agile in its movements and an excellent swimmer. When it feels threatened it raises its upper body, flattens its throat like a cobra, and darts at the opponent to bite in a flash. In the cool parts of its range it hibernates, and in warmer areas it takes a summer rest. Fish and frogs make up the bulk of its diet, though it sometimes eats mice as well. In keeping with its large distribution, mating periods vary and can occur any time of the year. Keelbacks lay from 8 to 87 eggs which hatch after about 3 months. The newborn snakes measure $6^1/2$ to 8 inches (17-21 cm).

CAPTIVITY AND BREEDING: The Checkered Keelback needs a terrarium with a large section of water. The bottom of the dry part is covered with a mixture of sand, forest soil, or peat. A few flat rocks and a tree stump supply hiding places. A bottom heater radiating gentle heat is necessary. The daytime temperature should be between 75° and 86°F (24°-30°C). There should be about 10 to 12 hours of daylight, but artificial lights are not necessary if the terrarium gets sunlight both in the morning and afternoon. Freshly imported Keelbacks are aggressive and bite, but they soon adjust and become more agreeable. This snake lives for a long time in a terrarium and is content to eat fish and frogs both dead and alive. It almost always retreats to dry ground to eat its prey.

Keelbacks have been bred in captivity. The eggs are placed in a mixture of slightly damp sand and peat. At 77° to 86°F (25°-30°C), incubation takes barely 3 months. The newborn snakes shed their skins a few days after hatching and soon eat baby fish, tadpoles, and small frogs. The Checkered Keelback does not need to hibernate in captivity.

Genus *Amphisema*
Oriental Gartersnakes

Amphisema mairii
Moluccan Gartersnake

PHYSICAL CHARACTERISTICS: Some herpetologists classify this snake under the genus *Natrix* and others count it among the genus *Amphisema*. The snake's head is only slightly set off from the neck. The scales are strongly keeled. The upper side of the body is gray, brown, olive, reddish, or black and has narrow, irregular crossbands or blotches. The belly is olive green, brown, or salmon-colored.

LENGTH: 20 to 40 inches (50-100 cm).

DISTRIBUTION AND BEHAVIOR: The Moluccan Gartersnake is native to the Moluccas, New Guinea, and the coastal regions of northern and northeastern Australia. It always lives close to water and spends time both in the water and on dry ground. Often it is found lying on branches overhanging the water. It is somewhat active in the daytime but more so at night, generally setting out in pursuit of prey in the late afternoon or in the evening. Its diet consists almost entirely of frogs, which it swallows hindlegs first. If it is discovered it immediately drops into the water. This snake is completely harmless and does not even resort to biting when it is teased.

CAPTIVITY AND BREEDING: This snake is imported only very infrequently. It requires an aqua-terrarium with a large section of water and a profusely forked tree branch to satisfy its need for climbing. It should have 12 to 14 hours of artificial lighting and daytime temperatures between 75° and 86°F (24°-30°C). Frogs are the only thing it will eat. This snake is extremely shy. It shares a trait with lizards the keeper should be aware of. When it is held by the tail, the tail comes off, sometimes as close to the anus as 1/2 inch (1.3 cm).

This species has reproduced in captivity. The female lays 5 to 12 eggs sometime between January and April. The young hatch 2 to 3 months later and measure about 7 inches (18 cm). For their first meals they can be given tadpoles or tiny frogs.

Amphisema stolata
Striped Gartersnake

PHYSICAL CHARACTERISTICS: The head is barely set off from the neck and the body is slender. The large eyes have round pupils. The scales are keeled. The ground color varies a great deal. Usually this snake is light gray to medium brown with 60 to 75 dark crossbars on the center of the back. Each of these crossbars on the neck and upper back ends in a light colored spot, and a light line runs down each side of the back, beginning behind the head and ending on the tail. These lines are broken about halfway down the body but then continue to the tail without any further breaks. The belly is white, becoming yellowish toward the throat.

LENGTH: Slightly over 28 inches (70 cm).

DISTRIBUTION AND BEHAVIOR: *A. stolata* has a large distribution reaching from Afghanistan eastward to Indochina and including Sri Lanka and the coastal provinces of southern China. It is quite a common snake that is found in lowlands, hilly country, and mountains, where it is met at altitudes up to about 6500 feet (1700 m). Unlike other related species it is not so dependent on water and inhabits wooded and grassy areas as well. It is frequently seen in damp valleys and lives on both wild and cultivated land. It is often seen along the edges of rice fields that are surrounded by the jungle. The snake's food consists of frogs, toads, and lizards. Generally the Striped Gartersnake is peaceful and seldom bites, but when it is very angry it flattens its throat somewhat. It is active during the day and likes to rest on branches overhanging the water. Sometimes it lurks in the water, and often it hides under logs and collections of leaves and rotting wood. It is quite often found along dry river banks and is especially fond of lying on the warm ground. In some areas of India it becomes dormant during the dry season, and in the cooler north it hibernates. Mating occurs during the dry season, and the eggs—up to 14—are laid any time from May to September. They take about 50 days to hatch, and the newborn snakes measure 5½ to 7 inches (14-18 cm).

CAPTIVITY AND BREEDING: The Striped Gartersnake has been imported into Europe repeatedly. It needs a fairly large water basin and a land area with completely dry bottom material and localized heat. The artificial lights should be on all day. Since this snake likes to sleep on branches, a climbing tree with many forks is important. The Striped Gartersnake needs a very even temperature between 77° and 82°F (25°-28°C). It can be given frogs to eat, and it has a very good appetite. According to Wall, a Striped Gartersnake consumed 131 toads in one year in captivity. *A. stolata* has been bred in captivity several times by snake fanciers in Germany.

Genus *Natriciteres*
African Marsh Snakes
3 species

Natriciteres olivacea
Olive Marsh Snake
2 subspecies

PHYSICAL CHARACTERISTICS: The oval head is set off only slightly from the neck. The eyes are not as large as those of the related *Natrix* species. The pupils are round and the irises golden brown. The body is slender, and the scales smooth. The anal plate is divided. The upper side of the body varies in color from olive green to bluish-black. A wide, dark band runs down the middle of the back from the neck to the end of the tail. This band may be flanked by light blotches. The sides of the body are olive green, reddish-brown, or bluish-gray. The belly is a uniform yellow to orange red.

LENGTH: Up to 24 inches (60 cm).

DISTRIBUTION AND BEHAVIOR: *N. olivacea* has a wide distribution from western Africa to eastern Africa and down to South Africa. It has adapted to life in the water and is found in the lowlands. But it has also been found on mountains as far up as 7000 feet (2100 m). Its main habitat, however, is in the savanna in the immediate vicinity of all kinds of different bodies of water. It also inhabits the equatorial African rain forests. It is at home on land as well as in the water, though it moves rather slowly on the ground. It is an excellent swimmer and likes to hide between aquatic plants. In its search of prey—frogs, toads, tadpoles, and fish—it often dives to the bottom. Occasionally it also feeds on caterpillars and grasshoppers. *N. olivacea* is primarily nocturnal and spends the day close to the water hidden under rocks, boulders, and dry tufts of grass. It is peaceful by nature and never bites when caught. If grabbed by the tail, it writhes around desperately, often breaking free by leaving the end of its tail behind the way lizards do. One quite frequently encounters Marsh Snakes with newly healed tails. During the rainy season in April these snakes often journey far. As a rule they lay 6 to 8 eggs. The month when this happens depends on the geographic location of the snake's biotope.

CAPTIVITY AND BREEDING: Being definitely aquatic in its habits, *N. olivacea* needs an aqua-terrarium with a generous water section. The dry area should have a layer of sand, gravel, and a little forest soil, and some pieces of bark and flat rocks are needed to provide hiding places. The air should be between 68° and 86°F (20°-30°C) during the day and a little cooler at night. Localized bottom heat is recommended, and lights should be on 8 to 12 hours a day. If the terrarium gets morning and afternoon sun or is next to a bright window no artificial lights may be necessary. This snake quickly adjusts to terrarium life, becomes hand tame, and can live long in captivity. It is fed frogs, fish, and strips of fish. There is no need for hibernation. Thus far there have been no reports of this snake reproducing in captivity.

Genus *Natrix*
European Watersnakes

Natrix maura
Viperine Snake (Viperine Watersnake)
(photo, page 68)

PHYSICAL CHARACTERISTICS: The head is clearly set off from the neck. The body is slender in the male and somewhat stouter in the female. The scales of the body are strongly keeled. The eyes are large, and the pupils round. The coloration and the markings vary considerably. The back is noticeably darker than the sides and may be any shade of gray, yellow, or green. A band of lozenge-shaped to round blotches runs down the back often combining into a zigzag pattern similar to that seen on the Common Viper. On the sides of the body there are oval spots that are often yellowish or white at the center. At the back of

the head and on the nape two blackish marks merge into each other. The yellowish sides of the head have more or less pronounced black dots and streaks. A dark stripe runs from the eye to the corner of the mouth. The olive colored to yellowish or brownish belly is irregularly speckled.

LENGTH: Rarely over 3 feet (1 m).

DISTRIBUTION AND BEHAVIOR: The Viperine Snake is found in southwestern Switzerland, northwestern Italy, southern France, on Sardinia, the Balearic Islands, the Iles-d'Hyères, the Pyrenean peninsula, and in northwestern Africa. Of all the European snakes of the *Natrix* genus, the Viperine Snake is best adapted to life in the water. It likes very weedy waters and is active during the day. It spends time between rocks of sea walls, hiding in washed-up debris, under overhanging banks, and often in the network of tree roots, leaving these refuges in the morning and afternoon to bask in the sun. It is extremely shy and takes to the water at the slightest sign of danger. If it is grabbed it hisses loudly. In its fright it sprays a stinking liquid from its anal glands but never tries to bite. The Viperine Snake is an excellent swimmer. It is much faster in the water than on land. It hovers on the water's bottom, ready to pounce on fish and amphibians, which it swallows still alive. Small prey it finishes off in the water, while larger frogs or fish are first dragged to shore. Around noon large numbers of these snakes can sometimes be seen in shallow water chasing after tadpoles and small fish. Young Viperine Snakes also eat earthworms. Depending on the weather and the geographic location, hibernation lasts from October to March or April. Mating occurs in March and April. Four to 20 eggs are deposited in June or July in loose soil, under stones, or under dense plants near the water's edge. The 6- to 8-inch-long (15-20 cm) young hatch in August or early September.

CAPTIVITY AND BREEDING: The Viperine Snake can be kept for years in a terrarium and gradually becomes so tame that it will take food from the keeper's hand. Because of this quality this snake can be recommended with good conscience for beginners. I keep my Viperine Snakes in my garden in a glassed-in outdoor terrarium. But modest to medium-sized terrariums with a sufficiently large water area will do quite well. These snakes spend hours and even days in the water before molting. Since they do not climb much, branches offering a good hold are not essential. The bottom is covered with a mixture of forest soil, sand, and gravel with a few flat rocks or a tree stub for hiding under. *N. maura* favors temperatures between 77° and 86°F (25°-30°C), which may drop by 18°F (10°C) at night. No artificial lights are necessary if the terrarium gets 6 to 8 hours of sunlight. Freshly captured Viperine Snakes are shy at first, hissing violently, drawing their necks back in an S-shape, and pretending to bite. If they are pestered too much, they fall into a rigidity of extreme fright. After the initial shock they soon become hand tame. They can be fed live fish, which they are quick and adept at catching, and consume in no time. They also eat dead fish and pieces of fish but are less fond of frogs, toads, and newts. These amphibians should not be used as food for this snake because they are shrinking in number. Another reason for not using newts as food is that there is a poison in their skins that sometimes makes snakes vomit. In imitation of natural conditions, the Viperine Snake should be allowed to hibernate 3 to 5 months at 40° to 47°F (4°-8°C) in moist forest soil and leaves. Animals that have hibernated eat better, and hibernation is a key factor in successful reproduction.

Several generations of this snake have been bred in captivity. The animals usually mate in the spring although the males can mate all year. The eggs are laid in June, generally 10 to 15 of them, though occasionally up to 32. They are placed in a mixture of peat and sand and kept slightly damp. If kept at 77° to 86°F (25°-30°C), they hatch after 40 to 45 days. The first skins are shed after 10 to 12 days, and soon thereafter the young snakes start eating

small fish, pieces of fish, and earthworms. The Viperine Snake is the only snake of western Europe that can be fed on earthworms for months. The snake reaches sexual maturity at 3 to 4 years of age.

Natrix natrix
Grass snake
10 subspecies
(photo, page 68)

PHYSICAL CHARACTERISTICS: The head, especially in the female, is flat and broad and clearly set off from the neck. The head of the male is longer and less set off from the body. The large eyes have round pupils. The scales of the body are strongly keeled. The ground color of the upper side is either uniformly grayish-green or has black blotches arranged in 4 to 6 rows running down the body. The subspecies *N. n. persa* has parallel white stripes down its back. The yellowish-white belly is more or less densely sprinkled with black or is entirely black. Some individuals have white, egg-yolk colored, or orange, moon-shaped blotches with black rims on the back of the head. There are some rare melanistic Ringed Snakes.

LENGTH: In exceptional cases over 5 feet (150 cm).

DISTRIBUTION AND BEHAVIOR: The Grass Snake is found in Europe, northwestern Africa, and western Asia. Its favorite haunts are the reedy and weed-infested shores of still or slowly moving waters. But it is also found away from water. It is a frequent denizen of abandoned quarries and sand pits, and it is encountered on mountain slopes, edges of woods, vineyards, and even close to human settlements. In the presence of danger the Grass Snake goes rigid for a while. It turns its belly side toward the attacker, opens the mouth from which saliva and sometimes even a little blood may drip, and lets the tongue hang out lifelessly. But it can also face danger quite differently, flattening the throat region, puffing itself up, hissing loudly, coiling itself up, and pretend-biting. Usually a foul-smelling liquid is emitted by the anal glands at the same time. The Grass Snake has many enemies among mammals and predator birds, but its main threat is man who, in his ignorance and irrationality, still wantonly destroys this snake. Grass Snakes eat frogs, toads, newts, salamanders, fish, and, less commonly, mice and lizards. They detect their prey by sight and smell. In the fall they search out hibernating dens under boulders and tree stumps, in holes in the ground, and even in manure heaps or other frost-free corners. In March or April they emerge from their winter dens and spend as much time as possible lying in the sun. After molting they mate. The male crawls over or along the female with twitching body motions and a strange nodding jerk of the head. Then the two animals wrap their tails around each other, and the male extrudes his paired penis and inserts one of the two hemipenes into the female's cloaca. The longish eggs—generally under 50—are usually deposited in decaying plant material and stick together in a clump. The young snakes hatch after about 6 to 10 weeks, measuring 6 to 7 $1/2$ inches (15-19 cm). Their first food consists of tadpoles, tiny frogs, toads, newts, and their larvae.

CAPTIVITY AND BREEDING: The Grass Snake is particularly well suited for terrarium life, often thriving for many years there if well cared for. It needs a terrarium and light conditions like those suggested for the Viperine Snake. Temperatures between 77° and 86°F (20°-25°C) during the day are sufficient, and at night it should be a few degrees cooler. Healthy Grass Snakes always show interest in food. They eat frogs, fish, and pieces of fish. Toads, newts, and salamanders should not be fed to them because some among them belong to protected species, and they contain mildly poisonous substances. Hibernation from October to March in a box with slightly damp forest soil, moss, and leaves is indicated; the snakes thrive better after cold conditions.

The Grass Snakes mate after their winter rest usually in March or April but sometimes not until fall. The eggs are usually laid in June or July. Place them in a canning jar with some sand and peat moss. They always have to stay slightly damp. Raising the baby snakes on small fish, tadpoles, and frogs presents no problems. This snake has been bred in captivity many times, and *N. n. natrix* and *N. n. persa* have mated together in a terrarium and produced viable offspring.

Natrix tessellata
Dice Snake
2 subspecies
(photo, page 86)

PHYSICAL CHARACTERISTICS: The longish head is moderately set off from the neck, and the body looks more slender than that of the Grass Snake. The eyes are large and have round pupils. The scales are strongly keeled. The ground coloration can be any hue of gray or brown. The back and sides are covered by 4 to 5 rows of irregular blotches that are staggered and may merge into crossbands. The belly is yellowish to reddish with black spots. On the neck there is sometimes a triangular mark with the apex of the triangle pointing forward. A subspecies *(N. t. heinrothi)* found on the island Serpilor in the Black Sea differs markedly from *N. t. tessellata*. It is bluish-black; the throat is yellowish and reddish; and the anterior body has a dotted pattern of the same colors. Black specimens of *n. t. tessellata* are sometimes found, too.

LENGTH: Up to 5 feet (150 cm).

DISTRIBUTION AND BEHAVIOR: The Dice Snake is distributed over a large area extending from central and southern Europe to northwestern India and western China. It is found in some places in West Germany, Austria, Czechoslovakia, Switzerland, Italy, and the Balkan peninsula, as well as in southern Russia, and in western and central Asia. This snake lives near all kinds of water but prefers banks overgrown with bushes and trees. Often it basks for hours on branches overhanging the water. It is an excellent swimmer and diver but is also quite at ease and quick on land. In the water it hunts for amphibians and fish, either lying in wait for them or swimming after them. Small fish are swallowed right away; large ones are dragged to shore first. Mating occurs in the spring shortly after waking from winter sleep. Between June and August, 5 to 25 oval eggs that often stick together in a clump are deposited in a pile of leaves, in some loose earth, under rocks, or in the roots of a tree. The young, which hatch after about 8 to 10 weeks, feed on tadpoles and small fish.

CAPTIVITY AND BREEDING: Being a true water snake (with eyes and nostrils placed on the side of the head and pointing upward), the Dice Snake needs a large terrarium with a sizable water section. As cover for the land area, a mixture of sand, gravel, and forest soil or peat is suitable, and flat rocks and a small tree bole provide hiding places. Since the Dice Snake likes to sun itself in tree branches, a climbing branch should be present in the terrarium. This snake usually adjusts quickly to captivity and soon becomes hand tame. It makes no great demands on the keeper and often lives for years in captivity. Generally it does not bite, but when it is picked up it emits an unpleasant odor. It does not need high temperatures; 68° to 79°F (20°-26°C) suffice during the day. If the terrarium gets several hours of sunshine no artificial lights are required. The Dice Snake likes little fish best, which it catches with great skill from the water basin. It is less fond of frogs. It should be wintered over from October to March at 40° to 50°F (4°-10°C) in a box filled with damp earth, leaves, and moss.
There are no reports of planned reproduction of this snake in captivity, but this should prove no more difficult than in the case of the Grass Snake or the Viperine Snake. One snake keeper had two females that were gravid when captured; between them they laid 21 eggs, which hatched in early August.

Genus *Nerodia*
American Watersnakes

Nerodia cyclopion
Green Watersnake
2 subspecies

PHYSICAL CHARACTERISTICS: The head is longish and only moderately set off from the neck. The body appears plump. The Green Watersnake differs from other American representatives of the same genus by having a row of scales between the eye and upper labials. The scales on the body and tail are clearly keeled. The back and the sides of the body are brown to olive colored with approximately 50 indistinct cross stripes. The brownish, whitish-gray, porcelain-colored, or yellowish belly has light blotches or half-moons. The underside of the tail is darkly mottled.

LENGTH: Up to 74 inches (188 cm).

DISTRIBUTION AND BEHAVIOR: *N. cyclopion* is native to the southeastern United States, occurring in South Carolina, Georgia, Florida, Alabama, Mississippi, Arkansas, Texas, Missouri, Tennessee, and Kentucky. It prefers weedy waters and is found on the edges of swamps, lakes, ponds, bayous, rice fields, canals, and slow-moving rivers. It loves basking in the sun along the shore on overhanging bushes, fallen trees, and on aquatic plants adrift in the water. At the slightest sign of danger it immediately retreats into the water. The Green Watersnake swims and dives with equal skill. If it is captured it always tries to bite. This snake is active both day and night. At night it is often found on and along roads eating frogs that may have been run over or warming itself on the asphalt still warm from the day's heat. *N. cyclopion* feeds on frogs, toads, newts, salamanders, and fish. In the northern part of its area of distribution it hibernates about 5 months. The Green Watersnake gives birth to fully developed young and is one of the most prolific snake species. Mating usually occurs in the first three weeks of April. At one birth as many as 101 young were counted. The baby snakes, which are usually born between June and August, measure 9 to 10 inches (22-25 cm).

CAPTIVITY AND BREEDING: The Green Watersnake thrives in a terrarium for a long time and eventually becomes hand tame. It needs plenty of space and a large water basin, which should take up about one third to one half of the area. A mixture of sand and gravel has proven a good bottom material, and some flat rocks and a tree root supply retreats. There is no need for bottom heating, and 5 to 8 hours of good light suffice. If the terrarium is placed near a window and gets the morning or afternoon sun, no artificial lights are needed. The air should be at 68° to 82°F (20°-28°C) during the day, and about 9°F (5°C) cooler at night. *N. cyclopion* happily eats dead and live fish as well as pieces of fish, which can be offered with tongs. A hibernation period of at least 3 months at lowered temperatures between 41° and 54°F (5°-12°C) is recommended, especially if there is an intention to breed the snakes.

Green Watersnakes have reproduced in captivity repeatedly. The young have to be separated from the mother immediately because females have been known to eat some of their offspring shortly after producing them.

Nerodia erythrogaster
Plainbelly Watersnake
4 subspecies

PHYSICAL CHARACTERISTICS: The head is barely set off from the neck. The scales are strongly keeled. The subspecies *N. e. erythrogaster* is known under the popular name of "copperbelly" in the United States. The back and head of this snake are light to chocolate brown with sometimes some gray or green on the sides of the body. The belly is unicolored red or orange red. The subspecies *N. e. flavigaster* has a gray to grayish-green back with faint crossbands, and the yellow belly has an orange tinge to it. The subspecies *N. e. transversa* is distinguished by dark brown saddle markings on the back and oval spots on the sides of the body. Its belly is pale yellow with a tinge of orange.

LENGTH: Up to 59 inches (150 cm).

DISTRIBUTION AND BEHAVIOR: The Plainbelly Watersnake is found along the Atlantic coast from Delaware to northern Florida and throughout Alabama, Mississippi, Louisiana, and Texas and the bordering states as far as northeastern Mexico. It is a typical aquatic snake, living in and next to all kinds of bodies of water. It inhabits primarily swamps and areas that flood regularly but is not as common as other North American *Natrix* species. In a shallow lake in Stone Mountain Park in southern Georgia I had a chance to observe a number of Plainbelly Watersnakes. The snakes were lying on the shallow bottom and seemed to be waiting for fish. I tried to catch some but had no luck. The snakes were very quick and escaped between my legs. When the weather is humid and sultry, the Plainbelly Watersnake undertakes journeys and is often found far from its home waters. If it is captured it bites aggressively. Its diet consists of fish, frogs, toads, salamanders, and crayfish. Depending on the climate, the Plainbelly Watersnake hibernates 6 to 8 months, a longer time than any other watersnake in North America. Mating takes place from May to June, and in September or October up to 27 young are born, measuring 11 to 12 inches (28-30 cm).

CAPTIVITY AND BREEDING: *N. erythrogaster* requires a sizable aqua-terrarium with large water section and a climbing limb. Requirements for light and temperature are the same as for the two previously described species. This snake survives for years in captivity and readily accepts fish and frogs. Five to 6 months of hibernation at lowered temperatures is recommended. Offspring have been produced in captivity both by females pregnant at capture and by others mated in the terrarium.

TOP: Gray-banded King Snake (*Lampropeltis mexicana*)
BOTTOM: Sonora Mountain King Snake (*Lampropeltis pyromelana*)

Nerodia fasciata
Southern Watersnake
6 subspecies
(photo, page 67)

PHYSICAL CHARACTERISTICS: In the past *N. fasciata* and its subspecies were all considered subspecies of the Northern Watersnake (*N. sipedon*) to which they are, in fact, closely related. The longish head is barely set off from the neck, and the body is moderately slender. The scales on the body are strongly keeled. Only very few snake species vary as much in coloration as the Southern Watersnake does. A dark band runs from the eye to the corner of the mouth. The body may be gray, grayish-brown, dark brown, blackish-brown, or reddish-brown to copper color with wide, yellowish-brown, blackish-brown, or reddish-brown crossbands that sometimes have light rims. The belly has reddish-brown, plain brown, or blackish-brown blotches. Most individuals darken with age. The black pigments intrude more and more, rendering the markings more indistinct until the entire snake appears a uniform blackish-brown.

LENGTH: In exceptional cases up to 63 inches (160 cm).

TOP LEFT: Pine Snake (*Pituophis melanoleucus*)
TOP RIGHT: Common King Snake (*Lampropeltis getulus*)
CENTER LEFT: Milk Snake (*Lampropeltis triangulum*)
CENTER RIGHT: California Mountain King Snake (*Lampropeltis zonata*)
BOTTOM LEFT: Tiger Ratsnake (*Spilotes pullatus*)
BOTTOM RIGHT: African Molesnake (*Psudaspis cana*)

DISTRIBUTION AND BEHAVIOR: This snake is native to North and South Carolina, Georgia, Florida, Alabama, Mississippi, Arkansas, Louisiana, Texas, Oklahoma, Missouri, Kentucky, Illinois, and Indiana, where it lives wherever there is water and moisture. It also inhabits open forests but almost always in the close vicinity of water. Sometimes it is found in holes in the ground, under piles of leaves and brush, or under toppled trees. In the water it is very agile, swimming and diving with great skill. This snake is active both day and night. The evening was an excellent time for catching specimens in the pine forests interlaced with swamps in Texas, South Carolina, and Florida. When captured they try to bite furiously, but with attentive care they become quite tame in the terrarium. *N. fasciata* hibernates from September to March. It lives on fish, frogs, toads, newts, salamanders, and earthworms. Mating takes place from March to May and always on dry land. Between May and August, up to 57 young measuring an average of 8 inches (20 cm) are born. In areas where the range of different subspecies overlaps, hybrid forms occur.

CAPTIVITY AND BREEDING: Being a truly aquatic snake, *N. fasciata* needs a big terrarium with a large part of it given over to water. A climbing tree should not be omitted because these snakes spend hours basking in the sun perched on a branch or some other elevated spot. They also like to lie in the water with only the head sticking out a little to permit them to breathe. Sand and gravel serve as bottom material, and some flat rocks provide hiding places. Artificial lighting should be provided for 5 to 8 hours a day unless the terrarium gets several hours of sunlight. For best results the Southern Watersnake should be kept at 68° to 82°F (20°-28°C) during the day and about 9°F (5°C) cooler at night. Live and dead fish and frogs are offered as food. A hibernating period of 3 months is necessary. This snake has reproduced a number of times in captivity. The baby snakes are easy to raise on small fishes, pieces of fish, and tadpoles.

Nerodia rhombifera
Diamondback Watersnake
3 subspecies
(photo, page 68)

PHYSICAL CHARACTERISTICS: The longish head is fairly clearly set off from the neck, and the body looks powerful. The large eyes have round pupils. The scales are strongly keeled. The male has several wart-like bumps on the underside of the chin, a peculiarity found only in this species. The upper side of the body is light brown to yellowish-brown. A large number of black blotches on the back and sides combine into a striking mosaic pattern. The belly is yellow with dark or black spots which may be crescent-shaped.

LENGTH: Up to 63 inches (160 cm).

DISTRIBUTION AND BEHAVIOR: This snake occurs along the Ohio and Mississippi Rivers from central Indiana south as far south and west as Texas and Mexico. In those parts of Mexico where their respective ranges overlap, the three subspecies N. r. rhombifera, blanchardi, and werleri interbreed to produce hybrids or intergrades. N. rhombifera is found primarily in lowlands and along rivers up to altitudes of about 2200 feet (670 m) above sea level. Its occurrence is essentially restricted to the vicinity of various kinds of waters, but it is also encountered in different terrains and sometimes even in fairly dry places. In many places this snake is quite common, and in Louisiana, for example, it is found in almost any good-sized puddle of water. The Diamondback Watersnake swims and climbs well. Often it is seen sunning itself on small trees and on branches overhanging the water. It drops back into the water at the slightest intrusion. This snake is active during the day and at night. In hot weather it moves about only at night, staying in its lairs under logs, rocks, piles of wood, leaves, or boards. Being of an aggressive temperament, it attacks and bites if it is cornered. Its diet consists of frogs, toads, fish, and crayfish, as well as young turtles.

Depending on the weather, the Diamondback Watersnake retires for its winter rest in October or November and does not reemerge until the end of March. Matings occur between April and June. N. rhombifera is quite prolific, producing up to 62 live young at a time. The young snakes are born between August and November and measure about 11 to 13 inches (28-32 cm).

CAPTIVITY AND BREEDING: N. rhombifera will thrive in an aqua-terrarium with a large water section and a climbing tree with many forked branches. It needs localized bottom heat and 6 to 10 hours of artificial light if it does not get sunlight both morning and afternoon. During the day, the air should measure between 72° and 86°F (22°-30°C). At night it should be a few degrees cooler. During the day this snake usually rests in the branches of the climbing tree. Before molting it often soaks in the water. It is very adept at catching fish in the water basin and is quite voracious in captivity. Toward its keeper it reacts with aggression and biting, becoming more docile only with time. Four months of hibernation in temperatures between 43° and 50°F (6°-10°C) are necessary. This snake has repeatedly been bred in captivity.

Nerodia sipedon
Northern Watersnake
4 subspecies

PHYSICAL CHARACTERISTICS: The Northern Watersnake is very closely related to the Southern Watersnake (N. fasciata), and the two snakes are very similar in build, but they differ widely in coloration. N. sipedon is the only water snake of any size in the northern United States. Further south its distribution overlaps with that of other large water snakes that look quite similar. The distinguishing marks of the Northern Watersnake are the dark crossbands on the neck and upper back. Farther down on the back and on the sides there are rows of blotches that alternate in a zigzag pattern. The dark blotches are wider than the intervals between them. The belly is covered with black or reddish crescent-shaped marks, and the underside of the tail has dark markings that combine into a connected pattern. The ground color can vary from a pale gray to a dark brown. The blotches are light rush-colored to black, and the crescent-shaped markings on the belly may be sparse, in clusters, or form a regular pattern or even be lacking altogether. *N. s. pleuralis* has a reddish hue and is a particularly pretty subspecies. *N. s. insularum* has paler colors, and the markings are fainter or absent, whereas *N. s. williamengelsi* is very dark or almost completely black.

LENGTH: Up to 56 inches (135 cm).

DISTRIBUTION AND BEHAVIOR: This snake is distributed from southern Canada (Quebec) and southern and eastern Maine across the Middle Atlantic states as far south as Florida, Alabama, and Mississippi. Its environmental requirements and behavior are largely similar to those of *N. fasciata*. Few snakes are as shy as the Northern Watersnake. If it is intercepted in flight, it flattens its body and angrily lashes out at its enemy with its teeth. If it is picked up it squirms around in one's hands and emits a foul-smelling secretion from its anal glands. It feeds on fish and amphibians. Up to 46 young are born at a time.

CAPTIVITY AND BREEDING: This snake requires exactly the same care as the Southern Watersnake *(N. fasciata)*. This species has reproduced a number of times in captivity, and these "domestic" offspring were always wintered over at cooler temperatures. There are reports of successful matings between *N. sipedon* and *N. fasciata* in captivity as well as of ones between so-called "intergrades" of various subspecies of *N. sipedon*. Raising the baby snakes on small fish and frogs presents no difficulty, but it is advisable to use a bottom heater that supplies some mild, localized heat because the young animals eat more and digest faster if they can rest on a warm bottom. If well fed, the young snakes can grow from 7 to 26 inches (18-65 cm) within 6 months.

Nerodia taxispilota
Brown Watersnake
(photo, page 86)

PHYSICAL CHARACTERISTICS: *N. taxispilota* occurs in the southeastern states of the USA and is the geographic counterpart of the more western *N. rhombifera*. These two snakes might perhaps be considered two geographic races of one and the same species. In any case, their habitats are practically identical. The head of the Brown Watersnake is more heart-shaped than that of just about any other water snake and is reminiscent of the head shape of certain poisonous snakes. It is clearly set off from the neck. The Brown Watersnake is the largest species of *Nerodia,* and its body can attain the thickness of a child's arm. The scales are strongly keeled, and the ground color is nut to chocolate brown, though there are many exceptionally dark individuals. Down the center of the back there are large, square, darker, and evenly spaced blotches, and down each side runs a row of similarly large and similarly colored blotches centered below the spaces between the dorsal blotches. The yellowish to brownish belly is also covered with square blotches. Because of its sturdy build and its brown coloration the Brown Watersnake is the *Nerodia* species most easily mistaken for the poisonous Cottonmouth *Agkistrodon piscivorus)*.

LENGTH: Up to 69 inches (175 cm).

DISTRIBUTION AND BEHAVIOR: The Brown Watersnake is native to Virginia, North and South Carolina, Georgia, Florida, Alabama, and Louisiana. It is restricted primarily to clear and still water. It is largely diurnal and likes to sun itself in bushes growing along the water's edge or high up in trees or branches overhanging the water or on small islands. If anyone approaches, it immediately drops into the water, dives, and swims away. The Indians believe that this snake is as poisonous as a rattlesnake. *N. taxispilota* bites wildly when it is cornered or grasped. Its food consists primarily of fish and frogs. This snake winters over in caves and hollows in the immediate proximity of water. Rising water drives it out of its winter quarters regardless of temperature. Large numbers of snakes driven from their lairs by rising water can sometimes be seen hanging in the bushes and sunning themselves for hours. When they have warmed up sufficiently they disappear again and look for new hiding places. Mating usually occurs in the latter half of May. The 14 to 58 young, measuring 7 to 10 inches (18-26 cm) are born between June and November. At birth the males are usually larger than the females, but by the time they are fully grown the opposite is the case.

CAPTIVITY AND BREEDING: The Brown Watersnake should be kept the same way as the Diamondback Watersnake, but it adjusts less well to life in captivity, is sometimes fastidious, and can present a feeding problem. Once it has adjusted, however, it eats voraciously, pouncing on frogs and especially fish and swallowing them immediately, often still underwater. It also likes ocean fish cut in strips. There are no reports of successful breeding initiated in captivity; all the offspring born in terrariums came from females that were pregnant when captured.

Genus *Regina*
Crayfish Snakes

Regina septemvittata
Queen Snake

PHYSICAL CHARACTERISTICS: The head is hardly set off from the neck, and the body is slender. The scales of the body are keeled. The back and sides are brown. There is a yellow stripe on both sides running from the tip of the snout to the tail. The back has three longitudinal lines that are black but sometimes not very clearly visible. The belly is yellow with four brown stripes, the outer ones of which are wider than the inner ones. In the southern range of this species one finds some Queen Snakes that are almost unicolored with only a suggestion of markings near the neck.

LENGTH: Up to 3 feet (92 cm).

DISTRIBUTION AND BEHAVIOR: This snake is native to southern Canada (Ontario) and the eastern United States south of the Great Lakes and as far south as the Gulf Coast. It prefers streams and small rivers with pebbly bottoms which offer good conditions to crayfish. However, it is not restricted to such habitats but is also found near water holes, ponds, lakes, bayous, and canals. It almost always stays close to the water. One of its favorite activities is to lie on willow branches overhanging the water— hence the common name "willow snake"— on bushes, toppled trees, and piles of twigs, branches, and leaves. At the slightest indication of danger it drops back into the water. This snake is extremely quick and often hard to catch. Individual snakes differ a great deal in temperament. Some are quite cooperative, others aggressive. In warm weather one sometimes comes upon fairly large numbers of Queen Snakes in shallow water with only the heads sticking out. Otherwise they are found under rocks, old driftwood, and in shrubbery along the banks. The diet of Queen Snakes consists mostly of freshly molted crayfish, but it also eats small dace, frogs, and newts. *R. septemvittata* usually retreats to its hibernating dens later than other snakes, i.e., in October or November, and reappears in March or shortly after the snow melts. Often many snakes hibernate in the same spot. Shortly after their winter rest they mate, and the young are born between July and September, measuring 7 and 9 inches (18-23 cm).

CAPTIVITY AND BREEDING: This snake requires an aqua-terrarium with a large water section as well as some climbing branches. The dry part of the terrarium is covered with a mixture of sand, leaf mold, and peat, and a few rocks, flat pieces of bark, and a tree root serve to supply hiding places. If the terrarium gets sun both morning and afternoons you can dispense with artificial lights which should otherwise be on 5 to 8 hours a day. Air temperatures should range between 68° and 79°F (20°-

26°C) during the day and drop a few degrees at night. The Queen Snake becomes quite tame in captivity. Sometimes it spends hours in the bottom of the water basin, coming up only for air. In contrast to other watersnakes, *R. septemvittata* is difficult to keep because it eats primarily crayfish. It therefore has to change its food habits and learn to accept minnows and small frogs. Natural hibernating conditions should be simulated, especially for animals from the north by allowing them to hibernate in damp leaves and moss at 39° to 41°F (4°-10°C). Hibernation should last about 4 months. As far as I know no attempts have been made to breed this snake in captivity, but several pregnant females have produced offspring in captivity.

Genus *Thamnophis*
American Gartersnakes
23 species

Thamnophis butleri
Butler's Gartersnake

PHYSICAL CHARACTERISTICS: This small snake has a narrow, longish head that is barely if at all set off from the neck. The large eyes have round pupils. The body is slender, the tail long and tapered. The dorsal stripe is whitish-yellow, the lateral stripes butter yellow to orange colored. The ground color of the back ranges from olive brown to black. Between the stripes there is often a double row of black blotches. Underneath the lateral stripes there is a coffee-colored band. The belly is grayish-green and mottled.

LENGTH: Up to 27 inches (69 cm).

DISTRIBUTION AND BEHAVIOR: *T. butleri* is native to the northern United States and southern Canada, being found in southwestern Ontario, Indiana, Michigan, Ohio, Wisconsin, and possibly Illinois. It inhabits lowlands and hilly country up to an altitude of 1600 feet (500 m). It prefers wet meadows, swamps, and lake shores, but it also occurs on dry ground and in clearings in the woods. Where the conditions suit it it is often found in large numbers. But in many parts of its distribution it is rare or lacking. It spends the day hiding under logs, old wood, and tucked between thick tufts of grass. In the summer it comes out into the open only at dusk. Its movements are slow and it hardly defends itself when it is captured. When it is excited or tries to flee it goes through curious motions that are not characteristic of any other *Thamnophis* species. It winds its body from side to side in exaggerated serpentine curves, expending a great deal of energy that is way out of proportion to the distance covered. This behavior makes it easy to spot and identify this snake in nature. Butler's Gartersnake lives on frogs, salamanders, fish, mice, earthworms, and insects. It hibernates from late September to March or early April. Mating occurs in April, and 4 to 16 young are born between June and September. The newborn snakes measure 5 to 7 inches (13-18 cm).

CAPTIVITY AND BREEDING: Because of this snake's modest size, the terrarium can be small but must have a proportionally large water section. The guidelines for setting up the terrarium and for looking after this snake are similar to those given for the Common Gartersnake. Small frogs, fish, and strips of fish are given as food, and in keeping with the climate of the natural habitat a hibernation period of five months is necessary. The hibernating box should be filled with damp forest soil, leaves, and moss and kept at 43° to 50°F (6°-10°C). This snake has reproduced in captivity a number of times. A pair of snakes in the Toledo, Ohio zoo was observed in different years to mate on March 23 and April 4. The young were born on July 2 and 3. Young snakes of this species may reach sexual maturity in their second year but more commonly not until the third.

Thamnophis cyrtopsis
Blackneck Gartersnake
6 subspecies
(photo, page 86)

PHYSICAL CHARACTERISTICS: The head is clearly set off from the neck, and the large eyes have round pupils. The body is slender, and the tail long and tapered. The scales are keeled. The top of the head is bluish-gray to black. On both sides of the throat there is a large, black blotch. A wide, orange stripe runs down the center of the back, starting behind the head and ending halfway down the tail. Two less distinct, light to butter yellow stripes run parallel to this orange stripe low on the sides of the body. Between these and the dorsal stripe there are large black or bluish-black blotches on a yellow background. In the subspecies *T. c. ocellata* these dark blotches run together into a wide black band. The belly is solid whitish-gray, brownish, or greenish.

LENGTH: Slightly over 3 feet (1 m).

DISTRIBUTION AND BEHAVIOR: The distribution of this snake extends from southwestern Utah and from Arizona and Texas to Mexico and as far as western Honduras. *T. cyrtopsis* is usually found near water, at springs and watering places for cattle, and in partially dry river beds as well as in mesquite brush in the desert, along mountainsides, and in open pine woods interspersed with slopes of loose rock. In Arizona it is by far the most common snake in the many canyons and mountain streams. In rainy weather it often travels for miles. It feeds primarily on amphibians like frogs, toads, and tadpoles. It rarely eats fish. Freshly captured specimens hardly ever bite but do secrete a bad-smelling substance. *T. cyrtopsis* usually starts to hibernate in September and reappears in March. Matings occur in March or April, and the 10 to 25 young are born sometime between June and August. They measure barely 8 inches (20 cm).

CAPTIVITY AND BREEDING: Like the species described just before this, *T. cyrtopsis* is a rewarding and easy snake to care for and modest in its demands for warmth and humidity. A medium-sized terrarium with a floor area of about 40 × 24 inches (100 × 60 cm) with a plastic water basin is quite adequate. Forest soil—or sandy or loamy soil mixed with forest soil or peat—can be used on the bottom, and a few flat rocks, some pieces of bark, or a small tree stump offer opportunities for hiding. Localized bottom heat is appreciated but not absolutely necessary, and if the terrarium gets the morning and afternoon sun, artificial lights, which otherwise should be on 10 to 12 hours a day, can be dispensed with. *T. cyrtopsis* is comfortable at daytime temperatures between 68° and 86°F (20°-30°C) but most so around 79°F (26°C). At night it should be a few degrees cooler. Four to 5 months of hibernation are advisable. The specimen I have initially ate frogs and toads but later changed to a steady diet of fish cut in strips. *T. cyrtopsis* has been bred in captivity, and it would seem that this snake is no harder to breed in captivity than *T. elegans*.

Thamnophis elegans
Elegant Gartersnake
4 subspecies

PHYSICAL CHARACTERISTICS: The head is only moderately set off from the neck and the large eyes have round pupils. The body is long and slender. The dorsal scales are keeled. In contrast to the water snakes of the *Nerodia* genus, all of which have divided anal plates, all *Thamnophis* species have a single, undivided anal plate. *T. elegans* has a clearly defined whitish-yellow dorsal line running from the center of the nape to the tip of the tail. Two less clear stripes run parallel to this line low on the sides of the body. The basic color of the body is brown, and the space between the stripes is black or has dark blotches and in places light specks. The subspecies *T. e. terrestris* has light red to orange dots on the flanks and the belly. Otherwise the belly is solidly grayish-white or in some cases with some white specks.

LENGTH: Slightly over 3 feet (1 m).

DISTRIBUTION AND BEHAVIOR: The Elegant Gartersnake is distributed over a wide area from southern Canada to the West Coast of the United States and as far south as northwestern Mexico. It lives in different biotopes on flat land and occurs as high up as 9000 feet (2800 m). It is found in savanna-like grasslands, land overgrown with low bushes, sunny, open woods, wet areas, and along the edges of bodies of water as well as in completely dry terrain. One of its favorite spots is river beds that dry out partially or completely every year. Here this snake is often found in large numbers. This indicates that *T. elegans* does not necessarily have to have moisture at all times to survive. Some subspecies are more terrestrial and others more aquatic. If danger threatens, the more terrestrial types immediately disappear into the thicket of plants or other crannies whereas the aquatic ones retreat into the water. The diet of *T. elegans* is extremely varied. It consumes frogs, toads, newts, salamanders, lizards, fish, shrews, mice, small birds, snails, spiders, ants, grasshoppers, and all kinds of other insects. Depending on the climate, it retires for hibernation in September or October and reemerges in March, April, or May. Large numbers of Elegant Gartersnakes often winter together in the same dens. These are usually caves and hollows underground. Mating takes place in the spring from March to May, and between late July and September an average of 10 young are born measuring between 5 and 7¹/₂ inches (12-19 cm).

CAPTIVITY AND BREEDING: *T. elegans* is quite an ideal snake for the terrarium; it does well, survives a long time in captivity, is easy to breed, and becomes remarkably tame. A specimen owned by the author let itself be taken out of the terrarium without visible signs of fear and would eat mice and fish from the keeper's hand. Depending on the size of the terrarium, one-fourth to one-sixth of the floor area should be taken up by the water basin.

The snakes like to spend hours at a time in the water especially before molting. A mixture of coarse sand and forest soil is used as bottom material. A pile of flat rocks or cork bark or a tree stump offers sufficient opportunities to hide. Because of the delicate build of this snake, some hardy plants can be kept permanently in the terrarium and will even grow. Localized bottom heat is recommended. The air should be 68° to 79°F (20°-26°C) during the day and a little cooler at night. Artificial lights should be turned on 10 to 12 hours a day unless the terrarium gets sunlight both morning and afternoon. Fish, pieces of fish, frogs, and small mice are offered as food. If the snake is to thrive it should be able to hibernate 4 to 5 months in a box with damp earth, leaves, and moss kept at 43° to 50°F (6°-10°C). The box should be placed in the dark.

This snake has repeatedly been bred in captivity. Before and during mating the male moves across the female's back with undulating movements. Some males copulate with several females in succession. Matings usually take place after the female's first molt in the spring. The female's moist skin secretion seems to stimulate the male. The gestation takes about 120 to 150 days. If properly cared for and given plenty of small frogs, fish, and pieces of fish, the young snakes grow very fast. Vitamin supplements help speed up the growth. In nature, the males usually do not reach sexual maturity until their third year, but one male in captivity matured much more rapidly and successfully mated when barely 12 months old.

Thamnophis sauritus
Eastern Ribbonsnake
4 subspecies
(photo, page 85)

PHYSICAL CHARACTERISTICS: The Eastern Ribbonsnake is distinguished from other gartersnakes *(Thamnophis* species) by its extremely slender body, a very long tail, and a belly devoid of markings. The head is hardly set off from the neck. The eyes are unusually large and have round pupils. A yellowish stripe that takes on an orange or greenish tinge toward the tail runs down the center of the back from the nape to the tip of the tail. Lateral stripes run parallel to this dorsal line. In the subspecies *T. s. nitae,* which is bluish-black, the dorsal stripe is faint or missing, and the lateral stripes are pale blue.

LENGTH: Up to 3 feet (1 m).

DISTRIBUTION AND BEHAVIOR: This snake is found in the eastern United States from Maine, New York, Michigan, and Ohio to Florida, Alabama, and Mississippi. It is more dependent on the proximity of water than the other gartersnakes of the eastern and central United States. It never moves far from the streams, rivers, canals, ponds, water holes, or swamps that form its exclusive habitat. The author collected several specimens of this snake in the swamps and flooded pine forests in Okeetee in South Carolina. The Eastern Ribbonsnake is active during the day and likes to sun itself on trees that have fallen into the water, on low bushes, and on dry reeds. When it senses an enemy's presence it takes to the water and swims off with remarkable ease. In contrast to snakes of the genus *Nerodia* it does not dive. Some Eastern Ribbonsnakes bite when they are caught while others produce a stinking liquid from their anal glands. This snake usually does not eat earthworms but lives on frogs, toads, and salamanders, with an occasional meal of fish, mouse, or insects. Depending on the weather it retreats to its winter quarters in October or November, and it is the first snake to reappear in the spring, usually in March but sometimes in February and once in a while as early as January. The mating takes place in the spring, and up to 20 young are born between July and November.

CAPTIVITY AND BREEDING: The Eastern Ribbonsnake needs an aqua-terrarium with a large water area. The land section is covered with forest soil mixed with sand. Bark, rocks, and a small tree stump provide hiding places, and a few forked branches offer opportunity to climb. The Eastern Ribbonsnake is very light, and it therefore does little damage to plants growing in the terrarium. No special lighting is necessary if the terrarium gets sun in the morning and afternoon. Otherwise artificial light should be provided 10 to 12 hours a day. Localized bottom heat is recommended, and daytime temperature should range between 68° and 86°F (20°-30°C). At night the temperature should drop a few degrees. The snakes eat frogs, and some quickly learn to accept fish while others are more reluctant to change their food habits. This snake needs 3 to 4 months of winter rest to thrive. Nothing has been reported about breeding this snake in captivity, though it should prove no more difficult than that of *T. elegans.*

Thamnophis sirtalis
Common Gartersnake
13 subspecies
(photo, page 85)

PHYSICAL CHARACTERISTICS: Both coloration and markings vary a great deal in the Common Gartersnake. Stripes or blotches may predominate. Externally, the snake resembles the European Grass Snake *(Natrix natrix).* The head is only slightly set off from the neck, and the large eyes have round pupils. The body is slender and the tail long and tapered. The scales are keeled. The top of the head is black or very dark. The ground color of the back and sides of the body may be black, dark brown, green, olive, or yellow. There is a dorsal stripe and a stripe on each side, all running the full length from head to tail and clearly visible. The stripes can be yellowish, brownish, greenish, or bluish. In the *T. s. annectens* the dorsal stripe is brick red. Between the stripes there is usually a double row of staggered black or very dark spots. Sometimes these dots stand out very clearly and sometimes they merge with the stripes. There are also individual snakes without lateral stripes. The subspecies *T. s. parietalis* has red dots on its side, and the belly is green or yellow with two rows of not very clearly visible black blotches, some of which are hidden by the shinglelike ventral plates.

LENGTH: Up to 50 inches (126 cm).

DISTRIBUTION AND BEHAVIOR: *T. sirtalis* is the most common and most widely distributed snake of its genus. It occurs from southern Canada throughout most of the United States and down to northern Mexico. Next to rattlesnakes, the Common Gartersnake is the best known snake in North America and is found almost anywhere. All the subspecies of this snake have a predilection for moisture and are therefore encountered near puddles, ponds, lakes, swamps, bayous, streams, rivers, and canals. But they also live along the edges of fields, in open woods, and on cultivated and uncultivated fields. *T. sirtalis* is primarily diurnal though it is to some extent also active in the evening. In southern Florida I found many *T. s. sirtalis* in the evening at a certain spot on the road and along paths that ran alongside ditches. Common Gartersnakes are not fussy about their food: They eat frogs, toads, salamanders, fish, mice, snails, earthworms, and insects. They are often found congregated in considerable numbers. They are among those snakes that are first to reappear in the open in March shortly after the snows melt. In the fall they retire late, sometimes not until November or December, for their winter rest. Large numbers of them often crowd together in good hibernating dens. Common Gartersnakes generally molt at frequent intervals of only 6 weeks. The Common Gartersnake is quicker to bite than other snakes of its genus. Captured individuals put up a fight by biting and giving off their characteristic obnoxious smell. Matings take place in April or May, and the young are born in July or early August. Common Gartersnakes are very prolific. Usually 14 to 40 are born at a time and sometimes up to 80. The young snakes measure about 7 inches (18 cm) at birth.

CAPTIVITY AND BREEDING: The Common Gartersnake is easy to keep in captivity, and if properly cared for will live for years. It has a pleasant nature and reproduces without difficulties. This snake can thus be whole-heartedly recommended for the beginner. Its demands in terms of setting up the terrarium and providing heat are comparable to those of *T. sauritus*. The Common Gartersnake becomes hand tame and it eats voraciously, accepting fish, strips of fish, frogs, and earthworms from its keeper's hand. Earthworms should be given only sparingly, however, because they can give rise to signs of poisoning. Two to 3 months of hibernation are advisable.

This species has frequently produced offspring in captivity. The fast-growing young snakes are easy to raise on small frogs, fish, and fish strips. Under optimum conditions they may grow to 29 inches (74 cm) within 2 years and reach sexual maturity in their second year.

Genus *Storeria*
Brown Snakes
4 species

Storeria dekayi
Brown Snake
8 subspecies

PHYSICAL CHARACTERISTICS: *S. dekayi* and *S. occipitomaculata* are both closely related to the snakes of the *Natrix* and *Thamnophis* genera. The Brown Snake has a slender body, keeled scales and the anal plate is divided. The ground color of the back and sides of the body varies from pale yellow to brown, gray to grayish-brown or a deep reddish-brown. Down the center of the back from the neck to the end of the tail runs a stripe that is flanked on both sides by 2 rows of dark blotches, and there is a pair of dark mirror-image marks on the back of the head. The belly can be yellowish, brownish, or pinkish.

LENGTH: Up to 19½ inches (49 cm).

DISTRIBUTION AND BEHAVIOR: This snake is distributed from northeastern Canada across the eastern United States to Mexico and Guatamala and as far as Honduras. It is found in all kind of biotopes ranging from wet to dry locations. Terrains it inhabits include hilly country, rock crevices, railroad embankments, pine woods, wet meadows, swamps, and the banks of ponds and lakes. Not infrequently this snake is also discovered in parks, cemeteries, and even in the green parts of large cities and very close to buildings—locations abandoned by any other snake. *S. dekayi* lives a hidden life and is active primarily at night. During the day it stays concealed under logs, old wood, rocks, boards, in collapsing cardboard boxes, underground, or in whatever other retreat it can find. Toward evening it wakes up and starts prowling, and then it is frequently seen on the road. When it is excited or senses danger it flattens its body and if it is then grabbed its anal glands secrete a liquid which, however, does not smell very strong. Among its prey are worms, snails, insects, small frogs and fish. Brown Snakes usually hibernate from October to March, many of them often congregating in one place. Their hibernating dens often include other snakes as well, such as *Thamnophis sirtalis* and *Natrix sipedon.* Matings occur generally in March or April but can also take place any other month. Gestation takes 105 to 113 days. *S. dekayi* gives birth to fully developed young that are about 3 to 4 inches (7-10 cm) long. The baby snakes are quite dark and have a white ring around the neck, thus resembling a Ringneck Snake, from which they differ, however, in having keeled scales.

CAPTIVITY AND BREEDING: A small terrarium suffices for this species. A mixture of sand and forest soil is used as bottom material, which should be lightly sprayed with water to keep it moist. Some rocks, pieces of bark, and moss clumps make good hiding places. The moss clumps have to be replaced periodically. A dish with fresh water must always be available. *S. dekayi* does not need artificial light or bottom heat. Daytime temperatures between 68° and 77°F (20°-25°C) are adequate. A windowsill is a good place for such a mini-terrarium. Here it will get sufficient daylight. The Brown Snake comes out of hiding in the eve-

ning when it can be fed earthworms, insects, and snails. No hibernation is necessary.
No reproduction in captivity has been reported, although females gravid at the time of capture quite commonly produce offspring in terrariums. The tiny snakes are raised on small earthworms and drosophila flies.

Storeria occipitomaculata
Red-bellied Snake

The small, 12-inch-long (30 cm) Red-bellied Snake *(S. occipitomaculata)* is very closely related to the Brown Snake and resembles it in body build and coloration. But it can easily be told apart by its light red belly and the absence of spots on the sides. *S. occipitomaculata* is found in approximately the same biotopes as *S. dekayi,* and the two snakes have the same requirements in captivity.

Subfamily Colubrinae—Rat Snakes, Racers, and Allies

RAT SNAKES

Genus *Coronella*
Smooth Snakes
2 species

Coronella austriaca
European Smooth Snake
2 subspecies
(photo, page 104)

PHYSICAL CHARACTERISTICS: The European Smooth Snake has a flat head that is only slightly set off from the neck. The large eyes have round pupils, and the scales are completely smooth. The coloration and markings vary with age and geographic location. The males are usually brown or reddish-brown and the females gray or brownish-black. Males have a brownish-red, females a grayish-brown belly. On the back there are 2 or 4 rows of blotches that may run together to some degree. A dark band runs from the nostril across the eye to the side of the neck. On the back of the head and the nape there is a dark patch that widens toward the back.

LENGTH: 30 inches (75 cm); rarely more.

DISTRIBUTION AND BEHAVIOR: The European Smooth Snake is found in northern and Central Europe from Sweden and Norway to northern Spain and Portugal and as far east as Asia Minor and even the Caucasus. It prefers sunny and dry, usually rocky terrain dotted with bushes, and it likes to lie concealed in piles of stones and loose rock, on rock faces, along the edges of woods and meadows, in loose stone walls, and similar places. *C. austriaca* is active during the day. Because of its camouflage color and quiet habits it generally goes undetected. It feeds on lizards and blindworms and sometimes snakes and mice as well, the latter of which it kills by constriction. Its movements are slow, but it is very supple. Hibernation usually lasts 5 months. It reappears early in the spring and mates as early as April. During pairing the male holds on to the head or neck of the female by biting and wraps himself around her. The young are born in August or September. The 5- to 6-inch-long (12-15 cm) newborn snakes push through the very delicate, transparent egg skins with their snouts and wriggle out of them immediately after birth. A few days later follows the first molt. Young European Smooth Snakes start out eating young lizards and sometimes grasshoppers and other insects. *C. austriaca* is quick to bite when captured. It digs its short teeth into your finger with chewing motions and at the same time evacuates a reeking liquid from its anal glands. Unfortunately, this totally harmless snake that is under environmental protection is still often slaughtered.

CAPTIVITY AND BREEDING: European Smooth Snakes can be kept unproblematically and for years in a small to medium-sized terrarium that has sand and loam at the bottom. Over this, some forest soil and pine needles are sprinkled and a few rocks and dry pieces of bark added to provide concealment. A tree stump overgrown with moss looks particularly handsome, and a flower pot with some ivy and blackberry canes as well as some moss clumps (which have to be replaced from time to time) give a nice natural touch to the whole set-up. A small water dish is not to be forgotten. *C. austriaca* has no special demands for temperature, but localized bottom heat is required. The snake often lies for hours on the heated spot. Artificial light is necessary only if the terrarium gets no sun. The air temperature should be between 68° and 77°F (20°-25°C) during the day and should drop at night. This snake always likes to eat lizards but most individuals can also be switched over to mice. If a given snake refuses mice at first let it go hungry for a while, but never make it fast until it loses weight. Once the snake is hungry enough it will usually take mice, especially ones with fur, crush them, and eat them.

I am not aware of any reproduction of this snake initiated in captivity, though females gravid at capture have frequently given birth in terrariums. Raising the young presents a problem because they eat only newborn lizards and tails of lizards. European Smooth Snakes, both juvenile and adult, need wintering over in a cool environment.

Coronella girondica
Southern Smooth Snake
(photo, page 104)

PHYSICAL CHARACTERISTICS: This species is identical in build to the species described above. It varies in color from yellowish, gray, and brown to pinkish. The back is covered from the neck to the base of the tail with dark transverse blotches that combine in places into a kind of ribbon. Centered on the neck is a mark shaped like a horseshoe with the ends pointing forward. A black stripe runs from behind the eye to the corner of the mouth. The belly has 2 rows of square blotches or two longitudinal stripes.

LENGTH: Only infrequently over 28 inches (70 cm).

DISTRIBUTION AND BEHAVIOR: The distribution of this snake reaches from the southern

Tyrol across Italy, southern France, and the Pyrenean peninsula to northwestern Africa. Its habitat largely resembles that of its northern relative. But unlike *C. austriaca,* which often basks in the sun, *C. girondica* is distinctly crepuscular and avoids intense sunlight. It likes to lie in stone heaps, loose rock walls, under boulders, and in crevices. Its diet consists almost purely of lizards. The Southern Smooth Snake is not as aggressive and ready to bite as *C. austriaca.* When it is picked up it generally does not struggle to get free. Otherwise its behavior closely resembles that of its northern cousin.

CAPTIVITY AND BREEDING: A terrarium for this snake is set up the same way as described under the previous entry. The care required is also the same except that *C. girondica* requires daytime temperatures about 5°F (2°-3°C) warmer than mentioned for the Smooth Snake. Lizards serve as food, and once in a while a mouse can be given. What I have said about reproduction in captivity in the previous entry also applies here.

Genus *Lampropeltis*
King Snakes
13 species

Lampropeltis getulus
Common Kingsnake
11 subspecies
(photo, page 122)

PHYSICAL CHARACTERISTICS: The oval head is barely set off from the neck, and the large eyes have round pupils. The ground color of the body is black. In the subspecies *L. g. getulus* the back and sides have a chain-link pattern made up of white to yellowish crossbands. These markings may be so much modified in some subspecies as to be hardly recognizable. The belly is mottled or striped. Often it is far from easy to tell the different subspecies apart. Not only are there all kinds of intermediate stages of coloration and markings, but there are also hybrid forms where the distribution of different subspecies overlaps. In addition all the species of the genus *Lampropeltis* seem to be in a stage of evolutionary transition. Of the subspecies *L. g. californiae* there exist two versions: one is black or dark brown with white to yellow crossbands; the other has the same ground color but with a white to yellow longitudinal stripe running down the center of the back. These are not two different subspecies because both variants can turn up in one and the same clutch. As already suggested, not all subspecies of *L. getulus* have chain-link markings. *L. g. niger* is almost entirely black with yellowish dots on the individual scales. In the case of *L. g. floridana* the stripes are less distinct, especially in older animals. The individual scales are light at the center. *L. g. holbrooki* lacks stripes altogether or has only a suggestion of them. Each scale has some white or yellowish-green on it.

LENGTH: Up to 5 feet (150 cm); in exceptional cases up to and over 6 feet (180 cm).

DISTRIBUTION AND BEHAVIOR: The Common Kingsnake ranges from southern Oregon and California to the eastern United States. This is its major area of distribution though it is also found in Mexico where it lives in Baja California, in Chihuahua, Sonora, San Luis Potosi, and Tamaulipas. It occurs primarily in lowlands and seldom ventures above 2600 feet (800 m). Its preferred habitats are moist pine forests with sandy knolls, thickets of palmetto trees, stretches along rivers, swamps, meadows, country roads, and streets, and mountain slopes with scree, clumps of low bushes, and occasional trees. In some places *L. getulus* occurs in considerable and even remarkable numbers. Along a road east of Savannah the author and his son once caught seven grown specimens within one hour. They had all been hiding under old wood, metal, and cardboard boxes. Other Common Kingsnakes were sunning themselves on old tree stumps that had rotted out at the middle. An American friend of mine was even luckier than we were and caught 86 *L. g. floridana* within a few hours near Lake Okeechobee in northern Florida.

Generally the Common Kingsnake lives well hidden. It suns itself only in the early morning and never moves far from its retreat into which it disappears at any sign of danger. If it is grabbed it does not always bite but winds itself around the hand and sprays a stinking liquid. Its diet consists of small mammals, birds, snakes, lizards, and eggs. It strangles its prey before eating it. Depending on the climate where it lives, *L. getulus* hibernates 3 to 6 months. Matings take place in the spring immediately after hibernation, and between 3 and 30 longish eggs are laid in June, July, or August. The young hatch after an incubation period of 60 to 120 days. They measure 10 to 12 inches (25-30 cm).

CAPTIVITY AND BREEDING: The Common Kingsnake is easy to care for. A terrarium measuring 32 × 16 × 16 inches (80 × 40 × 40 cm) is perfectly adequate. A layer of mixed sand and forest soil works well for the bottom, and a water dish is important because this snake drinks frequently. A few big pieces of bark, a hollow piece of decorative cork, or some rocks cemented together to form a cave provide adequate hiding. Localized bottom heat is beneficial for the snakes but not absolutely necessary. The lights should be on about 10 hours, and the temperature in the terrarium should be kept between 75° and 86°F (24°-30°C) during the day and at 68°F (20°C) at night. Mice and small rats are given as food, which the snake quickly spots with the aid of its eyes and especially its remarkable sense of smell. It does not take long to train a Common Kingsnake to take the prey, either dead or alive, from your hand. Since in nature Common Kingsnakes do eat snakes, including members of their own species, it is certainly advisable to keep these snakes singly to prevent losses. I had a small *L. g. splendida* that killed and tried to eat a Milk Snake (*L. triangulum*) that was twice its size. Depending on where given specimens were captured, Common Kingsnakes need to hibernate between 2 and 5 months at temperatures ranging from 41° to 59°F (5°-15°C).

Breeding these snakes in a terrarium is not particularly difficult and has been accomplished quite frequently. The author had a male *L. g. getulus* that mated with a female *L. g. floridana* on April 19, 1978. This resulted in 6 longish eggs that were deposited on June 4. From these eggs 6 healthy crosses between the two subspecies hatched from August 24 to 26. The eggs had been placed in a mixture of coarse sand and peat moss (coarse lava would be even better) and kept at temperatures between 72° and 86°F (22°-30°C). Adequate dampness was maintained through some spraying of water. Under artificial conditions the eggs usually hatch after 60 to 70 days. Once out of their shells the young snakes are seized by a strong urge to wander and immediately take off in search of hiding places. The first molt occurs after 10 to 14 days, and after that the snakes start eating young mice and lizards.

Lampropeltis mexicana
Gray-banded Kingsnake
4 subspecies
(photo, page 121)

PHYSICAL CHARACTERISTICS: The flat head is clearly set off from the neck, and the large, slightly protruding eyes have pinhole-shaped pupils. The moderately long body is very muscular. The scales are smooth, and the anal plate undivided. The subspecies *L. m. blairi*, one of the most colorful North American snakes, is roughly subdivided into three color variants. In general the ground color of the back and sides is some shade of gray ranging from light to dark. The top of the head may be solid black or show a horseshoe pattern of black dots and stripes. A black line runs from the lower edge of the eye to the corner of the mouth. The markings of the back and sides consist of 14 very conspicuous light to dark red saddle marks rimmed with black and white. The belly has light and dark blotches at regular intervals. From the cloaca on down to the tip, the tail has 4 to 5 black rings that are often reddish in the center. The subspecies are: *L.*

m. alterna, L. m. blairi, L. m. mexicana, and
L. m. thayeri.

LENGTH: 32 to 36 inches (80-90 cm) and up to
4 feet (120 cm).

DISTRIBUTION AND BEHAVIOR: The Gray-banded Kingsnake has a very narrowly defined
distribution. It is found in southwestern Texas
in the Trans-Pecos region west of the Del Rio
River to the Big Bend National Park. We also
know of two locations south of the Rio Grande
where it has been found in the Mexican state
Coahuila. *L. mexicana* is a typical creature of
the Chihuahua desert where it occurs in dry to
moderately moist biotopes. It inhabits both
flat land and mountainous country and seeks
out hiding places underneath rocks, along
slopes of loose rock, and especially rocky, dried
out riverbeds where opuntia, various hedge-hog and ocotillo cacti, mesquite, creosote, and
yuccas grow. *L. mexicana* used to be thought a
rare species, but in some locations it exists in
considerable numbers. Because of its secretive
and nocturnal habits one rarely sees this snake
during the day. It does not become active until
nighttime when it starts prowling ceaselessly.
Its diet consists of lizards and small mammals;
and, on occasion, it will also eat snakes and
frogs. It subdues its prey with its coils before
swallowing it. When the Gray-banded
Kingsnake is caught it wraps itself around the
person's hand forcefully but does not always
bite, instead exuding a reeking, salve-like
secretion from its anal glands. Matings take
place in the spring after a hibernation period
of 4 to 5 months.

CAPTIVITY AND BREEDING: *L. mexicana* is an
ideal snake for the terrarium, being very strik-ing both in shape and coloration. It also does
very well in captivity and reproduces without
problems. But it requires meticulous cleanli-ness. Unfortunately this snake is a very popu-lar pet and therefore is expensive ($300-$500
per animal). *L. mexicana* does not require a
very large cage. A terrarium measuring
20 × 16 × 16 inches (50 × 40 × 40 cm) is
adequate for two grown animals. I have been
using sandy loam for the bottom with good
success. A small water dish is essential. A bot-tom heater supplying very mild localized heat
contributes a great deal to the snakes' well-being and should definitely be supplied. The
temperature of the bottom and of the air is
kept between 77° and 86°F (25°-30°C) dur-ing the day; 81°F (27°C) is ideal. The lights
should be on 10 to 12 hours. *L. mexicana* eats a
lot; this snake should be fed once a week. It
takes live and dead mice as well as lizards. The
digestive process is completed in 2 to 3 days.
The skins are shed every 5 to 8 weeks and come
off in one piece.

This snake has been successfully bred in cap-tivity a number of times, but 3 to 4 months of
wintering over at 41° to 59°F (5°-15°C) are an
important prerequisite for this. The tempera-ture can drop even lower temporarily without
the snakes sustaining the slightest harm. My
snakes have mated in April, May, and June,
and about 4 to 5 weeks after mating between 4
and 6 eggs were deposited. Before laying her
eggs the female spends days digging in the
bottom and creating a depression for the eggs
in the dampest place. I place the eggs in a plas-tic box in a bed of damp earth through which
the air permeates. Then I cover the eggs with
some blotting paper that I keep slightly damp
by spraying it with water once a week. In the
past three years, 11 clutches of mine that were
kept this way at temperatures between 72°
and 82°F (22°-28°C) hatched. The incuba-tion takes 10 to 13 weeks. The 41 newborn
snakes measured between 8¼ and 9 inches
(21-23 cm) and shed their first skins after 10 to
12 days. After that, the young *L. mexicana*
will eat small lizards but only very few show
any interest in mice. Since most snake keepers
do not have small lizards readily available and
the snakes generally refuse newborn mice as
their first food, force-feeding is the only
answer. For this a newborn mouse is killed and
inserted into the snake's mouth very carefully
with some tongs. At that point the swallowing
motions of the snake take over and move the
mouse down to the stomach. Most snakes soon
decide to start eating on their own.

Lampropeltis pyromelana
Sonora Mountain Kingsnake
4 subspecies
(photo, page 121)

PHYSICAL CHARACTERISTICS: The head is hardly set off from the neck. The body is long but very strong. The large eyes have round pupils. The scales are smooth, and the anal plate is undivided. *L. pyromelana* is one of the most beautiful tricolored King Snakes. Its body is ringed with brick to bright red and sulphur yellow to white bands. These red and white bands or rings are set off from each other by wide black edges. The tip of the snout is white or yellow, and the top of the head and the areas immediately behind the eyes are black. The chin is white or yellow, and the yellowish belly is covered with square blotches.

LENGTH: Up to 42 inches (107 cm).

DISTRIBUTION AND BEHAVIOR: This species is distributed in the United States in northern central Utah, southeastern Nevada, Arizona, and southwestern New Mexico, and in Mexico in eastern Sonora and central Chihuahua. It lives in the mountains at altitudes between 3000 and 7500 feet (900-2300 m). It is found in open pine forests, canyons, beneath rocks, on slopes of loose rock, and along streams with ferns and occasional oaks. A friend told me he found Sonora Mountain Kingsnakes when he overturned large rocks at a height of 6500 feet (2000 m) above sea level. *L. pyromelana* is largely nocturnal. Very little is known about its life in the wild except that it lives on lizards and small mammals, which it strangles before eating them. This snake hibernates 4 to 6 months, and it reproduces by means of laying eggs.

CAPTIVITY AND BREEDING: The Sonora Mountain Kingsnake is easy to keep in a terrarium. Unfortunately it is rarely offered for sale, and when it is it fetches a high price. It can be kept in a fairly small cage but always has to have fresh water and needs some cavities made up of rocks or pieces of bark to hide in. The bottom of the terrarium is covered with a mixture of sand and loam. Artificial lights should be on about 10 hours a day, and localized bottom heat is required. During the day the air temperature should be between 77° and 86°F (25°-30°C), and it should not drop below 64°F (18°C) at night. My Sonora Mountain Kingsnake spends it days hiding under a flat rock or in a piece of pipe-shaped cork. It does not start moving until dusk but then starts prowling ceaselessly. It sheds its old skin every 2 to 3 months, and it eats 1 to 2 small mice a week. The digestive process is completed in 2 or 3 days. Every year it hibernates from mid-November to early or mid-March at lowered temperatures between 41° and 59°F (5°-15°C).

Thus far the only country where this snake has been bred in captivity is the United States. There, matings have been recorded on May 16, 17, and 20 and on June 1, 1975. The female then laid a clutch on July 9 consisting of 3 eggs all stuck together. The eggs measured $9/16 \times 2$ inches (15×50 mm) and $5/8 \times 2^{3}/8$ inches (17×60 mm). They were placed in a container with damp moss and kept at 68° to 91°F (20°-33°C). The young snakes hatched on September 28 and 29 of that year, weighing 4.94, 5.53, and 5.88 grams and measuring 9, 10, and $9^{1}/2$ inches (225, 255, and 240 mm). The coloration and markings of the baby snakes was identical with those of adult snakes. A few weeks after hatching, two of these young snakes were already eating baby lizards (*Urosaurus*). The third little snake ate only freshly killed newborn mice, a food its siblings refused to touch.

Lampropeltis triangulum
Milk Snake
23 species
(photo, page 122)

PHYSICAL CHARACTERISTICS: The various subspecies of this snake differ a great deal from each other not only in coloration and markings but also in length. But they are largely the same build. The slender animals have small, oval to longish heads that are not, or only barely, set off from the neck. Several subspecies have markings similar to those of the Arizona Coral Snake with the color sequence red, black, yellow or red, black, white. *L. t. triangulum* has dark red to chestnut brown saddle marks with black rims on the back. These saddle marks are seperated by white to yellow crossbands. The sides of the body have brown or black blotches, and the head is brown or black, too. Toward the back of the head there is a V-shaped white mark with a black rim, and across the top of the head there is a dark crossband running from eye to eye and continuing as a stripe to the corners of the mouth. The underside of the head and the throat are white to yellow, and the belly has black blotches or dark bands. The subspecies *L. t. elapsoides* has scarlet, black, and white or yellowish crossbands on the back, the sides, and the belly; and the part of the head anterior to the eyes is red. *L. t. annulata* and *L. t. arcifera* have black heads, whereas *L. t. amaura* and *L. t. gentilis* have heads that are black but with the tip of the snout white to yellowish. One of the handsomest subspecies of this snake is the *L. t. nelsoni*. Its head, too, is black; and it has wide, dark red crossbands alternating with narrow black and white to yellowish ones. As a general rule, young Milk Snakes are more brightly colored than adult ones, which darken some with age.

LENGTH: 24 to 51 inches (60–130 cm).

DISTRIBUTION AND BEHAVIOR: The Milk Snake is very widely distributed over almost the entire United States and as far south as Central America. The various subspecies require different biotopes and live in both wet and dry areas. *L. t. elapsoides* (formerly *L. t. doliata*) is often found in open pine forests. It stays on the ground and loves to hide in old, decaying tree stumps that have been chewed by termites, under toppled trees, and under loose bark. It will also make do with refuges located under rocks and in holes in the ground. After heavy rains and during floods the snakes crawl up dead but still standing pines, keeping out of sight under the loose bark of the trees. This affords them safety from the water and protection from enemies, and the sun-warmed bark offers them favorable conditions, namely warmth, dampness, and darkness. In addition they find ground skinks (*Lygosoma laterale*) there, which are this subspecies' favorite prey. When plowing up fallow land one often finds numerous Milk Snakes. In contrast to *L. t. elapsoides, L. t. syspila, L. t. amaura,* and *L. t. triangulum,* all of which live in flat lands and require similiar biotopes, *L. t. arcifera* and *L. t. nelsoni* like mountainous terrain and live well concealed in the Mexican Sierras. *L. t. gentilis* prefers a dry environment and lives under rocks and flat stones. Milk Snakes eat small mammals, lizards, small snakes, and sometimes insects. All the subspecies of this snake are largely nocturnal and are encountered only rarely away from their retreats (usually after heavy rains). Matings take place after a 3-to-6-month hibernation, and between June and August, 6 to 24 longish eggs are deposited under logs, bark, or in loose soil. The baby snakes usually hatch after 40 to 60 days.

CAPTIVITY AND BREEDING: Depending on the subspecies, Milk Snakes are kept in small-to-medium-sized terrariums. A mixture of sand and leaf mold with bits of bark and wood added to it works well for the bottom, and some large pieces of bark, flat rocks, or some decorative cork provide hiding opportunities in addition to the snakes' usual burrowing into the loose bottom material. My Milk Snakes often lie underneath some bark that is warmed by a heat lamp. Temperatures between 77° and 86°F (25°-30°C) should be supplied during the day, but a bottom heater

TOP: Horseshoe Whipsnake (*Coluber hippocrepis*)
BOTTOM: Red-headed Ratsnake (*Elaphe moellendorffi*)

is not absolutely necessary. Milk Snakes become active at dusk and then often crawl around for hours without stopping. During the day one catches only rare glimpses of these spectacular animals. It is best to keep these snakes singly because they compete for food and occasionally display cannibalistic impulses. Quite often two snakes fight over the same prey, and in the heat of battle the stronger animal may gulp down not only the prey but its rival as well. Captive Milk Snakes are offered newborn to medium-sized mice to eat. In the case of *L. t. elapsoides* there may be feeding problems because many individuals of this subspecies accept only lizards and persistently refuse to eat mice. A hibernation of 3 to 4 months at temperatures between 50° and 59°F (10°-15°C) is necessary.

This snake has frequently been bred in captivity. The eggs are incubated on a layer of damp peat or forest soil at temperatures between 75° and 82°F (24°-28°C). The young snakes usually hatch after 7 to 9 weeks, and after their first molt they accept young lizards, lizards' tails, and occasionally newborn mice as food.

Lampropeltis zonata
California Mountain Kingsnake
7 subspecies
(photo, page 122)

PHYSICAL CHARACTERISTICS: *L. zonata* closely resembles *L. pyromelana* in build, coloration, and markings. The markings consist of about 40 tricolored bands—brick to pomegranate red, black, and white—that form partial rings across the back and body sides. The white bands are the same width all across, but the black stripes are narrower on the sides than on the top, where they connect with each other in places. The red bands are wider on the sides than on the center of the back. The top of the head and the sides behind the eyes are black, and a white band encircles the back of the head. The belly is flecked with black.

LENGTH: Rarely over 38 inches (95 cm).

DISTRIBUTION AND BEHAVIOR: This snake is found in southern Washington, in Oregon, California, and in northern Baja California. It lives in the mountains at altitudes between 4250 and 8500 feet (1300-2600 m). Here it inhabits pine and oak forests interspersed with rocks. It usually stays hidden under stones during the day and emerges only at dusk. Its diet consists of mice, lizards, and small snakes. In California this species is often mistaken for the poisonous Arizona Coral Snake (*Micruroides euryxanthus*), a species that does not occur in California but resembles *L. zonata* very closely in coloration. *L. zonata* retreats to its winter quarters in September, October, or November, and reappears in March or April. The matings take place in the spring, and eggs are laid generally in June or July. The young hatch after 2 to 3 months.

CAPTIVITY AND BREEDING: This snake has the same requirements for captivity as the previously described *L. pyromelana*. Although the California Mountain Kingsnake is largely nocturnal it does, unlike the Sonora Mountain Kingsnake, occasionally venture out of its hiding place during the day. This splendid snake, too, needs to hibernate for 3 to 4 months at temperatures between 41° and 59°F (5°-15°C), if offspring are desired.

I have owned a pair of these snakes for about four years. In the spring of 1977 the male indicated readiness to mate by sliding over the female's back with twitching motions. I was unable to observe the mating, but on June 6, the female laid 3 longish eggs that were not stuck together. I place them in a plastic container with a mixture of sand and forest soil,

TOP LEFT: Desert Whipsnake (*Coluber ravergieri*)
TOP RIGHT: Dhaman (*Ptyas mucosus*)
CENTER LEFT: Stinking Goddess (*Elaphe carinata*)
CENTER RIGHT: Dione's Ratsnake (*Elaphe dione*)
BOTTOM LEFT: American Ratsnake (*Elaphe obsoleta*)
BOTTOM RIGHT: Amur Ratsnake (*Elaphe schrencki*)

covered them with blotting paper, and sprayed a little bit of water that measured 77° to 86°F (25°-30°C) every 3 to 4 days. I also keep the soil slightly damp. The temperature inside the plastic container was maintained between 74° and 82°F (23°-28°C) and the container covered with a top that had many small holes in it. Two of the eggs grew moldy after 3 weeks, but the third produced a healthy young snake on August 11, 1977, measuring about 9 inches (23 cm). Soon after hatching, the little snake burrowed into the damp soil in the incubator. Then it would crawl out of the tunnel system it had created in the soil and appear on the surface several times a day. The first molt was completed on August 18, and soon after that the snake started eating young lizards and newborn mice, which it strangled before eating. After a cool wintering over, the same female laid 4 eggs the following year on May 29. One egg again grew moldy, but the others produced young snakes about 9 inches long (23 cm) on August 14 (2) and August 23, 1978 (1).

Genus *Rhinocheilus*
Longnose Snakes
1 species

Rhinocheilus lecontei
Longnose Snake
4 subspecies
(photo, page 176)

PHYSICAL CHARACTERISTICS: The slender build of these snakes is very reminiscent of that of the tricolored King Snakes (*Lampropeltis*). The head with its large, black eyes is not set off from the neck. The snout is somewhat pointed, and the scales are smooth. The anal plate is not divided, and the scales under the tail—a few of which are keeled—are undivided as well. The black head and the neck region have a generous sprinkling of larger and smaller yellowish dots. The tip of the snout is whitish, pink, or reddish. The body and tail are covered with broad, saddle-shaped, red and black crossbands that are rimmed with yellowish borders. The red and yellow bands have a sprinkling of black scales, and the black saddle patches include some yellow scales. The whitish to yellow belly has only a few black speckles.

LENGTH: 20 to 32 inches (50-80 cm); rarely over 40 inches (1 m).

DISTRIBUTION AND BEHAVIOR: The Longnose Snake is at home in the southwestern United States and in Mexico. It occurs in the plains and in mountains up to 6000 feet (1800 m). It is active primarily at dusk and at night. If one hopes to collect this snake during the day one should look under rocks, boards, and old wood. This species prefers deserts and dry prairies dotted with low shrubs. But it also inhabits mountain slopes where it is found mainly in the rock debris at the foot of hills. With its pointed snout, smooth scales, and slender yet powerful body the Longnose Snake finds it easy to burrow through loose earth. Large numbers of these snakes are often turned up in the course of plowing fields. *R. lecontei* leaves its lair toward evening to hunt for lizards, small snakes, and small mammals. It is not aggressive but will bite if mistreated. When it is agitated it hides its head in the coils of its body and moves its trembling tail back and forth. When picked up it coils its body in the hand of the collector while the anal glands produce a foul-smelling secretion and a mixture of blood and excrement is emitted from the anus. But, strangely enough, only females excrete blood. In October or November the Longnose Snake goes into hibernation from which it sometimes reemerges as early as February or March. This snake is seen most often from April through June, and its period of greatest activity is in May. In the summer it is not so much in evidence. Matings take place in the spring, and in June or July an average of 6 to 7 eggs are deposited. The young snakes, which usually hatch in July or August, measure about 10 inches (25 cm).

CAPTIVITY AND BREEDING: A small-to medium-sized dry terrarium is adequate for *R. lecontei*. The bottom is covered with coarse sand mixed with some peat or forest soil. Some rocks provide cover. A small water dish is also important. Since the Longnose Snake spends most of the day in hiding, ordinary daylight is sufficient, but localized bottom heat is necessary. During the day the temperature in the terrarium should be 77° to 86°F (25°-30°C). At night it should drop a little. The Longnose Snake is an interesting snake to keep and survives well in captivity. A specimen of *R. l. lecontei* has been living in the San Diego Zoo for 18 years and was already mature when captured, and the Staten Island Zoo has had a *R. l. tessellatus* for the past 16 years. This animal, too, was already mature when captured. Young mice or, if necessary, lizards are offered as food. The snakes should always be fed at dusk. Two to 3 months of hibernation at 50° to 59°F (10°-15°C) are required. There are no reports of this snake being bred in captivity, but females gravid at the time of capture have laid eggs in terrariums, and the young snakes hatched after 65 to 80 days.

Genus *Cemophora*
Scarlet Snakes
1 species

Cemophora coccinea
Scarlet Snake
3 subspecies

PHYSICAL CHARACTERISTICS: The head is barely set off from the neck. The red snout is pointed, and the eyes small. The body is slender, and the scales not keeled. In coloration and build the Scarlet Snake closely resembles the Scarlet Kingsnake (*Lampropeltis triangulum elapsoides*). On the back and sides *C. coccinea* has brick-red saddle marks with black edges. The spaces between these marks are yellowish. The belly is solid white or yellowish.

LENGTH: 16 to 24 inches (40-60 cm); in exceptional cases up to 32 inches (82 cm).

DISTRIBUTION AND BEHAVIOR: The Scarlet Snake is distributed from New Jersey to Texas and Florida. Its prime habitat is a mixed forest of oak and pine. It is also found in fields and meadows but always very close to water. It favors sandy soil and lives a secretive life under piles of brush, under logs, bark, rocks, or in some similar hidden spot. Since it does not emerge into the open—or does so very rarely—it used to be considered a rare species, but this is not the case. At night Scarlet Snakes are often found on roads, and they can almost always be caught after sunset or before sunrise. *C. coccinea* lives on lizards, snakes, mice, salamanders, frogs, insects, and especially reptile eggs. Not much is known about the details of reproduction. The females lay 3 to 8 longish, soft-shelled eggs in the early summer. The snakes hibernate 4 to 6 months about 4 feet (1.2 m) down in the ground.

CAPTIVITY AND BREEDING: This quite colorful snake is imported into Europe only occasionally. No special size terrarium is required for this species, and because it is nocturnal it needs no artificial lighting. During the day, the air should be between 68° and 81°F (20°-27°C). The bottom is covered with sand that has some forest soil mixed into it, and on this a few pieces of bark are placed. The snakes spend the daytime underneath the bark and in the bottom material, through which they burrow constantly. Feeding this snake presents a problem. It is reluctant to accept food such as lizards, snakes, and naked mice, though it will happily eat snake eggs, both of its own and of other species. It chokes the eggs down, poking through the soft shell with its teeth in the process. But since snake keepers rarely have snake eggs available and, if they do, would rather not use them as snake food, there is another feeding method they can resort to that the River Ecological Laboratories of the University of Georgia in Savannah have developed. There, Scarlet Snakes are kept in cages without water. The egg yolk of a chicken egg is mixed with enough water to make it just drinkable. To induce the snake to drink this liquid during the night, it is placed together with the food dish in a separate box. Later it is returned to its normal terrarium where there is nothing to drink. The Scarlet Snake has not yet been bred and reproduced in captivity.

Genus *Elaphe*
Rat Snakes
36 species

Elaphe carinata
Stinking Goddess
2 subspecies
(photo, page 140)

PHYSICAL CHARACTERISTICS: The longish and somewhat triangular head is clearly set off from the neck, and the supraocular plate protrudes slightly over the eye on the side, lending the snake a mean look. The slightly elliptical pupils are vertical. The body is sturdy and the tail, long and tapered. In contrast to the other *Elaphe* species, this snake has strongly keeled scales, a feature which is reflected by the "carinata" of the Latin name. The ground color of the body ranges from light beige to olive gray with black rims on the scales. The markings, too, vary. The anterior body has crossbands, and the yellowish shields or plates on the head have wide black edges. The belly is porcelain-colored to yellowish-gray.

LENGTH: 60 to 68 inches (150–170 cm); rarely over 6½ feet (2 m).

DISTRIBUTION AND BEHAVIOR: This snake is found only in China and Formosa. It inhabits hilly country and especially mountains up to an altitude of 10,000 feet (3000 m) where is it encountered on slopes dotted with bushes, in woods, bamboo thickets, along fields, and not infrequently near human habitations. Its movements are quick, and it is aggressive toward humans, trying to bite as soon as it is caught. When it feels threatened it inflates its body, not its throat like other snakes. In a state of agitation it vibrates its tail, opens its mouth in a gesture of intimidation, and emits a loud hissing. Its anal glands are extremely well developed, and when the snake is seized, an ill-smelling secretion pours out of them. The smell of this secretion is so peculiar that one can recognize this snake by it from a distance. *E. carinata* feeds primarily on snakes—both venomous and nonvenomous—lizards, and occasionally rodents. We know very little about its reproductive habits in nature except that it lays whitish eggs stuck together in a clutch in decomposing plant material.

CAPTIVITY AND BREEDING: This snake is only rarely imported. Grown specimens need a large terrarium. Hollow pieces of bark or solidly cemented rocks provide retreats. The water basin has to be permanently installed because the snake will otherwise upset it. Plants cannot be included in the terrarium because they will almost inevitably be crushed sooner or later. Because the Stinking Goddess eats other snakes it has to be kept singly. The temperature should range between 68° and 82°F (20°-28°C) during the day and be lowered a few degrees at night. The snake usually stays out of sight during the day and emerges only at dusk. If the terrarium gets morning or afternoon sun or at least daylight no special lighting is required. Young snakes eat mice only reluctantly and since the keeper will generally not be in a position to offer the snakes their natural prey his is likely to have to resort to force-feeding. Young mice stuffed down the snakes are almost always readily digested. When it reaches a certain size, the Stinking Goddess will start looking for different prey, and when it is half grown it will eagerly consume mice and occasionally eggs. *E. carinata* does not make a friendly pet in captivity. It remains easily frightened and shy, and when it is disturbed it is quick to bite but lets go again quickly. A hibernation period from October to April at temperatures between 39° and 59°F (4°-15°C) is necessary.
This species has reproduced repeatedly in captivity. The male crawls over the female's back with twitching motions before mating. Stemmler placed the eggs which his snakes

produced in damp peat and kept them at 77° to 82°F (25°-28°C). The snakes hatched after 44 to 52 days and measured from 12 to 13 inches (30-33 cm).

Elaphe dione
Dione's Ratsnake
(photo, page 140)

PHYSICAL CHARACTERISTICS: The longish head is not, or only barely, set off from the neck, and the body and tail are long. This species resembles the *E. situla* in body build, and both species have similar markings on the head. The very shiny scales are smooth, and the back and sides of the body are pale gray to reddish-brown. The upper side of the body has 4 not very distinct longitudinal stripes, and the back and sides have dark transverse blotches. The distinguishing feature of this species is a horseshoe-shaped marking on the head. A dark line runs from the posterior edge of the eye to the corner of the mouth. The belly is dark gray speckled with black. There are some very dark specimens without markings, but they are rare.

LENGTH: Up to 40 inches (1 m).

DISTRIBUTION AND BEHAVIOR: *E. dione* is distributed over a large area extending from the southeastern part of the European USSR as far as Korea and China. It lives on flat land and in mountains up to an altitude of 5000 feet (1600 m) and is found in wet as well as dry biotopes, preferably in steppes and the oases of semi-deserts but also in woods and on cultivated land. It likes to hide in hollow trees, under rocks, in crevices, and in the burrows of small rodents. Sometimes it even lives concealed in houses that are lived in. *E. dione* feeds on small rodents, birds, lizards, bird eggs, and even frogs, snakes, and fish. It kills its prey either by constriction or by pressing it against the ground with its head until it expires. Dione's Ratsnake does not like to fight or bite. If theatened it raises up its anterior body but keeps the head and throat low. At the same time it vibrates its tail, producing a strange noise with it. Its movements are slow. Matings take place in the spring, and in June, July, or August, 5 to 16 eggs are deposited. The incubation period is short, not taking more than 2 to 4 weeks. Since this snake lives in regions where the weather varies we assume that the females are able to retain the eggs long enough to wait for temperatures conducive to the development of the embryos outside her body. It does not seem an outlandish idea to assume that Dione's Ratsnakes living at high altitudes may be truly ovoviviparous. The newborn snakes measure about 8 to 9½ inches (20-24 cm).

CAPTIVITY AND BREEDING: *E. dione* is a pleasant and interesting snake to have in a terrarium, and if it is housed properly in a cage with a dry bottom of sand and loam it is easy to care for. A few flat rocks, a tree stump, and some climbing branches and a small water container are essential. The snake often spends its days in the branches. Weak bottom heat improves its sense of comfort. During the day the air should measure 72° to 82°F (22°-28°C) and at night, 64° to 68°F (18°-20°C). If the terrarium does not get the morning or afternoon sun, artificial light should be provided for 8 to 12 hours a day. Small to medium-sized mice are offered as food. Four to 5 months of hibernation at temperatures between 41° and 59°F (5°-15°C) are necessary.
This snake has been bred repeatedly in captivity. The eggs are placed in slightly damp peat and kept at 72° to 82°F (22°-28°C). Raising the young snakes is unproblematical. They start eating newborn mice or pieces of larger mice after shedding their first skins.

Elaphe guttata
Corn Snake
3 subspecies
(photo, page 157)

PHYSICAL CHARACTERISTICS: The Corn Snake has a long, slender head that is hardly set off from the neck and a muscular body. The eyes and the pupils are large and round, and in bright light the smooth or slightly keeled scales glisten. The top of the body varies in color from rust red to orange or brick red. Brownish to brick red blotches partially or completely outlined in black run down the center of the back at regular intervals, and there are smaller spots of similiar shades on the sides. On the back of the head and the nape there is a V-shaped mark, and a line runs across the forehead connecting the eyes and running on to the corners of the mouth. The whitish belly is mottled with black, and the underside of the tail is striped. In *E. g. rosacea* the black color pigments are much reduced. The markings of *E. g. emoryi* are much like those of *E. g. guttata*, but the basic colors are shades of gray or brown.

LENGTH: Up to 72 inches (182 cm).

DISTRIBUTION AND BEHAVIOR: The Corn Snake is native to the eastern, southeastern, and central United States and to northeastern Mexico. Its favorite habitat is open, sunny pine forests where it is found both on the ground and on trees. Young snakes are particularly fond of hiding under the bark of dead pine trees as my own observations confirmed repeatedly. But Corn Snakes also live in rock piles, abandoned log cabins, barns, along roads, in and on the edge of corn fields, and they especially like abandoned orchards. Occasionally one will see a Corn Snake crawling out of the burrow of rabbits or cotton rats. In the spring these snakes are largely diurnal, but in the summer they are active more at dusk. Their diet is made up of all kinds of small mammals and of birds. They kill their prey before swallowing it either by constriction or by crushing it against the ground with their heads. Corn Snakes are not especially fast moving and can be caught quite easily. When they are grasped they fight, retracting the anterior body in an S-shape and striking with their teeth. In a state of high agitation they swish their tails back and forth. Matings take place in the spring, and 12 to 14 eggs, usually stuck together in a clump, are deposited usually between May and July. Depending on where the snakes live they hibernate 2 to 6 months. In southern Florida Corn Snakes can be caught any time of year if the weather is warm.

CAPTIVITY AND BREEDING: Corn Snakes are readily available and usually at relatively low prices. But albinos, which are occasionally offered for sale, are very expensive. *E. guttata* is a popular terrarium snake and for good reason. It is a striking looking animal, thrives without making great demands on its keeper, and can be bred in captivity. Its needs for space are moderate, and it feels just as happy in a small to medium-sized terrarium as in a large one. A mixture of sand and peat or sand and forest soil can be used as bottom material, and a water container, climbing branches, some rocks or decorative cork to hide under, and a weak bottom heater are required. If the terrarium gets no morning or afternoon sun or no natural daylight, 8 to 10 hours of artificial light have to be provided. This snake feels comfortable at 72° to 82°F (22°-28°C) during the day and 64° to 68°F (18°-20°C) at night. It will spend most of its day hiding in its retreat but come out now and then to bask on the heated bottom or under the lights. At night it often prowls around for hours. Always make sure that the terrarium door is securely locked. Corn Snakes are very good at hiding, and a snake might go undetected for weeks in an apartment before it is retrieved by chance during one of its nightly excursions. Corn Snakes become tame quickly. They will take live or dead mice from tongs. Young snakes grow fast and, when well fed, may reach sexual maturity after 2 years and in some exceptional cases even somewhat earlier. *E. guttata* should be allowed to hibernate at reduced temperatures of 41° to 59°F (5°-15°C) for about 2 to 3 months. Rasing young snakes is not difficult. I place the eggs in damp lava earth or peat and cover them with blotting paper. The young snakes hatch after 60 to 75 days and measure from 8 to 9½ inches (20-24 cm). After shedding their first skins they begin to eat newborn mice.

Elaphe hohenackeri
Transcaucasian Ratsnake
2 subspecies
(photo, page 158)

PHYSICAL CHARACTERISTICS: The longish head with the square snout is hardly set off from the neck, and the large eyes have round pupils. The body is slender and the tail long and tapered. The scales are smooth. The ground color of the body varies from gray to grayish brown, brown, and light brown. A row of irregular dark blotches, separated by lighter areas, runs down the spine. In the case of the subspecies *E. h. taurica* these blotches may form a broken, nut-brown, undulating band rimmed in black. On the back of the head there is a black mark that forks into two branches on the nape. Transverse blotches dot the sides at regular intervals. A black line connects the eye to the corner of the mouth, and a black spot under the eye extends to the edge of the mouth. The belly is yellowish to reddish with black blotches.

LENGTH: Rarely over 30 inches (75 cm).

DISTRIBUTION AND BEHAVIOR: *E. hohenackeri* is native to the Caucasus, to northwestern Persia, and to Turkey. It is found in mountains up to 8000 feet (2500 m) and above. Here it lives on sunny slopes with some boulders, short grass, and shrubs. According to the author's personal experience this rare snake can also be found in the crumbling stone walls enclosing old, abandoned orchards. During the day the snake hides under stones and rocks. Its diet is limited almost entirely to mice. In June or July, 3 to 7 eggs that stick together in a clutch are laid.

CAPTIVITY AND BREEDING: The Transcaucasian Ratsnake is very similar in behavior to the Leopard Snake. It, too, requires a dry terrarium with a bottom layer of sand and loam and with some large stones and hollow pieces of cork to hide under. In addition a small water dish is required as well as a climbing branch, where the snake will generally like to spend most of the day. The specimen I had, though, was usually hiding under a flat rock or a piece of bark. Artificial light should be provided all day, and localized bottom heat much improves the snake's sense of wellbeing. The temperature in the terrarium should be between 72° and 82°F (22°-28°C) and a few degrees cooler at night. Half-grown mice are offered as food. *E. hohenackeri* is a fickle eater; sometimes it will readily take the food it is given, and other times it will unpredictably go on a hunger strike. The prey is always killed before it is consumed. In keeping with the climate of the high altitudes at which this snake lives in the wild, a hibernation period of 4 to 5 months is a necessity. There have been no reports thus far of this snake being bred in captivity.

Elaphe longissima
Aesculapian Snake
3 subspecies

PHYSICAL CHARACTERISTICS: This snake has a slender body and tail and a longish head that is very little set off from the neck. The scales are smooth, and the top of the body gleams in all shades ranging from stray yellow to brown and black. The anterior body and the sides are lighter in color than the lower body. The scales of the back and sides have fine white streaks, and the belly is a solid yellowish-white. Melanistic specimens occur but are rare. On the back of the head, young snakes in particular often have a yellowish crescent-shaped mark that may be outlined in black. Because of this mark they are sometimes mistaken for young Ringed Snakes.

LENGTH: Up to 6½ feet (2 m).

DISTRIBUTION AND BEHAVIOR: *E. longissima* is distributed across northeastern Spain and large parts of central and southern Europe as far as Asia Minor and northern Persia. It occurs primarily on sunny slopes that are protected from the wind and have areas of loose rock and shrubs. But it is also found along the hedge-rows of fields and on the edges of open decidu-ous woods, and sometimes one comes upon it in the walls of old ruins and in the cracks of stone walls. The Aesculapian Snake emerges from its winter quarters in April or May, depending on the weather, and then spends almost all of its day in the open, sunning itself between rocks, in low bushes, or in dry grass. Its movements are slower than those of the Dark Green Snake (*Coluber viridiflavus*), which occurs in the same biotope. The Aescu-lapian Snake moves with agility in shrubbery and occasionally catches birds there, but its main diet consists of mice and rats. It kills its prey by wrapping its powerful upper body around it. Matings take place in May, and in June or July the female lays 5 to 8 or sometimes as many as 10 longish eggs. The young snakes, which hatch in September, are reminiscent in their coloration of young Ringed Snakes (*Natrix natrix*). They start out by eating lizards and small mice. *E. longissima* is not aggressive toward humans and does not necessarily bite when captured. It retires to its winter den in late September or in early or mid-October.

CAPTIVITY AND BREEDING: A fair-sized and tall dry terrarium with some climbing branches and a not too small water basin is necessary for *E. longissima*. Loam, or a mix-ture of sand, loam, and forest soil or peat is used for the bottom, and a suitable shelter is provided through a hollow piece of decorative cork, some flat pieces of bark, or a few rocks that are cemented together. Plants can be included in the terrarium. A large ivy is suit-able, which should be planted in a large plas-tic pot so that the soil and the root system can be kept damp. Localized bottom heat is required as well as 10 to 12 hours of artificial light unless the terrarium gets the morning and afternoon sun. Temperatures between 68° and 82°F (20°-28°C) are appropriate dur-ing the day. In the natural habitat the nights

are cooler than the days, and a drop in temper-ature of a few degrees is therefore desirable. During the day the Aesculapian Snake usually lies concealed in its shelter or basks in the sun or under a heat lamp. These snakes become tame quickly in captivity and take both dead and live mice from tongs. It is essential that this snake hibernate 4 to 5 months at tempera-tures between 41° and 59° (5°-15°C). As in the case of other snakes, hibernation is an important prerequisite for breeding.
Aesculapian Snakes have produced offspring in captivity a number of times. The eggs are placed in a litter of peat or vermiculite which is dampened from time to time, and the tem-perature in the incubator is kept at 74° to 78°F (24°-26°C). Under these conditions the snakes hatch after about 60 days. Raising them on newborn mice presents no special problems.

Elaphe mandarina
Jade-pattern Ratsnake

PHYSICAL CHARACTERISTICS: The oval head is barely set off from the neck, and the eyes are small and black, making it hard to see the pupils. In build this snake resembles the Corn Snake (*E. guttata*). It has smooth scales and a divided anal plate. The coloration varies from gray to light brown and salmon. The head is yellowish with three black cross stripes that run across the forehead and past the eyes. On the back there are 22 to 30 yellowish saddle patches with wide black edges that are in turn rimmed in yellow. The tail has black rings, and the yellowish belly has square black spots.

LENGTH: Over 3 feet (1 m).

DISTRIBUTION AND BEHAVIOR: *E. mandarina* occurs in upper Burma and in the Chinese provinces of Chekiang, Fukien, Kwantung, Kweichow, and Szechwan, where it lives in mountain forests up to an altitude of 7500 feet (2300 m). It is also found in dry fields and on slopes of loose rock. Little is known about its life in the wild except that it feeds on small mammals, birds, and bird eggs. It is likely that this snake, like other *Elaphe* species, lays eggs.

CAPTIVITY AND BREEDING: This snake is imported from Hong Kong only on rare occasions. It looks beautiful in a terrarium but is quite fussy and requires peace and quiet and a good shelter. It comes out into the open only rarely during the day. In the terrarium it is wild and nervous, and when it is disturbed, its tail trembles violently. A mixture of sand and forest soil is used for the bottom and a few flat pieces of bark or some rocks added to provide hiding places. A water dish is essential. Since this species is largely nocturnal, bottom heat is not necessary. Temperatures should range between 68° and 80°F (20°-27°C) during the day. If the terrarium gets no sun or daylight, a flourescent light should be installed and be on during the day. Mice are used as food, which the snake kills either by constriction or by crushing against a hard surface before swallowing them. *E. mandarina* has not so far been bred in captivity.

Elaphe moellendorffi
Red-headed Ratsnake
(photo, page 139)

PHYSICAL CHARACTERISTICS: The very long, lanciform head is clearly set off from the neck, and the large, reddish-brown eyes have round pupils. The body looks long and powerful. The scales on the back are slightly keeled and the ones on the sides, smooth. The gray to grayish-green ground color of the body becomes reddish-brown on the tail. The back is covered with about 30 nut brown saddle patches with black rims, and on the sides are spots of similar hue, also outlined in black, and some black speckles. The tail has longish, salmon-colored blotches, and the head and neck are a shiny rust brown. The porcelain-colored belly is covered with square black blotches.

LENGTH: Over 6½ feet (2 m).

DISTRIBUTION AND BEHAVIOR: *E. moellendorffi* occurs in the Chinese provinces of Kwangsi, Canton, Wuyung, and Kwantung, as well as in Tonkin. It is said to be not at all rare east of Canton and lives there at altitudes between 150 and 1000 feet (50-300 m) above sea level. We know next to nothing about its way of life in the wild. Its diet is made up of small mammals and birds.

CAPTIVITY AND BREEDING: *E. moellendorffi* is exported rarely. This handsome snake is apparently demanding and not easy to keep, but it is also quite conceivable that the animals that end up in terrariums spent weeks and months under miserable conditions before they were bought and that their resistance was so much lowered through infections that they soon expired after their owners acquired them. Whatever the case, I had no luck with this snake. In the San Diego Zoo, however, *E. moellendorffi* has not only been kept successfully but has also been bred. Five specimens were divided into 2 groups of 2 and 3 animals. The group of 3 was kept at 64° to 70°F (18°-21°C), the other 2 snakes at 75° to 81°F (24°-27°C). The group that was kept cooler thrived better and showed more interest in food than the second group, and all 5 snakes were therefore combined in the same terrarium (46½ × 30½ × 31½ inches [118 × 77.5 × 80 cm]) and kept at 64° to 70°F (18°-21°C). One snake died shortly thereafter, and two males and two females survived. On May 18, 1972 one of the males was observed going through a courtship display, but no eggs were deposited that year. On September 7, 1973, however, a female produced 6 elliptical eggs that were placed on some damp paper in an earthenware container. The container was covered with a pane of glass to keep the eggs from drying out. The incubating temperature was kept at 81°F (27°C), and the baby snakes hatched after 80 to 83 days between November 26 and 29. They looked very much like their parents and went through their first molt one week after hatching.

Elaphe obsoleta
American Ratsnake
8 subspecies
(photo, page 140)

PHYSICAL CHARACTERISTICS: The American Ratsnake is identical in build to the Corn Snake. Its scales are slightly keeled and the anal plate, divided. The coloration varies a great deal. The *E.o. obsoleta* is essentially black with the edges of the scales showing white spots and the skin showing brick red in between. The belly is whitish-gray, and the throat and chin are white. *E. o. quadrivittata, rossalleni,* and *bairdi* have 4 more or less well defined longitudinal stripes that start behind the head and end on the tail. The ground color is gray, yellow, brown, or reddish-brown. Other subspecies have more or less dark blotches on their backs and sides. The belly, too, is mottled to some extent.

LENGTH: Up to 101 inches (256 cm).

DISTRIBUTION AND BEHAVIOR: The American Ratsnake is distributed from northeastern Canada across the eastern, southeastern, and central United States and as far as Tamaulipas in northeastern Mexico. It also goes by the names of Pilot Snake and Mountain Black Snake and is found almost everywhere, both in flat and mountainous country and in dry and wet biotopes. It lives on the ground as well as in trees. During the day it can sometimes be seen in the open, but it mostly stays hidden under rocks, in rotting logs, piles of brush, burrows of cotton rats, and similar places. In the open pine forests of South Carolina and Florida I have collected a number of these snakes, including an exceptionally large specimen that I pulled out of an old, rusted refrigerator. I also found some under old pieces of metal lying alongside corn fields and in the rafters of collapsing wooden houses. Sometimes they are seen in barns. *E. obsoleta* is an excellent climber that often ventures far up into trees. Its diet is made up of all kinds of small mammals and birds. Sometimes it also eats amphibians. It crushes its prey before swallowing it. Depending on the geographic location the American Ratsnake hibernates for anywhere between 4 and 7 months. Matings usually take place in May or June. Combat dances between males are quite frequent. The 6 to 44 eggs are deposited in June or July, and the young snakes hatch after 53 to 109 days, depending on the temperature. They measure between 10 and 15$\frac{1}{2}$ inches (25-39 cm).

CAPTIVITY AND BREEDING: For an American Ratsnake one needs a large terrarium with climbing branches that offer good holds and a water container that has to be solidly anchored so that it cannot be knocked over. This snake requires the same conditions as the Corn Snake (*E. guttata*). Since it lasts very well in a terrarium it is an especially good choice for a beginner. Hibernation at reduced temperatures is recommended. *E. obsoleta* is often bred in captivity. The eggs are placed in an incubator with damp peat or some other litter. If kept at 77° to 81°F (25°-27°C) the eggs hatch after 2 to 3 months. The young start eating newborn mice immediately after their first molt. From then on rearing them presents no problems.

Elaphe quatuorlineata
Four-lined Ratsnake
5 subspecies

PHYSICAL CHARACTERISTICS: The longish head is set off only little from the neck, and the large eyes have round pupils. The body looks stronger and sturdier than that of any other European *Elaphe*. The scales on the back are slightly keeled. The top of the head is a uniform brown, and a dark stripe runs from the eyes to the corners of the mouth. The ground color of the body varies from light to dark brown. Four black longitudinal stripes or dark blotches on the back become paler toward the tail and eventually disappear altogether. Immature animals have a pattern of dark brown or black blotches on the back and sides and a dark mark on the back of the head as well as a black band across the forehead connecting the eyes. The belly has dark speckles.

LENGTH: Rarely over 6^1/$_2$ feet (2 m).

DISTRIBUTION AND BEHAVIOR: The Four-lined Ratsnake is widely distributed in southeastern Europe and Asia Minor. It inhabits different kinds of biotopes. Generally it is found on sunny, bushy slopes, on karst terrain, in open forests, and along still water. It is active both during the day and at dusk. In cloudy or hot, muggy weather preceding thunder storms it is more likely to emerge into the open than on bright, sunny days. Often it does not leave its hiding places until afternoon. If it is picked up from the ground it hisses loudly but does not always bite. Its diet consists of various small mammals, birds, and birds' eggs. Larger prey animals are strangled before they are eaten, but smaller ones are often swallowed alive. The mating season of the Four-striped Ratsnake is from spring to fall. In July or August the female lays 6 to 16 longish eggs under some rocks or in loose soil. The newborn snakes measure 9 inches (23 cm) and hatch in September or early October. They soon retire to winter quarters from which they reemerge in March, April, or May. In some areas the Four-striped Ratsnake has become rare or has disappeared altogether. In Italy this snake is caught for religious occasions and displayed at famous snake processions.

CAPTIVITY AND BREEDING: *E. quatuorlineata* is a quiet and rewarding snake to keep in a terrarium. It is not overly sensitive and survives for years in captivity. The terrarium should be large. The bottom is covered with a layer of sand, loam, and peat, and some rocks or hollow pieces of decorative cork are added to provide retreats. A few climbing branches should also be provided. During the day the snake often spends hours lying on the bottom heater that emits very gentle heat or on a branch exposed to the heat lamp. Artificial lights are not necessary if the terrarium gets morning and afternoon sun. Daytime temperatures should range between 77° and 86°F (25°-30°C), and at night it should be a few degrees cooler. The Four-lined Ratsnake soon becomes hand tame. It can be fed mice, rats, golden hamsters, young rabbits, guinea pigs, baby chicks, and sparrows, all of which the snake strangles before swallowing. Some individuals also eat eggs, which they crush with a tightening of the muscles after swallowing them. The egg shells are not digested and are eliminated as part of the excrements. The water container should not be too small because some snakes like to soak before shedding their skins. Four to 5 months of hibernation at about 50°F (10°C) are not absolutely necessary but are in keeping with the snakes' natural rhythm of life and therefore enhance their wellbeing. *E. quatuorlineata* has been bred in captivity. The eggs measure a little over 2 × 1 inches (60 × 30 mm), and they hatch after 30 to 60 days if kept in slightly damp peat and sand at an average temperature of 81°F (27°C). The newborn snakes measure about 14 inches (35 cm). Often they will eat young mice even before their first molt. If fed well they grow quickly and can reach 3 feet (90 cm) by the time they are one year old.

Elaphe scalaris
Ladder Ratsnake

PHYSICAL CHARACTERISTICS: The short head is barely set off from the neck, and the medium-sized eyes have round pupils. The body looks sturdy, and the scales are smooth. Coloration and markings vary with age. Young animals are yellowish- to grayish-green, mature ones, dark brown to reddish. The back has a regular, dark pattern of blotches that is flanked on both sides by a dark, longitudinal stripe. As the snake grows older the spots become lighter until finally the two longitudinal stripes are all that is left. The markings on the head fade, too, and finally disappear. The belly is a solid porcelain color.

LENGTH: Rarely over 5 feet (150 cm).

DISTRIBUTION AND BEHAVIOR: The Ladder Ratsnake occurs in southern France, on the Iles d'Hyères, on Menorca, and on the Pyrenean peninsula. It prefers dry spots with lots of sun and is found in the scree of mountain slopes, in rock piles, in dry terrain dotted with bushes, and in the remains of old stone walls. It is largely diurnal. In the spring it often spends the whole day sunning itself, whereas in the summer it is rarely seen in the open during the day and waits until evening or night to come out and roam. I once caught 6 of these animals on a country road near Barcelona one hot July night between 11 p.m. and 2 a.m. The Ladder Ratsnake is extremely quick on the ground and also a very agile climber. It is very shy and flees as soon as it catches sight of humans. If it is seized it usually bites. Its diet consists mostly of field mice, but it also eats birds and lizards. The prey is killed by constriction before it is swallowed. Matings take place in May or June. In July or August, 5 to 24 longish eggs are laid, which take 5 to 12 weeks to hatch.

CAPTIVITY AND BREEDING: The Ladder Ratsnake is a rewarding and long-lasting pet for the terrarium. Like the Four-striped Ratsnake (*E. quatuorlineata*) it requires a dry and warm terrarium. Care and feeding are also the same for the two snakes, with the exception that the Ladder Ratsnake does not eat eggs. When it first arrives *E. scalaris* is wild and fearful in the terrarium, but after a while it gets tame. Eggs laid by females gravid at capture have been incubated and have hatched in captivity.

Elaphe schrencki
Amur Ratsnake
2 subspecies
(photo, page 140)

PHYSICAL CHARACTERISTICS: This snake is very similar in build to the North American Ratsnake (*E. obsoleta*). Its longish head is barely set off from the neck, and the black eyes are of medium size. The dorsal scales are slightly keeled, those on the sides, smooth. The uniformly black top of the head has fine whitish or yellowish lateral lines on the shields of the upper and lower lips. The dark to blackish-brown or shiny ink black body has irregular, narrow, whitish or yellow crossbands that fork on the sides. The yellowish belly has black blotches.

LENGTH: Up to 67 inches (170 cm).

DISTRIBUTION AND BEHAVIOR: *E. schrencki* occurs in the Siberian Lowlands, in northeastern China, in eastern Manchuria, and in Korea. It lives in flat and hilly country and in mountains up to 10,000 feet (3,000 m). Its favorite habitats are forests, bushy landscapes, and clearings. Quite often it lives near human settlements, and sometimes it is found in orchards. It likes to hide under straw, piles of brush, or in hollow trees. It also climbs on trees to sun itself and to hunt for birds or search for bird eggs. But mostly it lives on small rodents. The females deposit 12 to 30 eggs between June and August, and the young snakes hatch in September measuring about 1 foot (30 cm).

CAPTIVITY AND BREEDING: This lovely snake is only rarely imported. It needs a large terrarium with several climbing branches and a small water basin. The bottom is covered with a layer of sand and peat or forest soil. If the terrarium gets no morning or afternoon sun or inadequate daylight, artificial lights should be on all day. *E. schrencki* is comfortable at daytime temperatures between 68° and 82°F (20°-28°C). The temperature should drop some at night. Since this snake spends most of its days on branches it is not absolutely necessary to install a bottom heater. If kept under the proper conditions, the Amur Ratsnake is a rewarding and long-lasting snake for a terrarium. It is fed mice, golden hamsters, young chicks, and sparrows. Three to 4 months of hibernation at reduced temperatures are essential if the snakes are expected to mate. This snake has reproduced a number of times in captivity. The incubation period is 48 to 50 days.

Elaphe situla
Leopard Ratsnake

PHYSICAL CHARACTERISTICS: The longish head is barely set off from the neck, and the large eyes have round pupils. The body is slender, and the scales are smooth. *E. situla* is one of the most colorful snakes of Europe. The ground color of the back and sides varies between light and dark shades of gray. Starting at the nape, the back is covered with square to roundish, strawberry red to brown blotches. On the tail these spots become smaller and eventually disappear farther down. These blotches on the back have dark rims and are clearly set off from the ground color. The sides also have dark spots. The underside of the upper third of the body is porcelain-colored, and the rest of the belly and the underside of the tail are speckled in black. The markings on the head consist of dark crossbands on both sides, and on the nape there is a triangular mark, the legs of which open toward the back and often meet at the front. A striped variant of this snake exists but is less common.

LENGTH: Up to 40 inches (1 m).

DISTRIBUTION AND BEHAVIOR: The Leopard Ratsnake is found in southern Italy, on Sicily, Malta, the Balkan peninsula, the Northern Sporades, the Cyclades, Crete, in the Caucasus, and on the Crimean peninsula. It lives in dry and rocky terrain that is dotted with low and thorny scrub. The Leopard Ratsnake loves warmth. During the day it is usually found under a rock or in the cracks of a stone wall. It does not move very fast but climbs with great agility on low bushes in the pursuit of young birds or just to sun itself. It lives mostly on mice, which it strangles before eating. It goes after lizards only rarely. Matings take place in May or June, and in July or August, 2 to 5 rather large eggs are deposited under rocks or in dry rotten wood or dry leaves. The young snakes measure 12 to 14 inches (30-35 cm) when they hatch. *E. situla* hibernates from October or November until April or May.

CAPTIVITY AND BREEDING: This snake has the reputation of being fussy, but if it is kept under proper conditions it presents no major problems. To be sure, it usually stays shy and does not give up biting. *E. situla* needs a medium-sized terrarium with a bottom layer of sand and loam, some rocks or decorative cork to provide a refuge, a fairly large water basin, and localized bottom heat. A climbing branch is essential because this colorful snake sometimes sleeps for hours in the fork of a branch. The specimen I keep sometimes hides for days under a flat rock. Before molting it sometimes soaks in the water basin. This is all the more remarkable because this species usually lives in quite dry regions. As a rule, Leopard Ratsnakes are good eaters, but sometimes they stop eating for weeks or months. This is nothing to worry about if the animal is healthy. Depending on the size of the snake it can be given medium-sized or newborn mice. Newborn mice are swallowed alive; larger and fully grown ones are strangled first. Twelve to 14 hours of artificial light should be provided. Leopard Ratsnakes are especially fond of the sun and often will enjoy the morning or afternoon sun lying on a branch. Temperatures between 72° and 82°F (22°-28°C) are appropriate during the day, and at night it should be a few degrees cooler. A winter rest of 3 to 4 months at 41° to 59°F (5°-15°C) benefits the general health of the snake and is a prerequisite if offspring are desired. *E. situla* has reproduced in captivity. The eggs are about $1\frac{1}{2} \times \frac{3}{4}$ inches (4 × 2 cm). They are placed in some slightly damp peat and sand and kept at 75° to 82°F (24°-28°C). Under these conditions they will hatch after 60 to 70 days. The newborn snakes measure about $10\frac{1}{2}$ to 14 inches (27-35 cm) and soon start eating newborn mice.

Elaphe subocularis
Transpecos Ratsnake
(photo, page 175)

PHYSICAL CHARACTERISTICS: The spatulalike head is set off very clearly from the slender neck, and the projecting eyes are very large and have round pupils. The body is slender but very muscular. In the United States this snake is also known under the name of "H Snake" because of the H-shaped markings on its back. The ground color of the body is yellowish-brown, yellow, or olive, and the head is solid yellow to yellowish-brown. Two black, parallel stripes start just behind the head and go down about a quarter of the snake's length on either side of the spine. Between these stripes there are dark crossbands at fairly even intervals. The markings farther down the back and on the tail are H-shaped and are clearly outlined with black. The belly is all whitish without spots. Because of the noticeably keeled scales the surface of the body looks somewhat rough.

LENGTH: Up to 66 inches (167 cm).

DISTRIBUTION AND BEHAVIOR: *E. subocularis* occurs in southern New Mexico and in southwestern Texas as well as in the state of Coahuila in northern Mexico. At altitudes between 1600 and 3200 feet (500-1000 m) it is quite frequent, and it is found up to about 5500 feet (1700 m). The Transpecos Ratsnake is a typical snake of the Chihuahua desert, living on slopes with some rocks and overgrown with yuccas, mesquite, creosote, and, above all, opuntia cacti. *E. subocularis* is largely nocturnal. During the day it hides in rock piles, crevices, and the burrows of rodents. At night it prowls around in search of prey. It eats mostly rodents but also bats and birds. The young eat lizards. Matings take place in the spring, and the eggs are deposited from June to August. The hatchlings are about 11 inches (28 cm) long and look like miniature adults.

CAPTIVITY AND BREEDING: This snake is only rarely kept by hobbyists. It is usually difficult to keep healthy and shows little interest in food. Absolute cleanliness is of utmost importance because this snake easily gets infections of the stomach and intestines. A dry terrarium with a small water container and a few flat rocks to provide cover is necessary. The bottom is covered with a layer of sand and loam, and a well functioning bottom heater that gently warms part of the bottom to 82° to 86°F (28°-30°C) is essential. The animals I had sometimes spent the whole day on the bottom heater. If there is not enough daylight, artificial lights should be on 10 to 14 hours. The Transpecos Ratsnake sometimes stays out of sight practically all day and comes to life only at night when it prowls around for hours. As food it is given mice, which it strangles before eating. If the temperature of the environment is adequate, the digestion takes 3 to 4 days. *E. subocularis* has on occasion reproduced in captivity. The snakes mate at night, and the whitish to yellowish eggs measure about 2 by a little over 1 inch (5 × 3 cm). They are placed in slightly damp litter inside a plastic container. At temperatures ranging from 75° to 86°F (24°-30°C) they hatch after 80 to 90 days. The first molt is due after about 10 days, and after that young snakes start eating newborn mice.

Elaphe vulpina
Fox Snake
2 subspecies

PHYSICAL CHARACTERISTICS: The head is set off a little from the neck, and the medium-sized eyes have round pupils. This species looks plumper than the other *Elaphe* snakes of the United States. The tail is short and thick, and the scales are lightly keeled. The ground color of the body varies from yellowish to light brown. A row of roundish, chocolate-colored to black blotches runs down the center of the back, and there are dark spots on the sides as well. The top of the head is brown and does not have any special markings. A dark band runs across the forehead, connecting the eyes and running on to the corners of the mouth. The belly is yellowish and covered with large, black blotches.

LENGTH: Up to 6 feet (180 cm).

DISTRIBUTION AND BEHAVIOR: *E. v. vulpina* occurs in Indiana, Illinois, Iowa, Kentucky, Michigan, Minnesota, Missouri, Nebraska, and South Dakota; the subspecies *E. v. gloydi*, in Ontario, Ohio, and Michigan. Although this snake is one of the more common snakes in the Midwest, less is known about its way of life than of other American *Elaphe* species. Local people often refer to the Fox Snake as "Pine Snake" or "Spotted Adder." When it is startled it trembles violently with its tail so that it is often mistaken for a Copperhead (*Agkistrodon contortrix*) or a Timber Rattlesnake (*Crotalus horridus*) and all too often killed. If it is seized it secretes a powerful and foul-smelling substance from its anal glands that is reminiscent of the smell of a fox den. This is what gave the snake its name. *E. vulpina* is found at altitudes between 550 to 1600 feet (170-500 m), where it lives on cultivated fields, at the edge of woods, in forests, in brushy areas, near farms, and in river valleys. The subspecies *gloydi* lives in the swamps surrounding Lakes Erie and Huron. This species is largely terrestrial in its habits and is found on bushes and trees only rarely. Since it is plumper than most of its relatives it climbs less well. But it is a good swimmer. *E. vulpina* lives mostly on mice, rats, young rabbits, birds, and birds' eggs, and when young it also eats insects. Matings generally take place in May and June, and during copulation the male often keeps hold of the female with his teeth. The 7 to 29 longish eggs that stick together in a clutch are deposited during June or July under rotting tree stumps, in decayed wood, in holes in the ground, or similar spots. The young, which measure between 10 and 12 inches, hatch between August and October.

CAPTIVITY AND BREEDING: The Fox Snake survives for years in a terrarium and becomes hand tame. The care it requires is like that for a Ratsnake (*E. obsoleta*) or a Corn Snake (*E. guttata*). Mice, rats, and chicks are offered as food, and the prey is killed by constriction before being eaten. Four to 5 months of hibernation at 41° to 59° (5°-15°C) are necessary. This snake has reproduced more than once in captivity. Raising the baby snakes on newborn mice is unproblematical.

Genus *Pituophis*
Pine Snakes, Gopher Snakes, and Bull Snakes
2 species

Pituophis melanoleucus
Pine Snake, Gopher Snake, and Bullsnake
10 subspecies
(photo, page 122)

PHYSICAL CHARACTERISTICS: This large, powerfully built species has a longish head that is only moderately set off from the neck. The large eyes have round pupils. The scales are keeled, and the anal plate is undivided. The coloration of the back varies from grayish-white and yellowish to reddish-brown. The sides of the body are lighter. Down the spine there is a row of dark blotches that are black on the anterior body and get brownish toward the tail. The belly is whitish, yellowish, brownish, or black, either uniform or mottled. There is a great deal of variation in color. The subspecies *P. m. mugitus* is cream-colored to rust brown and almost without markings. *P. m. lodingi* is a melanistic (i.e., darkly colored) subspecies. *P. m. catenifer* and *P. m. sayi* have highly contrasting markings and are called Bull Snakes. *P. m. catenifer* used to be considered a separate species but is now counted as a subspecies.

LENGTH: 6 feet (180 cm); in exceptional cases, over 8 feet (250 cm).

DISTRIBUTION AND BEHAVIOR: This snake has a broad distribution ranging from southern Canada to Mexico. With the exception of some eastern, midwestern, and southern states, it is found all over the United States. It lives both on flat land and in the mountains and is at home as much in wild as in cultivated country. It inhabits the prairie, abandoned fields, and open, sunny pine and oak forests. In wet forests this snake is seen almost exclusively on gently rising, sandy knolls where the ground is usually dry. In the western sections of its distribution *P. melanoleucus* even penetrates into the deserts and high up in the mountains. The species is mostly diurnal, but in hot weather it is active at night as well. It is a ground-dwelling snake that climbs into bushes and trees only rarely. It likes to burrow into loose soil and often takes over the burrows of pocket gophers, which are also its favorite prey. Otherwise its diet consists of all manner of small mammals, birds, lizards, and birds' eggs. Its reaction to humans varies. In South Carolina I saw a newly captured individual that was perfectly peaceful while others put up quite a fight when they were caught. When defending themselves, these snakes inflate their throats, hiss loudly, and bite vigorously and repeatedly, and their tails tremble with agitation. *P. melanoleucus* hibernates from 4 to 7 months depending on its geographic location. Usually it comes out in the open in March or April and retires for the winter in October or November. Matings take place in April or May and occasionally later. The eggs are laid in May, June, or July, and the young, which measure between $12^{1}/_{2}$ and 16 inches (32–40 cm) hatch after 2 to 3 months.

CAPTIVITY AND BREEDING: This snake is an impressive and striking animal that is, however, rather fussy about the conditions in the terrarium and requires conscientious care. In keeping with its size this snake requires a large terrarium, the bottom of which is covered with a mixture of sand and good forest soil. The bottom is then covered with pine and spruce needles. A small water dish can be supplied but is not absolutely necessary if the terrarium is sprayed with water twice a week. This snake likes to drink water in the form of drops. *P. melanoleucus* should otherwise be kept dry.

Twelve to 14 hours of sunlight or artificial light are required as well as a bottom heater that produces some mild local heat. The temperature should be between 77° and 86°F (25°-30°C) during the day and a few degrees cooler at night. A good hiding place, such as a hollow piece of decorative cork, drainage tile, some heavy rocks cemented together, a hollow log, or a small wooden box is essential. *P. melanoleucus* reacts badly to disruptions, and it is best to keep each animal separately. If the snake is disturbed too much it will often refuse to eat. A climbing limb should also be provided. The snakes I had often lay on a forked tree limb under the heat lamp. Recently captured specimens often display a wild temperament during their first weeks in captivity, but in time most of them become completely tame and eat readily both inside their cage and outside. Mice and rats as well as chicks and eggs are offered as food. The snake swallows the eggs, crushing them inside the body with its powerful muscles. Living prey is strangled before eating. Three to 4 months of wintering over at low temperatures are required.

This snake has reproduced in terrariums a number of times. Charles E. Shaw managed to get several snakes of this species to produce offspring year after year in the San Diego Zoo. Some females under the care of this outstanding herpetologist even produced two clutches a year.

Corn Snake (*Elaphe guttata*)

Genus *Arizona*
Glossy Snakes
Arizona elegans

Glossy Snake
9 subspecies
(photo, page 104)

PHYSICAL CHARACTERISTICS: The longish head, which is not set off from the neck, is tapered toward the snout. The rostral shield is prominent. In bright light the round pupils contract to a tiny dot. The body is fairly slender but powerful. The scales are smooth and the anal plate is undivided. The light brown to reddish-yellow back has marks running across it that are brown at the center and black at the rim. The sides of the body have two rows of staggered small dots. A dark line runs from the eye to the corner of the mouth. The belly is a uniform whitish-yellow.

LENGTH: Up to 50 inches (125 cm).

DISTRIBUTION AND BEHAVIOR: This snake occurs from Nebraska, Oklahoma, and Texas to California and northwestern Mexico. It lives in various biotopes and is found on rock-strewn slopes as high up as 6500 feet (2000 m), in dry grassland, in open, sunny woods, in dry waste land, and in cactus deserts. It always favors open country. The Glossy Snake is mostly nocturnal and spends its days burrowed in the ground or hidden under rocks. It is often turned up in the course of plowing or clearing land. In the eastern part of its distribution it is often found away from its retreat during the day. It is very peaceful and does not

TOP LEFT: Transcaucasian Ratsnake (*Elaphe hohenackeri*)
TOP RIGHT: Speckled Racer (*Drymobius margaritiferus*)
CENTER LEFT: Longnose Vinesnake (*Ahaetulla nasuta*)
CENTER RIGHT: Mud Snake (*Farancia abacura*)
BOTTOM LEFT: Mangrove Snake (*Boiga dendrophila*)
BOTTOM RIGHT: (*Philodryas olfersii*)

bite when caught. Its food consists of lizards, snakes, and small rodents, which it kills by constriction before swallowing. Matings occur in the spring, and the female lays 3 to 23 longish eggs. After about 68 days young snakes $9^1/2$ to $11^1/2$ inches long (24-29 cm) hatch in August or September.

CAPTIVITY AND BREEDING: This species needs needs a dry terrarium with sand and clay at the bottom into which it burrows during the day. A pile of rocks or pieces of bark provide additional opportunity to hide. A water container is also necessary. The temperature should be between 77° and 86°F (25°-30° C) during the day and drop to 64° or 68°F (18°-20°C) at night. *A. elegans* does not come alive until evening. It is easy to keep and long-lived in captivity. Mice, both dead and alive, are offered as food. Four months of hibernation are recommended. The Glossy Snake has not thus far been bred in captivity, but females gravid at capture have laid eggs in terrariums from which little snakes hatched after 68 days.

SAND SNAKES

Genus *Chionactis*
Shovelnose Snakes
2 species

Chionactis occipitalis
Western Shovelnose Snake
4 subspecies

PHYSICAL CHARACTERISTICS: The head is hardly set off from the neck. The upper jaw protrudes quite a bit beyond the lower one. The body looks slender but strong. The scales are not keeled. Back and sides are grayish-white or greenish-white to straw-colored, and the belly is solid grayish or greenish-white. Twenty-one or more dark to blackish, saddle-shaped crossbands cover the back and reach halfway down the sides. Between these dark bands there are often, though not always, more saddle markings that are orange to red in color. A dark crossband covers the top of the head and extends down to the eyes.

LENGTH: Slightly over 14 inches (35 cm).

DISTRIBUTION AND BEHAVIOR: *E. occipitalis* is distributed from southwestern Nevada to northwestern Mexico, where it lives in desertlike regions and often seeks out the driest spots. It is found mostly in sandy plains with scant vegetation composed of cacti, mesquite and creosote scrub, and desert grasses and is especially frequent in sand dunes and near rocks surrounded by windswept sand. This species has adapted completely to life in the desert and in loose sand. The streamlined head with its protruding upper jaw is ideally suited for burrowing. The snake can glide through the sand effortlessly with its smooth scales while the angled belly plates supply the necessary push to move ahead. Thus this small desert snake is able to disappear into the sand in no time in the presence of danger. It stays underground during the day but comes to the surface at night, leaving behind its characteristic tracks. Being so small in size, this snake eats only tiny creatures such as insects, spiders, scorpions, centipedes, and occasionally a small lizard. Hibernation lasts 4 to 5 months, and mating takes place between March and May. From the 2 to 9 eggs, little snakes measuring 4 to 5 inches (10-12 cm) emerge.

CAPTIVITY AND BREEDING: *C. occipitalis* can be kept in a small terrarium with a sandy bottom and a few rocks. During the day the temperature should be between 77° and 86°F (25°-30°C) and at night, between 64° and 68°F (18°-20°C). A heater underneath the terrarium is desirable to heat one area of the sand to 86°F (30°C) or slightly above. There should always be fresh water in the water dish. Since this snake is nocturnal one hardly ever gets a chance to see it during the day, but it comes out of hiding in the evening, at night, and in the early morning. It eats readily in captivity and thus usually lasts quite well. A diet of mealworms, grasshoppers, crickets, and freshly hatched lizards is suitable for it. Three to 4 months of winter rest at 50° to 59°F (10°-15°C) are recommended. To my knowledge this snake has not been bred in captivity.

Genus *Eirenis*
Dwarf Snakes
10 species

Eirenis modestus
Asia Minor Dwarfsnake
2 subspecies
(photo, page 104)

PHYSICAL CHARACTERISTICS: The head is barely set off from the neck, and the large eyes have round pupils. The body and the tail are long and slender. This Dwarf Snake is solid gray, brown, or cream-colored on the back and sides and porcelain to a dirty white on the belly. The top of the head has two clearly marked, dark brown crossbands, and the neck is encircled by a gray, brown, or black ring that may be quite indistinct. The smooth scales have light centers and dark rims.

LENGTH: Rarely above 20 inches (50 cm).

DISTRIBUTION AND BEHAVIOR: This snake is native to the extreme southeastern parts of Europe and to western Asia. It occurs primarily in mountainous regions where it favors sunny slopes with sparse vegetation and rocky ground. It spends the hot part of the day underneath rocks, among loose stones, and in crevices. Sometimes it lies in the sun in the early morning or in the evening. Depending on the altitude at which it lives and on the weather *E. modestus* leaves its winter den in March or April. The mating takes place after the spring's first molt, and in June or July, 4 to 8 eggs are laid. The young measure about 4 inches (10 cm) when they hatch. The Asia Minor Dwarfsnake lives on grasshoppers, beetles, spiders, and occasionally lizards.

CAPTIVITY AND BREEDING: A small terrarium will do for this snake. Loam or garden soil with some sand are a good bottom material. Some stones and pieces of bark can be piled up in imitation of the scree at the foot of a slope and provide places of concealment, and some potted plants will lend a natural look to the terrarium. A small dish with fresh water is essential, and now and then some water should be sprayed in the terrarium because this snake likes to lick up the drops of water. If no morning or afternoon sun is available, 8 to 10 hours of artificial light should be provided, and localized bottom heat is necessary. During the day the air should be 77° to 86°F (25°-30°C) and at night 64° to 68°F (18°-20°C). *E. modestus* is an easy snake to keep and is not fussy about its food. It can be given grasshoppers, crickets, and small lizards. The latter is held by the snake in a tight embrace before swallowing. In the summer the Asia Minor Dwarfsnake usually does not emerge from its retreat until early evening. A hibernation of 4 to 6 months—depending on where the snake was captured—is necessary. There is no information on breeding this snake in captivity.

Genus *Phyllorhynchus*
Leafnose Snakes
2 species

Phyllorhynchus decurtatus
Spotted Leafnose Snake
5 subspecies

PHYSICAL CHARACTERISTICS: The tapered, spatula-shaped head is not set off from the neck, and the grotesquely enlarged rostral shield curls up in front and sticks out on the sides. The eyes are large. *P. decurtatus* is one of only a handful of North American colubrids with slitlike pupils. The dorsal scales are generally smooth. Only the males sometimes have faintly keeled dorsal scales. The ground color of the body varies from yellowish-brown to reddish, yellowish, or pale gray with up to 60 brown blotches along the spine and smaller spots along the sides spaced between the dorsal blotches. The belly is a uniform white.

LENGTH: Up to 20 inches (50 cm).

DISTRIBUTION AND BEHAVIOR: *P. decurtatus* occurs in southern Nevada, southeastern California, western and southern Arizona, and in the Mexican states of Sonora and Sinaloa. It lives in deserts up to altitudes of 3000 feet (1000 m) where creosote and mesquite bushes and saguaro cacti grow. This snake is active exclusively at night and leads a secretive existence hidden in crevices, under rocks, and in the burrows of rodents. For this reason it was in the past thought to be quite rare. In actuality, however, it is one of the most common species in its native regions and is often run over in considerable numbers at night on the highways. With the aid of its well-developed rostral shield it is able to burrow easily in the ground. Its diet consists of lizards, especially geckos of the *Coleonyx* genus. But it also eats lizards' eggs and insects and considers the tender gecko tails a special treat. Any collector of reptiles roaming the southwestern United States should therefore be careful not to put geckos in the same bag with this snake. Very little is known about the reproductive habits of the Spotted Leafnose Snake except that it lays 2 to 4 eggs. The snakes are about 6¼ to 7 inches (16-18 cm) long when they hatch.

CAPTIVITY AND BREEDING: *P. decurtatus* is rarely kept in captivity. To feel comfortable it needs a small desert terrarium. The setup and environmental requirements are the same as for the Glossy Snake (*Arizona elegans*), but since the Leafnose Snake feeds exclusively on lizards and geckos it is not a likely choice for many snake fanciers. *P. decurtatus* has not yet been bred in captivity.

RACERS

Genus *Masticophis*
American Whip Snakes
7 species

Masticophis flagellum
Coachwhip
7 subspecies
(photo, page 103)

PHYSICAL CHARACTERISTICS: The long, narrow head is barely set off from the neck, and the large eyes have round pupils. The body and tail are long and slender. The scales are smooth and the anal plate divided. The head and anterior body of *M. f. flagellum*, which is found in the eastern and southeastern states, are more or less brown to black. This color gradually changes into a dark brown and lightens visibly on the tail. The coloration of the belly resembles that of the back and body sides. Sometimes one finds entirely black individuals or ones with a black body and a red tail. The western subspecies *M. f. testaceus* is a light yellowish-brown or dark- or reddish-brown. There are animals of a solid color and ones with narrow or wide crossbands.

LENGTH: Up to 102 inches (260 cm).

DISTRIBUTION AND BEHAVIOR: This snake is distributed widely from North Carolina across the eastern, central, western, and southern United States and far into Mexico. It inhabits dry and wet areas and is found in forests with sandy soil, in the prairie, in shrubby country, and in mountains as high up as 8500 feet (2600 m), as well as in cactus deserts and along swamps. The Coachwhip is a lively and extremely fast-moving animal that often crawls along with its head in the air. It is difficult to catch. If it is surprised on its own turf it makes for some bushes or a thicket of cacti like an arrow, and if it finds itself cornered it puts up an active defense, coming right up to the attacker. In its excitement it vibrates its tail and creates a sound in the dry leaves or grass that is reminiscent of the noise of a rattlesnake. If it is caught it reacts vehemently and bites fiercely, digging its teeth deep into the flesh and tossing its head and upper body back and forth and causing painful, deep wounds. Coachwhips are diurnal and dwell not only on the ground but frequently move along bushes and trees, too. They are very little bothered by dry weather and survive the hot summer days that are common in their range better than most other reptiles. Small mammals, young birds, snakes, lizards, and in some rare cases young turtles and frogs constitute their diet. Coachwhips hibernate from September or October to March or April, often together with rattlesnakes. Matings usually take place in April or May, and between June and August 10 to 20 elliptical eggs with small tubercles are laid. The little snakes generally hatch after 50 to 60 days and measure 12 to 16 inches (30-41 cm).

CAPTIVITY AND BREEDING: *M. flagellum* is very tense at first in a terrarium and sometimes tries to bite anyone who passes near its cage, but this changes with time. This snake needs a large terrarium with hiding places, climbing branches, and a small water dish. This last item is especially crucial because the Coachwhip frequently drinks from the dish even though it otherwise tolerates no moisture and needs to be kept absolutely dry if it is to thrive. Localized bottom heat is a must, and 12 to 14 hours of artificial light should be supplied. During the day the air temperature should lie between 77° and 86°F (25°-30°C); at night it can drop somewhat. *M. flagellum* is a voracious eater and can be offered a diet of mice, small rats, and chicks. If offspring are desired a hibernation period of 3 to 4 months at lowered temperatures is necessary. This snake has been bred repeatedly in captivity. Under these artificial conditions the eggs take 76 to 79 days to hatch.

Genus *Coluber*
Racers
19 species

Coluber constrictor
American Racer
12 subspecies

PHYSICAL CHARACTERISTICS: The head of this slender but strong snake is a longish oval and hardly set off from the neck. The large eyes have round pupils. The scales are smooth, and the anal plate divided. Coloration varies considerably from subspecies to subspecies. In the subspecies *C. c. constrictor* the head and the top of the body are olive colored to black. Juveniles are gray and have brown blotches on the back and black dots on the sides. The belly is dark gray to greenish-yellow. *C. c. anthicus* is black on top with extensive white speckling.

C. c. foxi is blue with a dark band on both sides of the head, and *C. c. flaviventris* has a yellow belly and is brown on the top and sides.

LENGTH: 4 to 5 feet (120-150 cm); rarely up to 6½ feet (2 m).

DISTRIBUTION AND BEHAVIOR: This Racer ranges from southwestern and southeastern Canada almost throughout the entire United States and across Mexico all the way to Guatemala. It is considered one of the most common North American snakes and inhabits dry and wet regions and flat lands as well as mountains, where it can be found as high up as about 6500 feet (2000 m). It likes wasteland grown over with scrub, dry and wet forests, meadows, edges of fields, sand dunes, mountain slopes, and cultivated as well as wild land. It is very agile both on the ground and in the branches of trees and bushes. The Racer flees at the slightest sign of danger, often escaping with great speed up into bushes and trees. But if it is cornered it bites furiously and whips the tip of its tail, creating sounds in the dry leaves similar to the noise produced by rattlesnakes. The diet of Racers consists of small mammals, birds, lizards, snakes, and occasionally frogs and insects. It does not kill its prey by constriction but by pressing it against the ground with its head. It hibernates for 4 to 6 months, often together with snakes of different species. Matings take place in the spring. While mating, the male often hangs on the female by biting her in the neck. The female generally lays up to 42 longish eggs in June in a protected spot, and the young snakes hatch anytime from July to September. They measure 8 to 12 inches (20-30 cm) at birth.

CAPTIVITY AND BREEDING: The American Racer is not always easy to take care of in a terrarium. Some individuals quickly adjust to life in captivity and become tame while others stay nervous and timid, languishing and gradually wasting away. For a Racer one needs a large terrarium with a layer of sand and forest soil at the bottom and, most important, with a good hiding place. A large enough water basin is also important since these snakes like to bathe now and then. Artificial lights are necessary for 8 to 10 hours a day unless the terrarium gets morning and afternoon sun. Localized bottom heat is also necessary. The temperature should range between 68° and 82°F (20-28°C) during the day and 64° to 68°F (18-20°C) at night. A tree stump or some branches should also be provided because the Racer likes to climb. In a terrarium the Racer is active, particularly during the day. It can be fed with mice and chicks. Three to 4 months of wintering over at temperatures between 41° and 59°F (5°-15°C) are necessary.

It is apparently not difficult to breed this snake in captivity and offpsring have been produced a number of times in terrariums. If kept at 75° to 82°F (24°-28° C), the eggs take 51 to 63 days to hatch. The young snakes are fed newborn mice or possibly small lizards after the first molt.

Coluber hippocrepis
Horseshoe Whipsnake
(photo, page 139)

PHYSICAL CHARACTERISTICS: The head is barely set off from the neck, and the large eyes have round pupils. The body looks moderately slender and strong, and the tail is long and tapered. The scales are smooth and the anal plate undivided. Depending on age the color of the Horseshoe Whipsnake is grayish-green, yellowish, or orange. A dark band runs across the center of the head, and a horseshoe-shaped mark is formed by light and dark colors on the back of the head. A row of dark, lozenge-shaped blotches with light rims runs down the center of the back from the neck to the tip of the tail. The sides also have regularly spaced spots. The belly is a uniform yellowish to orange color with some black blotches especially toward the tail.

LENGTH: 4 to 5 feet (120–150 cm); occasionally up to 6½ feet (2 m).

DISTRIBUTION AND BEHAVIOR: The Horseshoe Whipsnake is at home on the Pyranean peninsula, in northwestern Africa, and on Pantellaria. It inhabits flatlands as well as mountains and prefers dry, rocky terrain dotted with a lot of brush. It is a lively and aggressive snake that is quick to bite. At the slightest disturbance it flees, but it will defend itself ferociously if attacked. It displays no great tendency to climb and is more of a ground dweller that likes to spend its time in the burrows of rodents, under stones, and among bushes. The Horseshoe Whipsnake is active during the day as well as at night. In the morning it likes to sun itself; then it withdraws to its retreat around noon and often does not reappear until dusk. It feeds on small mammals, birds, and lizards and crushes its prey before eating it. Mating season is in April or May after a hibernation period of 4 to 5 months. In the summer, 5 to 10 eggs are laid, which hatch between July and September.

CAPTIVITY AND BREEDING: This handsome snake presents no problems to its keeper if it is kept in a terrarium with completely dry bottom material. A water dish is essential. For the bottom, a mixture of sand and loam is used, and a retreat is provided under some flat rocks or a tree stump. The snakes like to lie on a bottom heater that radiates very mild warmth. Lights should be on 10 to 12 hours a day if there is no morning and afternoon sun. The Horseshoe Whipsnake is comfortable at 72° to 82°F (22°-28°C) during the day. At night the temperature should drop a little. *C. hippocrepis* overcomes its shyness only slowly in captivity. If it is disturbed it immediately withdraws to its hiding place. As food, mice, chicks, and sparrows are offered. Prey is accepted both dead and alive. The Horseshoe Whipsnakes I have eat 4 to 6 mice in the course of one or two weeks. A hibernation from November to March is necessary. This species has reproduced in captivity.

Coluber jugularis
Caspian Whipsnake
4 subspecies

PHYSICAL CHARACTERISTICS: The head of this powerful snake looks longish and is set off only slightly from the neck. The tail is long and tapered. The large eyes have round pupils, and the scales are smooth. The coloration of the back and the sides can vary considerably and ranges from olive gray to light or dark brown and black. The scales have dark upper and lower edges and yellow median lines which form parallel longitudinal stripes. The top of the head has regular dark blotches. The belly is yellowish, brown, reddish-yellow, brick red, or black.

LENGTH: 6 feet (180 cm); occasionally up to 10 feet (3 m).

DISTRIBUTION AND BEHAVIOR: The Caspian Whipsnake is found in southeastern Europe and Asia Minor. It likes steppelike wasteland and mountain slopes with bushes where it hides away in rock crevices and thick scrub. *C. jugularis* is diurnal and likes to sun itself in the morning and afternoon. The name Whipsnake is quite appropriate because the movements of this snake are extremely fast. When there is any sign of danger the snake shoots down a mountain slope into some scree, a crevice, or some other hiding place in a flash. If it is cornered or held fast it fights ferociously. When it bites it does not let go but keeps clamping down with chewing motions. The bite of a large Whipsnake can cause serious wounds. The snake's diet consists of various small mammals, birds, lizards, and snakes. Small prey is consumed alive, and larger animals are killed by being squeezed against the ground. Matings take place in early May, and usually 7 to 10 oval eggs are laid sometime between the end of June and early August.

CAPTIVITY AND BREEDING: A large terrarium is required for this snake with some good opportunities for hiding among rocks, in a tree stump, or a hollow piece of decorative cork. A climbing tree with many branches and a built-in water container are also required, as well as localized bottom heat. If there is no access to morning and afternoon sun, 10 to 12 hours of artificial light have to be provided. A mixture of coarse sand and loam or limestone can be used for the bottom. *C. jugularis* is active during the day in a terrarium. It likes to climb onto branches and bask under a heat lamp. During the day it needs temperatures between 77° and 86°F (25°- 30°C), and at night between 64° and 68°F (18°- 20°C). The Caspian Whipsnake adjusts only slowly to life in captivity and it becomes really tame only in rare cases. Young animals work out best for a terrarium. Depending on the size of the snake it can be offered rats, mice, sparrows, or chicks. Since *C. jugularis* has been known to eat other members of its own species it is best to keep this snake singly. It needs 3 to 5 months of hibernation. Apparently nobody has yet succeeded in breeding this snake in captivity and obtaining offspring.

Coluber najadum
Dahl's Whipsnake
3 subspecies

PHYSICAL CHARACTERISTICS: The head is only barely set off from the neck, and the extremely slender and pliable body is hardly thicker than a pencil. The tail is thin and long. The large eyes have round pupils, and the scales are smooth, though on the tips there are small pits with tactile spots. The upper side of the body is fawn-colored to reddish-brown. Head and neck are light gray, the tail region is greenish-gray, and the belly porcelain-colored to yellowish. On both sides of the neck there are between 3 and 20 oval, dark dots, which are rimmed with white or pale yellow and get progressively smaller toward the back. A dark stripe runs from the nostril across the eyes and to the corners of the mouth.

LENGTH: Rarely over 52 inches (130 cm).

DISTRIBUTION AND BEHAVIOR: *C. najadum* is widely distributed across the Balkan peninsula, Asia Minor, Syria, and northwestern Persia. It lives both on flatlands and in mountains, where it is found in rocky and craggy terrain with a lot of bushes. Dahl's Whipsnake loves warmth and is active during the day. It likes to bask in the sun near bushes and among rocks. If it is disturbed it dashes away like an arrow and is difficult to catch. Sometimes it climbs into the bushes and hides cleverly. When it is seized it tries to free itself by writhing wildly and biting. Like the Ringed Snake it sprays a foul-smelling liquid in the process. Dahl's Whipsnake lives almost exclusively on lizards and occasionally eats some insects. They chase their prey with remarkable speed and swallow it while it is still alive. In October they retire to their winter quarters and do not reappear until late March or early April. Matings usually take place in April or May, and between June and August a few long and thin eggs—usually no more than 3 to 5—are deposited in holes, crevices, and under stones.

CAPTIVITY AND BREEDING: *C. najadum* needs a large desert terrarium with weak bottom heat. The bottom is covered with a mixture of sand and loam, and a few flat rocks are added to supply hiding places. A small water dish should also be provided. Climbing branches are not absolutely necessary because the Dahl's Whipsnake spends most of its time on the ground. If the terrarium does not get the morning and afternoon sun, artificial lights should be on 10 to 12 hours. Some individuals adjust only poorly to captivity, are fussy, and are reluctant to accept food. For this reason it is best to keep this snake singly. Wall lizards (*Lacerta*) or other lizards of comparable size are offered for food. If kept under the proper conditions, Dahl's Whipsnake is quite voracious. A winter rest of 3 to 5 months at temperatures lowered to between 41° and 59°F (5°- 15°C) is necessary. So far no reproduction in captivity has been reported.

Coluber ravergieri
Desert Whipsnake
4 subspecies
(photo, page 140)

PHYSICAL CHARACTERISTICS: The head looks longish but is clearly set off from the neck. The moderately large eyes have round pupils. The body is sturdy, and the scales lightly keeled.

The back and sides are grayish-brown to olive gray. On the uniformly gray top of the head there are sometimes a few dark stains, and a dark brown stripe with light borders runs across the forehead from eye to eye. Another stripe connects the eye to the corner of the mouth and runs on toward the neck region. The markings on the back consist of regularly spaced lozenge-shaped blotches. Some individuals look as though they had been sprinkled with a fine, dark powder. The dark markings may be faint and hardly visible, or they may stand out prominently. The belly is grayish-white with brown spots.

LENGTH: Over 3 feet (1 m).

DISTRIBUTION AND BEHAVIOR: *C. ravergieri* is distributed from Rhodos to Central Asia. It lives in semiarid regions and on brush-covered mountain slopes. It is an agile and shy diurnal snake that likes to sun itself in the morning and afternoon close to a protective bush, a boulder, or a pile of rocks. If it is seized it is quick to bite. Its diet consists of small mammals, birds, and lizards, which it strangles and then swallows head first. Matings take place in the spring. In July, 5 to 10 oval eggs are laid. The young hatch in September and already measure up to 9½ inches (24 cm).

CAPTIVITY AND BREEDING: *C. ravergieri* presents no special problems to the keeper. A medium-sized terrarium is needed with a bottom of sand and loam, several flat rocks and pieces of decorative cork to provide hiding places, a small water dish, and localized bottom heat. Eight to 10 hours of artificial light are required and daytime temperatures between 72° and 86°F (22°-30°C). A nightly drop of several degrees benefits the health of the snakes. My Desert Whipsnake was at first quite wild, scared easily, and was quick to bite. But it calmed down soon and began to eat white mice which it always strangled first. From its natural habitat *C. ravergieri* is used to hibernating for 4 to 5 months. Thus far this snake has not reproduced in captivity.

Coluber viridiflavus
European Whipsnake
2 subspecies

PHYSICAL CHARACTERISTICS: This snake is slender with a long, tapered tail and a longish head that is only moderately set off from the neck. The scales are smooth, and the ground color of the body is black. The subspecies *carbonarius* is solid black whereas *C. v. viridiflavus* has a network of yellowish-green crossbands and speckles on the upper body and middle. On the lower third the black and green markings gradually change into parallel longitudinal lines. The belly is yellowish gray. Juveniles are a more or less uniform yellowish-gray. The ventral plates have some dark spots on the sides. The head is mottled with yellow and black dots with black dominating on the top and yellow on the sides of the neck and around the eyes.

LENGTH: Up to 6 feet (180 cm).

DISTRIBUTION AND BEHAVIOR: This snake occurs in northeastern Spain, France, southern Switzerland, Italy, and northwestern Yugoslavia, as well as on Sicily, Malta, Pelagosa, Sardinia, Corsica, and Elba. It is encountered primarily in dry and rocky terrain with low shrubs. It moves extremely fast and is therefore hard to catch. When it is grasped it bites immediately and holds on with chewing motions, often turning around its own axis in the process. The European Whipsnake is primarily diurnal. It often climbs up on low shrubs to sun itself there and lie in wait for birds. It eats various small mammals, lizards, blindworms, snakes, and frogs, as well as grasshoppers, beetles, and snails. Depending on the size of the animal it either strangles the prey first or swallows it alive. Matings take place in April or May. The two snakes intertwine their bodies for mating, and the male often holds onto the female's neck with his teeth. The eggs are deposited between late June to early September. Generally a clutch consists of 8 to 15 eggs, sometimes more. They take 6 to 8 weeks to hatch. The newborn snakes measure about 10 inches (25 cm).

CAPTIVITY AND BREEDING: *C. viridiflavus* is kept in a terrarium exactly the same way as *C. jugularis*. Keeping them singly is recommended because the European Whipsnake sometimes develops cannabilistic tendencies in captivity. They should therefore also not be combined with snakes of different species. They are offered mostly mice and chicks as food rather than lizards and frogs. The Dark Green Racer tracks its prey down mostly with the help of its eyes. It then strikes at the prey animal very fast and kills it by constriction or by pressing it against the ground. Different animals respond very differently to captivity. Some individuals adjust rapidly and accept food offered to them from the beginning while others are frantic at first, refuse to eat, and calm down only gradually. Several females that were caught gravid have deposited eggs in terrariums, but there are no reports so far of reproduction that was initiated in captivity.

Genus *Spalerosophis*
Desert Racers
2 species

Spalerosophis diadema
Diadem Snake
4 subspecies

PHYSICAL CHARACTERISTICS: The longish, slightly triangular head is noticeably set off from the neck, and the large eyes have round pupils that contract into a tiny point in bright light. The body is slender, and the scales are lightly keeled. The anal plate is undivided. Coloration varies considerably. The upper side of the body is gray, ochre, yellowish, or reddish. Red or brown blotches run down the middle of the back. The head has a pattern of dark, irregular blotches. The subspecies *S. d. atriceps* is covered with irregular black blotches or black all over. It seems possible, however, that this subspecies is nothing more than a variation of *S. d. diadema* caused by age because the young of the two races are practically, if not altogether, indistinguishable from each other and occur in the same range. In the subspecies *S. d. atriceps* the black blotches do

not start to show up until the snakes are half grown. The belly is reddish or whitish and either partially blotched or unicolored.

LENGTH: 5 feet (1.5 m); rarely 6 1/2 feet (2 m).

DISTRIBUTION AND BEHAVIOR: *S. diadema* has a huge distribution reaching from northern Africa across Asia Minor and the Arabian peninsula all the way to Pakistan and India. It inhabits lowlands and mountains up to about 6500 feet (2000 m). The favorite habitat of this snake is various kinds of desert. I caught two specimens of this species in a sand desert in southern Tunisia and caught sight of another one in a rocky desert in southern Morocco. The Diadem Snake lives hidden under rocks, in crevices, and especially often in the tunnels of rodent burrows. In the spring *S. diadema* is largely diurnal whereas in the summer it wanders about at night. It feeds on lizards, small birds, and rodents, killing its prey by strangling it or by crushing it against the ground. Matings usually occur in the spring. Then 3 to 16 eggs, measuring about 3 by 1 1/4 inches (80 × 30 cm) and all stuck together in a clutch are laid. Occasionally a female will deposit two clutches in one season.

CAPTIVITY AND BREEDING: To be comfortable this snake needs a medium to large desert terrarium with a layer of sand on the bottom, a small water dish, and some flat rocks for hiding under. A well functioning bottom heater is an absolute must. Air temperatures during the day should measure 77° to 86°F (25°-30°C) and can drop to about 75°F (24°C) at night. Twelve to 14 hours of artificial light should be provided. This snake is also particularly fond of direct sunlight. Mice, young rats, chicks, and sparrows are offered as food. If properly cared for, *S. diadema* lasts for a long time in captivity. It usually eats without problems though it will occasionally fast for a while. Depending on where a given snake was captured it should be allowed to rest for 2 to 3 months in a cooler environment of 50° to 61°F (10°-16°C). This species has reproduced in captivity.

Genus *Dasypeltis*
African Egg-eating Snakes
5 species

Dasypeltis scabra
Common Egg-eater

PHYSICAL CHARACTERISTICS: The head is small and hardly set off from the neck, and the eyes have vertical slits for pupils. The snout is rounded. There are 3 to 9 very small non-functional teeth embedded in the tissue of each half of the upper mandible. The longish scales are clearly keeled. Thorn-like extensions of the vertabrae covered with something like tooth enamel penetrate far into the esophagus. The ground color of the body is gray, yellow, or brown, and there is a row of black blotches running down the spine. These blotches sometimes merge together and form a broken zigzag band. The sides of the body also have fairly regularly spaced blotches. On the head there are two dark marks that meet at an acute angle. The belly is whitish to yellowish, either solid or with dark blotches.

LENGTH: 28 to 36 inches (70-90 cm).

DISTRIBUTION AND BEHAVIOR: The Common Egg-eater is found in southern Arabia as well as from eastern and central Africa down to South Africa. This species, which is both terrestrial and arboreal in its habits, lives in dry forests and bushy regions. *D. scabra* is an expert climber and is often seen near birds' nests. It feeds exclusively on birds' eggs, which it steals mostly at night, the time of its greatest activity. The head of a fully grown Common Egg-eater is barely as thick as a finger, but the animal manages to dispose of a chicken egg without the slightest difficulty. When it finds an egg it opens its mouth very wide, pushes the egg against a firm surface, and begins to ingest it pointed end first. The skin of the throat and the walls of the oral cavity expand enormously in the process. Propelled by the snake's muscles the egg is choked down past the hard extensions of the vertebrae, which slit

the shell. The inside of the egg then moves on to the stomach while the shell is regurgitated. Occasionally a snake may find a plaster egg in a chicken house, and because this fake egg has taken on the smell and the body temperature of the hen the snake may mistake it for a real egg and try to swallow it. In such a case the snake has to disgorge the fake egg or die. Common Egg-eaters do not attack humans. In situations of danger they roll and unroll their bodies, thus creating a rasping noise. When angry they inflate their bodies and strike out ferociously at the intruder, but they are completely harmless. Because they resemble the Night Adder (*Causus rhomeatus*) in their coloration and behavior, they are often mistaken for this snake and killed. *D. scabra* lays 12 to 15 eggs in December or January and sometimes as late as April or May. These eggs are deposited singly and not, as is usual for most snakes, in a clutch that sticks together. When the young hatch after 3 to 4 months they measure about 9 inches (23 cm).

CAPTIVITY AND BREEDING: If kept under the proper conditions the Common Egg-eater does well in a terrarium and may live over 10 years. Even though it may be hostile at the beginning it rarely bites, and its tiny teeth do not break through the skin. In time it gets so tame that it will take chicken eggs (use only small ones) and pigeon eggs from the keeper's hand. The best feeding time is evening. Sometimes *D. scabra* goes on a fast in the spring and summer. This snake should be kept in a medium-sized, dry terrarium with a sandy bottom, some rocks and climbing branches, a potted plant, and a small water dish, from which it will drink regularly. Localized bottom heat is required. Lights should be on 10 to 12 hours a day. The temperature should range between 72° and 86°F (22°-30°C) during the day and drop a few degrees at night. This snake has been bred in the Lincoln Park Zoo in Chicago, and eggs laid by females gravid at time of capture have, after artificial incubation, hatched on a number of occasions.

Genus *Salvadora*
Patchnose Snakes
7 species

Salvadora grahamiae
Mountain Patchnose Snake
2 subspecies

PHYSICAL CHARACTERISTICS: The head is hardly set off from the neck, and the large rostral plate forms a patch that curves up and extends over the tip of the snout and protrudes slightly on the sides. The large eyes have round pupils. With its long, thin body and tail this snake is reminiscent of the whipsnakes of the *Masticophis* genus. The scales are smooth, and the anal plate is divided. The body is whitish, pale gray, yellowish, or brownish, and two rather wide and dark brown or almost black stripes run down the back starting on the sides of the snout and ending on the sides of the tail. The subspecies *S. g. lineata* has a fine black line running parallel to and underneath these stripes. The band on the back is lighter than the sides of the body. The belly is a uniform grayish-white.

LENGTH: Up to 38 inches (95 cm).

DISTRIBUTION AND BEHAVIOR: *S. grahamiae* is found in the mountains of Arizona, New Mexico, Texas, Oklahoma, and northeastern Mexico at altitudes between 4000 and 8200 feet (1300-2500 m). It lives on rocky slopes and in grassy clearings with a few scattered pines or cedars. This very fast snake is active primarily during the day and usually spends the afternoon away from its retreat. With its broad rostral plate it can dig in the loose sand, but sometimes it also climbs onto low bushes. When it is taken by surprise it dashes under a large rock or some flat stones like an arrow. Its food consists mostly of lizards, but it will also eat small mammals and birds. The Mountain Patchnose Snake comes out of hibernation as early as February or March and mates soon after. The eggs are laid in April or May, and the young snakes hatch in August measuring 8 to 10 inches (21-25 cm).

CAPTIVITY AND BREEDING: The Mountain Patchnose Snake should be kept in a dry terrarium of generous proportions and with a sandy bottom. A few flat rocks and a small water dish are required, as well as bottom heat and 12 to 14 hours of artificial light. These warmth loving snakes are also very fond of the morning or afternoon sun. Daytime temperatures should range between 77° and 86°F (25°-30°C) and drop a little at night. *S. grahamiae* becomes tame quite quickly in captivity. Although its active period is really during the day this snake has the peculiarity of not going after mice and lizards offered as food until dusk or night. Often it is hard to entice it to eat. In nature it is used to hibernating for 3 to 4 months in cooler weather, and a winter rest is therefore in order in captivity as well.

There are no reports of this snake reproducing in captivity, but in several instances females that were gravid when captured laid eggs in terrariums. One snake keeper had a female that laid 10 eggs on April 1, 1941, which hatched between August 4 and 10. The young snakes were very lively, crawling around the terrarium and biting when disturbed. The first molt took place between August 12 and 26.

Genus *Opheodrys*
Green Snakes
3 species

Opheodrys aestivus
Rough Greensnake
(photo, page 103)

PHYSICAL CHARACTERISTICS: *O. aestivus* is a very long, thin snake with a narrow head that is barely set off from the neck. The large eyes have round pupils. The scales are keeled, and the anal plate divided. The back is grass green, turning lighter on the sides. The belly is porcelain-white, yellowish, or pale green.

LENGTH: Up to 46 inches (116 cm).

DISTRIBUTION AND BEHAVIOR: This snake lives in one connected area reaching from Connecticut to Florida in the east, from Ohio and Indiana to Kansas and Texas in the west, and to Tampico, Mexico in the south. It is a truly arboreal species that spends most of its time in low trees, bushes, and tall grass. Its color is so well adapted to its environment that it is generally overlooked unless it moves. Its favorite haunts are the dense vegetation along the banks of moving and still water. Sometimes it enters the water and then lives a partially aquatic existence. The Rough Greensnake is not a rare species, and it is particularly common on the little islands of thick growth, or hummocks, of the Everglades in Florida. There it lies draped over the branches of bushes and trees and slithers from one tree to the next with amazing ease. This snake sometimes sticks its tongue out of its mouth and leaves it out without flicking it. Its diet consists of all kinds of insects, spiders, and even snails and frogs. It begins its active period in March or April and goes into hibernation in October or November, depending on the geographic and climatic conditions of its environment. Matings take place in the spring and sometimes in the fall as well. Up to 12 eggs, all stuck together in a clump, are deposited between June and August. The 6- to 8-inch-long (15-20 cm) snakes hatch after 1½ to 3 months.

CAPTIVITY AND BREEDING: This snake requires a medium-sized terrarium with many climbing branches that offer good holds as well as plenty of creeping plants, rocks, and pieces of bark. A mixture of sand and forest soil is used for the bottom. About a third of the floor area should be taken up by water. No bottom heat is necessary, but artificial light should be provided for 12 to 14 hours. The air should measure between 77° and 86°F (25°-30°C) during the day and about 9°F (5°C) less at night. *O. aestivus* thrives much better in captivity than *O. vernalis*. It can be fed all kinds of insects, such as grasshoppers, cockroaches, hover flies, crickets, dragonflies, and spiders. This small snake sees extremely well and is good at catching its prey in the air. It is mostly diurnal. Often it lies on branches and makes undulating movements with its anterior body without moving forward. If this snake is excited, blue blotches appear on its body. Three to 4 months of hibernation are required.

This lovely snake has not thus far been bred in captivity, but a female that was gravid at capture laid 10 eggs on June 27, 1963. The eggs were placed in moss, sprayed with a little water every day, and kept at a temperature between 81° and 90°F (27°-32°C). Little snakes hatched out of them on August 2 of that year.

Opheodrys vernalis
Smooth Greensnake
2 subspecies

PHYSICAL CHARACTERISTICS: This snake is not as long and slender as the one described above, but its somewhat shorter head is hardly set off from the neck at all. The eyes with their large pupils are especially large. The tail is shorter, and the scales smooth. The anal plate is divided. The top of the body is dark green, and the color of the belly is somewhere between porcelain-white and yellowish.

LENGTH: Up to 26 inches (66 cm).

DISTRIBUTION AND BEHAVIOR: The Smooth Greensnake occurs from southern Canada to as far south as Texas. But its area of distribution is continuous only in the Northeast. In North Carolina, Tennessee, Oklahoma, Texas, New Mexico, Colorado, Nebraska, and Kansas the snake exists only in isolated areas. *O. vernalis* is found on flat land but more often in hilly country and even in mountains up to 10,000 feet (3000 m). In contrast to the Rough Greensnake, this species dwells on the ground and has little inclination for climbing. It lives in dry as well as in wet locations. Likely places to find it are in dry meadows, open forests, clearings, old, abandoned fields, wet grassland, and swamps. During the day it often hides under rocks, old wood, boards, cardboard boxes, old linoleum, etc. In April or May it emerges from its winter retreat to which it returns in October. Its main food consists of insects, especially caterpillars, but it also eats spiders, centipedes, snails, and even salamanders. In color it is beautifully adapted to its surroundings, but it does not move anywhere as quickly as the Rough Greensnake. Matings take place both in the spring and the summer. The 3 to 11 eggs are laid in June or July, and the young snakes, measuring 5 inches (12 cm), hatch in August or September.

CAPTIVITY AND BREEDING: This pretty snake is not as easy to keep in a terrarium as *O. aestivus*. It usually refuses to accept food and wastes away. A terrarium for this snake should have a mixture of sand and forest soil on the bottom, and some rocks and pieces of bark should be provided to hide among. Ten to 12 hours of light should be supplied as well as an optimum temperature of 77° to 81°F (25°-27°C). At night the temperature should drop a few degrees. This snake does not crush plants, and some potted climbing plants can therefore be included in the terrarium to add to its attractiveness. Usually caterpillars, spiders, and crickets are offered to this snake as food. If it refuses to eat after a short acclimating period you should try to force-feed it. Stuff it with small fish and strips of meat. This is not in keeping with the snake's natural diet, but the animals digest fish and meat well and are at least kept from starving to death. Hibernation is necessary.

The Smooth Greensnake has not been bred in captivity. Females gravid at capture have occasionally laid eggs in captivity which were then artificially incubated and produced offspring.

Genus *Drymarchon*
Indigo Snakes
1 species

Drymarchon corais
Indigo Snake
8 subspecies

PHYSICAL CHARACTERISTICS: The head is set off only little from the neck. The body looks very powerful and is somewhat flattened on the upper sides so that there is a faint ridge along the spine. The scales are smooth, and the anal plate is undivided. When excited this snake inflates its throat and head, which, being puffed out like this, present a flat vertical surface. The brown, dark brown, or bluish-black upper side of the body has a wonderful glossy and metallic look, especially after a molt. The belly may be olive gray, dark green, or bluish-gray. The throat and the chin are sometimes orange to coral red.

LENGTH: Up to 105 inches (270 cm).

DISTRIBUTION AND BEHAVIOR: The Indigo Snake is found from the southeastern United States all the way to Argentina. *D. c. couperi*, the subspecies most commonly kept as a pet, comes from South Carolina, Georgia, Florida, Alabama, and Louisiana. The Indigo Snake is a creature of the flat land and lives in both dry and wet locations. Some of its favorite environments are flat pine and oak forests and sandy elevations with low palmetto trees. It is found less frequently near swamps. Sometimes it is seen in the water. This snake is active mostly during the day and likes to spend hours lying in the sun especially in the morning. Like the Eastern Diamondback Rattlesnake (*Crotalus adamanteus*) the Indigo Snake likes to disappear into the holes of gopher tortoises (*Gopherus polyphemus*) and is therefore commonly called "gopher snake" in Florida. Its quick movements indicate how strong and active this snake is. *D. corais* lives mostly on the ground and climbs onto bushes and low trees only occasionally, though sometimes it is found stretched out full length on some branches. It has a peaceful disposition and is therefore the most popular snake in Florida to be exhibited or kept as a pet by children. Its diet is surprisingly many-sided. It eats small mammals, birds, nonpoisonous as well as poisonous snakes, lizards, turtles, frogs, fish, and eggs. It catches hold of its prey with its jaws, holds it fast, and squeezes it against the ground. Indigo Snakes mate in the spring and sometimes in the winter. The eggs measure 4 × 1¼ inches (10 × 3 cm), and the hatchling snakes are 24 to 26 inches (60-65 cm) long.

CAPTIVITY AND BREEDING: A large terrarium with a layer of coarse sand and peat at the bottom is required for this species. Localized bottom heat is indicated because these snakes clearly enjoy mild warmth from below. My Indigo Snakes spent most of their time cuddled together in the gently heated spot in the terrarium. Eight to 10 hours of lighting are adequate. During the day the temperature should be between 77° and 82°F (25°-28°C) and at night between 68° and 72°F (20°-22°C). A water container is essential. You cannot keep plants in the terrarium because Indigo Snakes always crush them in no time, but you do have to supply hiding places. This is usually done by including in the terrarium a solidly cemented structure of rocks, a hollow piece of cork oak of appropriate size, or a small wooden box. Proper temperatures and opportunities to hide are the key requirements for keeping Indigo Snakes in captivity. Freshly caught animals adjust quickly if these conditions are met. At first they will spit and quiver their tails with agitation, but after a few weeks these signs of excitement subside. Indigo Snakes are incredibly greedy eaters, but they do show some preference for certain prey animals. While some individuals consume only mice and rats, others prefer chicks, frogs, or fish. Each of my Indigo Snakes would eat up to 10 chicks at one meal or fully grown mice that they would take alive or dead from tongs or from my hand. Indigo Snakes molt at short intervals of 4 to 6 weeks. They do not need

extensive hibernation, but the temperature should be lowered to 64°-68°F (18°-20°C) during December and January.

D. c. couperi has successfully reproduced a number of times in captivity. The individuals owned by the author mated on November 26, 1974. The male crawled over the female's back with twitching motions and rubbed her back with his chin until he finally took a permanent hold of her neck with his teeth. Unfortunately the female died before it was time to deposit the eggs. Eggs that are laid are then placed in some moderately damp material and kept at temperatures between 68° and 79°F (20°-26°C). Incubation takes 12 to 14 weeks. At higher temperatures the embryos develop faster, but then they are too small when they hatch, show malformations, or are not viable.

Genus *Leptophis*
American Tree Racers
8 species

Leptophis ahaetulla
Parrot Snake
12 subspecies

PHYSICAL CHARACTERISTICS: The long head is only little set off from the neck, and the strikingly large eyes have round pupils and point forward to allow for three-dimensional vision. The upper back fangs are elongated. The body looks very slender, and the tail is long and tapered. A ventral plate is lacking. The scales on the back are more keeled in males than females. The anal plate is divided. The grass green upper side of the body of this splendidly colored snake has a metallic sheen. Sometimes a bluish-green longitudinal line runs down the middle of the back, and the sides of the body may be bronze colored. The scales on the back have a more or less black edge, and the sides of the tongue have greenish rim. The belly is whitish to yellowish-green.

LENGTH: 5 feet (1.5 m).

DISTRIBUTION AND BEHAVIOR: *L. ahaetulla* is distributed in Central and South America from southern Mexico to central Argentina. It prefers areas rich in vegetation near water and is diurnal, spending most of its time on low bushes and moving more rarely on the ground or in the tops of trees. Its dainty body moves with remarkable speed and agility. When *L. ahaetulla* feels attacked it does not always respond immediately by biting but instead opens its mouth wide, spreading its lower jaw far apart and thus creating the illusion of a much broader head. It often keeps up this threatening stance for a while. The diet of this snake consists of tree lizards and frogs. Now and then it also eats birds. Although *L. ahaetulla* is nonvenomous and has non-grooved fangs, its bite nevertheless has a mildly poisonous effect and can be very painful. But the symptoms are not very dangerous and usually disappear quickly because the poison is diluted with saliva when it enters the wound. Not much is known about the reproduction of the Parrot Snake except that it lays sticky eggs measuring $1\frac{1}{8} \times \frac{1}{2}$ inches (29 × 12 mm). In the Amazon region these snakes supposedly lay eggs at any time of year, and in one case eggs were found in some Spanish moss that had freshly fallen from a tree. This would seem to suggest that *L. ahaetulla* lays its eggs in suitable locations even on trees. These particular eggs not only survived the fall but even hatched. The little snakes measured $10\frac{1}{2}$ inches (24 cm).

CAPTIVITY AND BREEDING: The Parrot Snake is often listed in catalogues of dealers in reptiles, and since in the wild it often lives in banana plantations and hides in banana bushes, this lovely snake would in the past sometimes turn up in Europe in a shipment of bananas. As a creature of the tropics this snake needs a large and tall, humid and warm terrarium with plenty of opportunity for climbing. Consequently it makes sense to include plants in the terrarium, especially because this very light snake will not bother them much. The bottom is covered with forest soil high in organic matter and with several pieces of bark. The snakes should also have a large water basin where they will sometimes soak. *L. ahaetulla* stays on the ground most of the time and often hides under a piece of bark. Artificial lights should be on all day. These snakes are not particularly fond of direct sunshine and, in fact, tend to avoid it. Air temperatures should range between 75° and 86°F (24°-30°C) during the day and drop a little at night. Lizards and frogs are offered food and quickly succumb to the snake's poisonous saliva. Every so often Parrot Snakes enter a longish fasting period. If kept properly, these snakes are long-lived in captivity. They should, however, never be held by the tail because, as in a number of other snake species, the tail may tear off. So far *L. ahaetulla* has not reproduced in captivity.

Genus *Drymobius*
Speckled Racers
4 species

Drymobius margaritiferus
Speckled Racer
4 subspecies
(photo, page 158)

PHYSICAL CHARACTERISTICS: The head is moderately long and hardly set off from the neck. The body is slender and the tail long and tapered. The large eyes have round pupils. The dorsal scales are faintly keeled, and the anal plate is divided. The top of the head is shades of fawn to dark brown, and a black stripe runs from behind the eyes to where the neck begins. The upper and lower labials are yellowish. On the upper body and the tail the scales are bluish-green, those at the center of the body more yellowish. All scales have black rims. The belly is white to yellowish, and the ventral plates are black on the anterior rim.

LENGTH: 28 to 36 inches (70-90 cm); rarely over 52 inches (130 cm).

Descriptions of Species

DISTRIBUTION AND BEHAVIOR: The distribution of this snake extends from southern Texas along the eastern coast of Central America down to northern South America. *D. margaritiferus* lives in the plains as well as in mountains up to 5000 feet (1500 m). It prefers areas of dense vegetation near water. In July 1973 I saw a specimen of this lovely snake in the mountains of the state San Luis Potosi in Mexico. This snake, which is depicted in illustration 55, was crossing a country road around noon. This fact is all the more remarkable because the Speckled Racer is reputed to be crepuscular and nocturnal. The rocky slopes on both sides of the road were overgrown with rain forest including thick vines and ferns. The way of life in the wild of this snake has not yet been studied sufficiently. Its diet is assumed to consist of frogs, lizards, mice, and small birds. *D. margaritiferus* lays eggs measuring about $1^3/8 \times {}^1/2$ inches (3.5 × 1.5 cm). These eggs, which do not stick together, are deposited between April and August.

CAPTIVITY AND BREEDING: The Speckled Racer is a lively animal but does not bite. In the wild it supposedly dwells on the ground, but in the terrarium it likes to climb. It should be housed in a medium-sized terrarium with dry litter and a few rocks, climbing branches, and a water basin. As a nocturnal animal it stays mostly hidden during the day and comes to life at dark. If there is not adequate daylight, artificial lights should be supplied. The daytime temperatures should be kept between 75° and 86°F (24°-30°C). Frogs, lizards, mice and chicks are offered as food. In the winter the temperature should be lowered a few degrees for about 6 weeks. *D. margaritiferus* has not yet been bred in captivity, though females gravid at capture have deposited eggs. The young snakes hatched after about 50 days.

Genus *Spilotes*
Tiger Rat Snakes
1 species

Spilotes pullatus
Tiger Ratsnake
5 subspecies
(photo, page 122)

PHYSICAL CHARACTERISTICS: The Tiger Ratsnake is one of the largest and most conspicuous colubrids of South America. The conically pointed head is slightly set off from the neck, and the black eyes with their round pupils stand out clearly against the yellow to orange color around them. The sides of the body are flattened so that the snake is not round but more triangular in cross-section. The body of the snake is slender, and the tail long and tapering. Bluish-black to black crossbands that slant backward stand out clearly against the yellow to yellowish-green ground color. The yellow scales of the body are rimmed with black, and the tail is ringed with broad black and narrow orange bands. The areas behind the eyes, and the underside of the head, and the underside of the anterior body are yellowish to orange. The belly is yellow, and some of the ventral plates have black edges.

LENGTH: 10 feet (3 m); in exceptional cases up to 13 feet (4 m).

DISTRIBUTION AND BEHAVIOR: This snake has a huge distribution which extends from southern Mexico across Central and South America as far as Argentina. It lives in rain forests and areas with bushes and scrub. It is never far from water and is often found in the rafters of abandoned huts and houses. *S. pullatus* is largely diurnal. During the day it likes to rest in the branches of trees and bushes. It lives on

TOP: Transpecos Ratsnake (*Elaphe subocularis*)
BOTTOM: Red-tail Tree Racer (*Gonyosoma oxycephalum*)

all kinds of small mammals, birds, lizards, and snakes, grabbing its prey with its mouth and crushing it either by constriction or by pressing down on it against a hard surface. The Tiger Ratsnake responds with quick aggression to humans, inflating head and throat vertically. When it is furious it moves its tail back and forth quickly and noisily in a manner reminiscent of the rattling of rattlesnakes. *S. pullatus* lays eggs that adhere to each other in a sticky clutch.

CAPTIVITY AND BREEDING: The Tiger Ratsnake can be a demanding terrarium animal. Because of its huge length it needs a terrarium that also has to be tall. A large water section and numerous climbing limbs are essential. A mixture of sand and leaf mold is used for the bottom of the dry part and a few large rocks added. Artificial lights should be on 12 to 14 hours a day. Air and bottom temperatures are kept between 77° and 86°F (25°-30°C) during the day and allowed to drop just a little at night. The Tiger Ratsnake spends most of its day lying on branches. Anyone wanting to have plants in his or her terrarium has to choose extremely hard and sturdy ones if they are not to be crushed immediately. Large rubber plants and philodendrons are a possibility. Coming from a rain forest environment, *S. pullatus* likes high air humidity and an occasional showering with lukewarm water. Mice, rats, and chicks are offered for food; the best time to feed these snakes is toward evening. This snake continues to be wild and unruly in the terrarium for a long time, and sometimes it never changes. The keeper should watch to make sure that a freshly acquired snake does not rub itself sore by pushing against the front glass panel. *S. pullatus* has been successfully bred in the Moscow zoo.

TOP: Spotted Skaapsteker (*Psammophylax rhombeatus*), a dangerously *venomous* snake.
BOTTOM: Texas Longnose Snake (*Rhinocheilus lecontei tessellatus*)

Genus *Ptyas*
Oriental Ratsnakes
2 species

Ptyas mucosus
Dhaman
2 subspecies
(photo, page 140)

PHYSICAL CHARACTERISTICS: The short, oval head is barely set off from the neck, and the large eyes have round pupils. The slender body looks compressed on the sides and is triangular in cross-section. The scales are smooth. The body is yellowish to olive gray. The anterior body is unicolored but farther back there are dark crossbands. Coloration varies a great deal. There are some black individuals whose posterior bodies and tails are yellowish. Albinoes are rare among this species.

LENGTH: 6$^1/_2$ to 10 feet (2-3 m); occasionally up to 12 feet (3.6 m).

DISTRIBUTION AND BEHAVIOR: The distribution of the Dhaman is huge. This snake is found from east of the Caspian Sea to China and Formosa, and in central Asia from India to Ceylon, and in Southeast Asia in Indochina as well as on Java and Sumatra. It lives in all kinds of habitats but mostly in flat or hilly country and less frequently in mountains. Gemerally it prefers open terrain. Quite often it is found close to human settlements. This largely diurnal, lively snake likes to climb on trees and often lives close to water where it hunts frogs and toads, which form the bulk of its diet. It also eats rats, bats, birds, snakes, and lizards, prey it crushes against the ground before swallowing. The Dhaman is fearful of humans and flees when disturbed. If it is cornered it raises its anterior body, puffs up its throat, produces strange noises, and bites wildly. In India and Indochina rural poor people eat Dhamans. Mating season is usually from April to August, but depending on the geographic and climatic origin of the animals it can extend over the entire year. Some females even produce 2 clutches a year. The newborn snakes measure 14 to 18¹/₂ inches (36-47 cm).

CAPTIVITY AND BREEDING: This snake is kept in a sizable terrarium with a large water basin. Sand and loam make a good bottom material, and hollow pieces of cork or a few rocks that are cemented in place provide cover. Localized bottom heat is necessary, and lights should be on 12 to 14 hours a day. The wellbeing of the snakes is improved if they can be exposed to the morning and afternoon sun. During the day the air is kept at 77° to 86°F (25°-30°C) and at night a little cooler. Sometimes Dhamans are not very cooperative in captivity and continue to bite for a long time. *P. mucosus* is fed primarily frogs in captivity though it also eats rats and mice, which it presses down against the ground with its head until they die. Sometimes this snake has trouble digesting warmblooded prey and regurgitates it. Some individuals will get used to eating dead fish. Depending on where a given snake comes from a short hibernation at reduced temperatures may be in order. This snake has been bred in captivity. The young snakes reach sexual maturity after 20 months.

Genus *Gonyosoma*
Oriental Tree Racers
1 species

Gonyosoma oxycephalum
Red-tail Tree Racer
2 subspecies
(photo, page 175)

PHYSICAL CHARACTERISTICS: The Red-tail Tree Racer is one of the most beautiful of large snakes. It has a long head that tapers toward the snout. The eyes have round pupils, and the slender, muscular body is somewhat compressed on the sides. A black line runs from the tip of the snout across the eyes and fades away on the sides of the neck. The smooth scales are either uniformly green or green with black edges. The tail is yellowish-brown. Some animals have a light red line down the center of the tail. The belly is yellowish.

LENGTH: Up to 7¹/₂ feet (2.3 m)

DISTRIBUTION AND BEHAVIOR: This snake is distributed in southeast Asia from the eastern Himalayas across Burma, Thailand, Laos, and Cambodia to South Vietnam and Malaya as well as on the Malaysian archipelago, and the Philippines. It prefers thickly wooded regions in wet valleys and along rivers. In South Vietnam it is found with special frequency along the banks of the Mekong. It often lives on bushes near brackish water. Since it is almost completely arboreal it has taken on a green coloration that camouflages it so well that even a careful observer often overlooks it when it sleeps all curled up on a forked branch and some twigs. Young snakes are said to hide by themselves under logs. *E. oxycephala* responds with quick biting when disturbed. Its movements are remarkably fast, and it even catches birds in mid-air. But it also eats small mammals. This snake lays eggs.

CAPTIVITY AND BREEDING: Red-tail Tree Racers are considered difficult to keep and short-lived in captivity. This is certainly the case if the animals one acquires were already sick when imported. Healthy snakes, however, can thrive in captivity. A large and thickly planted terrarium with lots of branches to climb on is needed for them to feel comfortable. Forest soil, which keeps the moisture well, is used on the bottom, and a large water basin that always contains fresh water is also required. Lights should be on 12 to 14 hours a day. Since the snakes spend most of their time lying on branches a bottom heater can be dispensed with. Air temperatures should range between 81° and 90°F (27°-32°C) during the day and should drop at night, but not below 72°F (22°C). High air humidity from 80 to 100% is desirable, and for this reason the plants and the snakes should be sprayed with lukewarm water every day. Mice, baby chicks, and sparrows are offered as food. The Red-tail Tree Racer has been bred in terrariums several times, and eggs laid by females gravid at capture have hatched in captivity. If kept at about 82°F (28°C) the eggs hatch after 14 to 17 weeks, producing little snakes 18 to 18½ inches (45-47 cm) long.

TREE SNAKES

Genus *Ahaetulla*
Oriental Vinesnakes
8 species

Ahaetulla nasuta
Longnose Vinesnake
(photo, page 158)

PHYSICAL CHARACTERISTICS: The head is clearly set off from the thin neck. It is lanciform, and the snout has an elongated, proboscislike tip. The eyes are strikingly large with slit-like horizontal pupils that narrow toward the center of the head and are reminiscent of a keyhole in shape. The Longnose Vinesnake perceives objects with both eyes and therefore has three-dimensional vision. The eyes are generally focused for distance. The body of this snake is extremely thin and looks like the lash of a whip, hence its vernacular name. The scales are smooth. The top of the body is a magnificent yellow green that becomes more yellow on the sides. On each edge of the belly there is a sharply defined, yellowish-white stripe beginning at the neck and disappearing toward the tip of the tail. The belly itself is yellowish-green to yellow. Some specimens are yellow, brown, or cream colored on the top and lead gray or pink below. The underside of the head is white.

LENGTH: Sometimes over 5 feet (150 cm).

DISTRIBUTION AND BEHAVIOR: *A. nasuta* is native to tropical Southeast Asia from Sri Lanka across much of India and as far east as Indochina. It lives mostly in trees and descends to the ground only rarely. Often it lies motionless on branches and twigs with much of its body hanging in thin air, and it moves from branch to branch effortlessly and without ever losing its hold. The Longnose Vinesnake is diurnal. Its diet is made up almost exclusively of lizards. It sometimes eats mice and birds and is said to feed, on rare occasions, even on snakes. When it catches a lizard it does not strangle it in the coils of its body but instead holds on with its teeth until the prey is dead. *A. nasuta* is mildly poisonous and does not bite so that caution is in order with this snake as with all other Boiginae. *A. nasuta* gives birth to between 8 and 23 fully developed young, usually between March and December.

CAPTIVITY AND BREEDING: For the Longnose Vinesnake to feel comfortable it should be housed in a large and tall terrarium that simulates the conditions of a rain forest and includes many forked climbing branches and plenty of plants. Leaf mold or peat is used on the bottom. A bottom heater is not needed because this snake leaves the branches only seldom if at all, but a large water basin is necessary. This snake also likes to be sprayed 2 or 3 times a day. It should get artificial light all day and also likes sunlight. Daytime temperatures between 72° and 82°F (23°-28°C) are required. As food it should be offered 1 to 3 lizards the size of wall lizards every week. The snake will strike at these lizards with amazing accuracy from its typical attack position, in which the upper body is folded in S-curves and bobs up and down. Sometimes this snake will also accept small mice and fish. The prey dies within about 10 minutes after the poison is injected through the grooved rear fangs. *A. nasuta* has been bred in captivity, and females that were imported pregnant have given birth to young in terrariums. The baby snakes measure an average of 17½ inches (44 cm) and undergo their first molt after about 2 weeks. They eat young common frogs and lizards and after a while even newborn mice. After about 3 months they measure 22½ inches (57 cm).

Genus *Chrysopelea*
Flying Snakes
5 species

Chrysopelea ornata
Ornate Flyingsnake
2 subspecies

PHYSICAL CHARACTERISTICS: The longish, flat head with its square snout is clearly set off from the neck, and the strikingly large eyes have round pupils. The slender and elegant shape of the body indicates that this species dwells mostly in trees. The scales are smooth or only faintly keeled. The head is black and yellow mottled or has transverse stripes of those colors. The green scales of the back and sides of the body have black rims. *C. o. ornata* has red markings of varying shapes running down its back. These are lacking in *C. o. ornatissima*. In this subspecies the individual scales have black lines in the middle. In contrast to adult animals, juveniles always have light, transverse stripes on their bodies. The belly is pale yellow to greenish-yellow.

LENGTH: Rarely over 56 inches (140 cm).

DISTRIBUTION AND BEHAVIOR: This snake is native to Sri Lanka, India, southern China, and Southeast Asia, including the Malay Peninsula. It is a fairly common reptile and climbs extremely well. It lives on trees and bushes, though young animals are sometimes found in the grass and at the foot of trees. Dense forests are avoided by this snake, but old trees often harbor one or more of them even in urban areas. Coconut palms and the rafters of old houses are favorite haunts. *C. ornata* moves with amazing agility and is able to crawl up the vertical trunks of trees. It cannot take flying leaps like the closely related *C. paradisii*, which can flatten its body, but it moves easily from one branch to the next. The diet of *C. ornata* consists of lizards—primarily geckos—mice, bats, snakes, and insects. It snatches its prey, holds on to it with its jaws, coils its upper body around it, and swallows it

head first. Matings take place in June, and the 6 to 12 longish eggs are usually deposited in trees.

CAPTIVITY AND BREEDING: *C. ornata* requires the same conditions and care as *Boiga dendrophila* with slightly lower daytime temperatures between 72° and 82°F (22°-28°C), and it should be kept a little less moist than *B. dendrophila*. The largely diurnal Ornate Flyingsnake needs 12 to 14 hours of artificial light and preferably morning and afternoon sun. Although this snake tends to bite there have been no reports of poison symptoms in humans. If the snake refuses to eat mice, it is fed lizards. *C. ornata* has been bred in captivity. The eggs, which were kept at 86° to 88°F (25°-26°C) hatched within 70 to 92 days. The hatchlings measured about 8 inches (20 cm).

Genus *Oxybelis*
American Vinesnakes
4 species

Oxybelis aeneus
Mexican Vinesnake
2 subspecies

PHYSICAL CHARACTERISTICS: The longish, narrow head is clearly set off from the neck. There is no pointed extension of the snout as in the case of *O. fulgidus*. The large eyes have round pupils. The body looks exceptionally thin, and the tail is long and tapered. The dorsal scales are smooth or faintly keeled, and the body's basic color is a glistening yellowish-gray to reddish-brown. The back and sides may be a solid color or have brown or black blotches. A black line runs across the eye on the sides of the head, and the upper and lower labials as well as the throat and belly are whitish and look somewhat rouged. Sometimes there is a fine, dark line running down the sides of the belly on the edges of the ventral plates, and there may be a light line running down the center.

LENGTH: 5 feet (150 cm); in exceptional cases up to 75 inches (190 cm).

DISTRIBUTION AND BEHAVIOR: The Mexican Vinesnake is found from southern Arizona to the northern parts of South America, and it also occurs on Trinidad, Tobago, and the Huevos Islands. It lives mostly on plains and more rarely in hilly country. This species is active more during the day than at night and spends all its time on bushes and low trees near water. *O. aeneus* is common in almost all wooded areas. The placement of the eyes on the sides of the head enables the snake to see what is happening both above and below. This species' diet consists of lizards, frogs, and young birds, prey it quickly paralyzes with its venom and then swallows head first. But this snake represents no danger to humans. It bites only rarely even when disturbed, usually only opening its mouth wide. When it feels threatened it secretes a strong smelling substance from its anal glands. *O. aeneus* produces a clutch of about 6 eggs in June.

CAPTIVITY AND BREEDING: *O. aeneus* requires a terrarium suitable for arboreal snakes with many climbing branches, plenty of growing plants, a layer of leaf mold rich in organic matter on the bottom, and a water container. There is no need for bottom heat. Lighting should be provided all day. Daylight and especially sunlight have a beneficial effect on this snake. The Mexican Vinesnake is used to essentially constant temperatures between 77° and 86°F (25°-30°C) and catches cold easily if subjected to fluctuations in warmth. Lizards, small frogs, and nestling sparrows are offered as food. The terrarium should be sprayed with lukewarm water from time to time because the snake likes to drink the drops of water. Thus far this species has not reproduced in captivity.

Oxybelis fulgidus
Green Vinesnake

PHYSICAL CHARACTERISTICS: The long, narrow head with its rigid, strikingly pointed rostral shield is noticeably set off from the head. The large eyes have round pupils. The body gives an impression of unusual thinness and delicacy with a tail that is long and threadlike. The dorsal scales are smooth or faintly keeled. The gorgeous grass-green on the upper side of the body is set off from the yellowish-green of the belly by a white line on the edges of the ventral plates. The upper and lower labials are yellowish-green, and the tongue is the same green as the back.

LENGTH: 5 to 6 feet (150-180 cm); in exceptional cases up to 84 inches (213.5 cm).

DISTRIBUTION AND BEHAVIOR: *O. fulgidus* is distributed from Mexico to Argentina. It occurs in plains and at altitudes up to 3300 feet (1000 m) above sea level and is quite numerous in places. It is active both during the day and at night and lives exclusively on bushes and low trees, avoiding the ground altogether. With its green coloration and vine-like build it mimics its environment perfectly and is often impossible to detect in a network of branches. Its diet is made up of lizards, nestling birds, and, to a lesser degree, of frogs. If it is disturbed it puffs out its upper body so that the scales are spread apart and the bright green color stands out especially vividly. If one grabs hold of this snake it strikes, but the bite is harmless. *O. fulgidus* is oviparous.

CAPTIVITY AND BREEDING: Like the previously described species, *O. fulgidus* is rarely imported. It requires the same conditions in captivity as *O. aeneus* and is fed lizards the size of wall lizards. Some individuals will also accept frogs and small birds. Thus far *O. fulgidus* has not reproduced in captivity.

Genus *Philothamnus*
African Greensnakes
8 species

Philothamnus irregularis
West African Greensnake
2 subspecies

PHYSICAL CHARACTERISTICS: The rather flat and longish head is set off noticeably from the neck. The snout is rounded, and the large, golden yellow eyes have round pupils. The body is slender and the tail long and tapered. The scales are smooth and the anal plate is divided. The back and sides are a uniform light to olive green with black-rimmed scales on the anterior body. Sometimes there is a stripe down the back.

LENGTH: 28 to 36 inches (70-90 cm); rarely over 40 inches (1 m).

DISTRIBUTION AND BEHAVIOR: *P. irregularis* occurs in western, central, eastern, and southern Africa. It lives both on flat land and in mountains up to 7500 feet (2300 m). Usually it is found near water, where it hunts for frogs and toads. It also eats lizards, small birds, and sometimes snakes. This Greensnake is largely diurnal. Its movements are surprisingly fast and agile. It is a superb climber and likes to sun in shrubbery. It is also a good swimmer, and when it swims it keeps its head and neck above the water. On the ground it also moves with ease and speed. When the West African Greensnake gets excited it inflates its throat and flattens it vertically. Six to 16 eggs are laid between December and February, and the baby snakes measure about 8½ to 10 inches (22-26 cm) when they hatch after 2 months.

CAPTIVITY AND BREEDING: *P. irregularis* is shy and nervous in a terrarium and takes some time to become more relaxed. A medium-sized terrarium with a large water basin and some climbing branches is recommended for this snake. Forest soil is used for the bottom and a suitable retreat provided in the form of a piece of decorative cork, a tree stump, or some flat rocks. This is not a heavy snake, and it is therefore possible to have plants in the terrarium. Artificial light should be provided 12 to 14 hours a day, and the temperature is kept between 75° and 82°F (24°-28°C) during the day and a few degrees cooler at night. Frogs and lizards are offered as food. This snake accepts mice only in rare cases. *P. irregularis* has been bred in captivity. The eggs are longish and oval and have fine longitudinal grooves. At an average temperature of 75°F (24°C) they take about 65 days to hatch.

Genus *Boiga*
Cat Snakes
21 species

Boiga dendrophila
Mangrove Snake
7 subspecies
(photo, page 158)

PHYSICAL CHARACTERISTICS: The oval head is only slightly set off from the neck, and in bright light the pupils narrow down to vertical slits in the large eyes. The body is somewhat flattened on the sides, and there is the suggestion of a ridge running down the center of the back. The "Ularburong," as the Malayans call this species, has magnificent colors and markings. Sulphur yellow, transverse bands stand out brightly against the bluish-black of the body. The bands are broken over the spine and widen toward the belly, which is either uniformly black or mottled with yellow. The upper and lower labials and the throat are yellow with black rims on the scales.

LENGTH: Slightly over 6½ feet (2 m).

DISTRIBUTION AND BEHAVIOR: The Mangrove Snake is native to southern Asia, Indonesia, and the Philippines. It lives in tropical rain forests and is active at dusk and at night. It is an arboreal snake and descends to the ground only rarely. Birds, snakes, and lizards make up most of its diet though it occasionally eats bats and fish as well. This snake is very hostile toward humans. When an enemy approaches it immediately gets ready to attack, bending its head back and vibrating the tail in agitation. As a rule, the bite of this snake is harmless, but in a number of cases it has led to severe poisonings; therefore, this snake should always be approached with great caution. *B. dendrophila* generally lays between 7 and 10 eggs.

CAPTIVITY AND BREEDING: *B. dendrophila* is a tree-dwelling snake and should therefore be kept in a very large terrarium with sturdy climbing branches and plenty of plants. The bottom of the terrarium is covered with a mixture of leaf mold and sand and lots of decaying leaves, and the inside of the terrarium as well as the snake should be sprayed with lukewarm water every day. A large water basin is required. Ideal temperatures lie between 77° and 86°F (25°-30°C) during the day and around 72°F (22°C) at night. Birds, lizards, fish, and mice, too, are offered as food. The Mangrove Snake has to be kept singly because otherwise one individual may simply eat its companion. During the day these snakes lie on the branches and barely move. They rarely descend to the ground. *B. dendrophila* has been bred in the Baltimore Zoo. The eggs were placed in a sterile litter, and the young snakes hatched after 108 days.

Genus *Crotaphopeltis*
African Herald Snakes
3 species

Crotaphopeltis hotamboeia
Red-lip Snake
3 subspecies

PHYSICAL CHARACTERISTICS: The flat, short head is clearly set off from the neck, and the large eyes have vertical slits for pupils. The body is somewhat compressed on the sides, and the scales are smooth or faintly keeled. The color varies from grayish-brown to olive brown, grayish-green, or blackish. The snake may be unicolored or have white blotches. Usually there are whitish dots on the edges of the scales which form fine transverse stripes. The top of the head is dark blue to black, and the upper labials are orange red, yellowish, or white. The belly is solid white, the throat and the tip of the tail, sometimes black.

LENGTH: 28 inches (70 cm); sometimes up to 44 inches (110 cm).

DISTRIBUTION AND BEHAVIOR: *C. hotamboeia* is distributed over wide areas of tropical Africa and in South Africa from the western half of Cape Province eastward. *C. hotamboeia* lives from just above sea level up to about 6500 feet

(2000 m). Because of its wide distribution it is one of the best known African snakes. This snake was given its name by J. M. Leslie who first discovered it in the so-called "Herald district" of the eastern part of Cape Province. *C. hotamboeia* is largely nocturnal and is often confused with the Night Adder (*Causus rhombeatus*). *C. hotamboeia* favors a humid environment. During the day it stays hidden under logs, old wood, rotting bark, leaves, and rocks. If it is disturbed it reacts with hostility, hissing loudly, flattening head and body, and striking fiercely at the intruder. Its favorite prey is frogs and toads which it grabs by whatever part of the anatomy it can get a hold of and chokes down while still living. But it also consumes lizards and small mammals, especially mice. Its bite is generally not harmful to humans because the poison fangs are located far back and the poison is not very strong. In late spring or early summer *C. hotamboeia* lays 6 to 12 eggs measuring $1^{1}/4 \times {}^{1}/2$ inches (30 × 12 mm). These eggs, which are usually deposited in some decaying plant material, require about 3 months to hatch. The young snakes measure about 3 to 4 inches (8-10 cm).

CAPTIVITY AND BREEDING: This snake adjusts rather quickly to captivity, becomes hand tame, and accepts food from its keeper's hand. It is quite a good snake for a beginner, thriving in a small to medium-sized terrarium with a layer of sand and forest soil on the bottom and a few pieces of bark and rocks to hide under. A fair-sized water container is also necessary. Since this snake is largely nocturnal it seldom comes out in the open during the day. *C. hotamboiea* requires temperatures between 77° and 86°F (25°-30°C) during the day and a few degrees cooler at night. There are no reports of this snake reproducing in captivity. There has been a report of a two-headed specimen that lived in the Port Elisabeth Snake Park. This snake ate with both heads with the food progressing into one stomach. The two heads competed for food and often grabbed the same frog and fought over prey.

Genus *Dispholidus**
Boomslangs

Dispholidus typus
Boomslang

PHYSICAL CHARACTERISTICS: The head is short, somewhat thicker toward the back, and clearly set off from the neck. The very large eyes have round or sometimes horizontal pupils. The body is slender and slightly compressed on the sides. The narrow scales are clearly keeled. The Boomslangs are not divided into different subspecies, but they do vary widely in their coloration. The top of the body may be light or dark brown, grass to olive green, or even black. Some specimens are unicolored, others are mottled with brown or black, and still others have a dark line down the center of the back. Green Boomslangs may have black rims on their scales. The belly can range from brown to yellow or green and be of a solid color or mottled. All these variations occur not only in the forms mentioned but also in all kinds of transitional stages so that Boomslangs are often not recognized as such but mistaken for completely different species. As a general rule Boomslangs that are brown are females and the differently colored ones are males.

LENGTH: 52 to 60 inches (130-150 cm); rarely over 6 feet (180 cm).

DISTRIBUTION AND BEHAVIOR: Boomslangs are widely distributed in Africa ranging from Senegal and Ethiopia all the way to South Africa. They live in savannas and bushy regions, and their favorite environments are trees and bushes. With their slender bodies they move with ease through the branches. Not only does their coloration help camouflage them, but they are also able to remain motionless in a tree or bush with raised body for some time and thus blend in so well with their environment that even birds often fail to notice them. Sometimes they descend to the ground, but here they are not anywhere as

*These snakes are dangerously venomous.

agile as up on trees. At the slightest disturbance they make for the next tree or bush and disappear. Boomslangs also swim very well. *D. typus* feeds on arboreal lizards, especially chameleons. It also eats frogs, mice, birds, and birds' eggs. Boomslangs do not strangle their prey but hold it in their jaws until the venom takes effect. The bite of this snake can also be very dangerous to humans. The poison fangs are farther front in the upper jaw than is the case with other Boiginae and thus quite likely to come into play when the snake bites. The poison is very strong, being more potent in fact than the same amount of venom of a mamba (*Dendroaspis*) or a cobra (*Naja*). It affects both the nervous system and the blood and can easily be fatal to humans. Human fatalities have occurred more than once, and extreme caution in handling this snake is therefore in order. However, *D. typus* is not an aggressive snake and bites are uncommon. But if it is cornered and has no way to escape it inflates the throat region and upper body vertically. Boomslangs mate in trees and bushes rather than on the ground like most other snakes. After about 4 months the female deposits between 8 and 23 eggs in a hollow tree, the nest of a woodpecker, or in a place in the ground where warmth and humidity will aid the maturing of the embryos. The baby snakes, which hatch after 4 to 7 months, are about 13 inches (33 cm) long.

CAPTIVITY AND BREEDING: The Boomslang has a great urge to move and therefore needs a large terrarium with plants and many climbing branches. Sand is used on the bottom, and a water container is required. No bottom heat is necessary because the snakes spend almost all of their time on the branches. Only sturdy plants can be used in the terrarium because more delicate ones will not stand up to the snakes' crawling around. If the terrarium gets no morning or afternoon sun or adequate daylight, artificial light should be provided all day. *D. typus* requires daytime temperatures between 77° and 86°F (25°-30°C) and nighttime temperatures between 68° and 72°F

(20°-22°C). Since in nature this snake eats mostly chameleons, providing food for it presents some difficulties. Some individuals consistently refuse to accept mice and may therefore have to be force-fed. Most Boomslangs, however, will sooner or later start eating mice and then can be long-lived in a terrarium.

D. typus has reproduced in captivity. The eggs are placed in damp peat moss or some similar litter and kept between 77° and 82°F (25°-28°C). The baby snakes molt 7 to 11 days after hatching. Often they refuse to eat the food offered them and may have to be force-fed at the beginning. But usually they will soon start eating small mice on their own. Although *D. typus* belongs to the family Colubridae, and is thus not a venomous snake in the common sense of the term, there is always a possibility that a bite from this snake may have tragic consequences as it did in the case of the renowned American herpetologist Karl Patterson Schmidt, who died of being bitten by a Boomslang. Boomslangs should therefore be kept privately only by very experienced snake fanciers, and any force-feeding has to be undertaken with the greatest of care.

Genus *Thelotornis**
African Bird Snakes
1 species

Thelotornis kirtlandii
Bird Snake
3 subspecies

PHYSICAL CHARACTERISTICS: *T. kirtlandii* has a long, pointed head that is clearly set off from the very slender neck. The large eyes have horizontal pupils that narrow toward the center of the head and thus resemble the shape of a keyhole. The body is thin and the tail long and tapered. The scales are longish and faintly keeled. The dark gray to grayish-brown body has irregular light crossbands with dark edges. On the neck there are one or two large, black transverse blotches. The head is grayish-green, violet, or reddish-brown with a varying number of brown to black spots. In places the spots merge together in a Y-shaped pattern. A reddish-violet to black stripe runs from the corners of the mouth across the eyes and ends on the sides of the neck. The belly is reddish-white with dark gray blotches.

LENGTH: 48 to 68 inches (120-170 cm).

DISTRIBUTION AND BEHAVIOR: As its vernacular name suggests, *T. kirtlandii* makes its home in trees and seldom descends to the ground. Its primary habitat is the savanna. In its coloration it is more perfectly adapted to the environment than almost any other African snake. Up in the trees or bushes it takes on its typical resting position in which the upper third of the body is raised up diagonally and remains motionless like this for a long time. When it is cornered it immediately assumes an impressive threatening stance with the throat and upper body inflated vertically and the head held horizontally. Since the fangs of the Bird Snake are quite far back in the mouth bites are usually harmless although the venom is as potent as that of the Boomslang and causes similar symptoms—almost uncontrollable internal bleeding. In August 1975 the well-known and respected herpetologist, Dr. Robert Mertens, was fatally bitten by a Bird Snake. The preferred diet of *T. kirtlandii* consists of lizards and especially geckos and chameleons, but it also eats snakes, frogs, and toads. Thanks to its excellent spatial vision made possible by the keyhole-shaped pupils this snake perceives prey both when the prey moves and when it is still. The snake grabs its victim and holds on with its jaws until the prey animal succumbs to the venom. Bird Snakes lay 6 to 10 eggs, usually in December or January. The hatchlings measure between 9 and 10 inches (23-25 cm).

CAPTIVITY AND BREEDING: *T. kirtlandii* requires the same care and conditions as *Dispholidus typus*. Lizards and frogs are offered as food, and some individuals also eat birds and mice. Extreme caution is in order with this

*These snakes are dangerously venomous.

snake. *T. kirtlandii* has produced offspring in the Lincoln Park Zoo in Chicago.

Genus *Telescopus*
Tiger Snakes
8 species

Telescopus fallax
European Tigersnake
8 subspecies

PHYSICAL CHARACTERISTICS: The broad and flat head is well set off from the neck, and the medium-sized eyes have vertical slits as pupils. The body looks compressed on the sides and is taller than it is wide. The scales are smooth. The ground color of the European Tigersnake is light to dark gray. The top of the head can have dark dots or blotches. From behind the head a row of black spots runs down the middle of the back to the tail. The sides of the body also have dark, evenly spaced spots. The belly is porcelain colored, yellowish, or pale pink and usually is mottled. Cat Snakes have venom glands and grooved fangs, but these fangs are set so far back that they cannot injure humans.

LENGTH: Up to 40 inches (1 m).

DISTRIBUTION AND BEHAVIOR: The European Tiger Snake is native to the Balkans, the Aegean Islands, and the Near East. Here it lives on plains as well as in mountains and especially likes dry, rocky terrain with a growth of low bushes. This snake, which becomes active at dusk, leaves its refuge toward evening or at night. It feeds on lizards and less commonly on mice. It first coils itself around its prey and then kills it by biting and injecting its venom. Hibernation lasts about 4 to 6 months. In the summer the female lays 7 to 8 eggs measuring about 1¼ to 1⅜ inches (33-36 mm) by slightly over ½ inch (14 mm). The young snakes usually hatch in the late summer and are about 6 to 8 inches long (15-20 cm). They start out by eating larger insects and small lizards.

*These snakes are dangerously venomous.

CAPTIVITY AND BREEDING: This small, rear-fanged colubrid is rarely kept by fanciers. It needs a dry, small to medium-sized terrarium. A mixture of sand and loam is used for the bottom and some flat limestone rocks or some hollow pieces of cork are supplied as hiding places. A small water basin and a few branches must also be provided, as well as localized bottom heat. There is no need to do without plants since this snake does not weigh much. *T. fallax* requires daytime temperatures between 77° and 86°F (25°-30°C). Artificial light should be provided 12 to 14 hours a day if there is no morning or afternoon sun or not enough daylight. The snake is fed lizards. Some individuals also eat young mice. Three to 4 months of hibernation are required. Thus far *T. fallax* has not been bred in captivity.

Telescopus semiannulatus
Banded Tigersnake
2 subspecies

PHYSICAL CHARACTERISTICS: The broad, flat head is clearly set off from the neck, thus lending this snake a viper-like appearance; and the moderately large eyes have vertical slits as pupils. The somewhat compressed sides make the body look taller than it looks wide. The scales are smooth, and the ground color of the back and sides of the body varies from dark pink to yellowish and to reddish-brown. The subspecies *T. s. semiannulatus* has between 24 and 46 dark brown to black blotches on the back, whereas *T. s. polystictus* has between 52 and 75 of them. The belly is porcelain colored.

LENGTH: 28 inches (70 cm); rarely over 40 inches (1 m).

DISTRIBUTION AND BEHAVIOR: *T. semiannulatus* is distributed from Kenya and the Congo southward across Tanganyika as far as South Africa. This largely nocturnal snake is mostly ground-dwelling and climbs onto bushes and trees only rarely. Now and then it is found in the nests of weaverbirds. *T. semiannulatus* feeds primarily on geckos and other lizards and less frequently on nestling birds and small mammals. It holds its prey in its jaws until the venom has taken effect. Toward humans the Tiger Snake behaves with considerable aggressiveness. When threatened it hisses furiously and bites. But it represents no danger to people. It is a rather sluggish snake, and its fangs are located far back in the mouth and rarely penetrate when it bites. The venom is very weak, causing no more than a slight swelling in the bite area and a light burning sensation. *T. semiannulatus* lays 6 to 10 eggs measuring 1 × ³/₈ inch (25 × 10 mm).

CAPTIVITY AND BREEDING: This snake, rarely imported, should be kept in a small to medium-sized terrarium with sand and loam at the bottom, some rocks to provide a refuge, a climbing tree with lots of branches, and a small water dish. Localized bottom heat is recommended. Since this snake leaves its hiding place only rarely during the day ordinary daylight is sufficient. The temperature should range between 77° and 86°F (25°-30°C) during the day and drop a few degrees at night. This snake likes to eat lizards and accepts mice only in some cases. Sometimes *T. semiannulatus* refuses food for a long time before it starts eating regularly. This extremely quiet snake has not yet been bred in captivity.

Genus *Trimorphodon*
Lyre Snakes
11 species

Trimorphodon biscutatus
Lyre Snake

PHYSICAL CHARACTERISTICS: The broad head is clearly set off from the slender neck and body, and the large eyes have vertically elliptical pupils. The scales are smooth, and the ground color of the body looks gray or brown. The top of the head has a lyre-shaped mark, and down the center of the back there is an average of 35 (the number can vary from 28 to 43) dark brown spots that are more or less hex-

agonal in shape. Each of these spots has a light transverse area at the center. The grayish-white to yellowish belly has a sparse scattering of brown blotches. Lyre Snakes that come from desert areas have lighter coloration than those from the mountains.

LENGTH: 20 to 32 inches (50-80 cm); occasionally slightly over 40 inches (1 m).

DISTRIBUTION AND BEHAVIOR: This snake is found in southwestern California and in northwestern Baja California from sea level up to about 3300 feet (1000 m). It is active at night and likes rocky terrain. *T. biscutatus* is found both in the coastal mountains of California and in deserts. During the day it stays hidden under rocks and in deep, well-protected crevices. Only at night or in the early morning does it venture out from hiding, and then it often crosses roads and is run over by cars. Its main diet consists of lizards, which it kills with its venom. But it also eats mice and small bats. *T. biscutatus* hibernates for only 2 or 3 months, disappearing in October or November and emerging again in January or February. This species lays eggs. The baby snakes, which hatch after about 11 weeks, measure about 8 inches (20 cm).

CAPTIVITY AND BREEDING: The Lyre Snake does well in a heated dry terrarium with a few large chunks of rock and a climbing branch. It requires the same care as the Night Snake. Lizards offered as food are readily accepted either live or dead. Mice are crushed before they are swallowed. *T. biscutatus* comes alive at dusk when it starts crawling around. If it is bothered it reacts quite aggressively, hissing, trembling with its tail, and biting. Although it is rather helpless in the bright daylight, it strikes with great accuracy in the dark. Apparently the bite of this snake is not harmful to humans. As far as we know *T. biscutatus* has not been bred in captivity, but females that were gravid when captured have deposited eggs in terrariums with the young snakes hatching after 79 days.

INDEX

Index